LLEWELLYN'S 2023

Sabbats
ALMANAC

Samhain 2022
to
Mabon 2023

D0104608

Llewellyn's 2023 Sabbats Almanac
Samhain 2022 to Mabon 2023

Cover art © Carolyn Vibbert
Editing by Hanna Grimson
Interior Art © Carolyn Vibbert

You can order annuals and books from *New Worlds*, Llewellyn's catalog. To request a free copy, call 1-877-NEW WRLD toll-free or order online by visiting our website at http://subscriptions.llewellyn.com.

ISBN: 978-0-7387-6399-6

Llewellyn Worldwide Ltd.
2143 Wooddale Drive
Woodbury, MN 55125-2989
www.llewellyn.com

Printed in the United States of America

2022

JANUARY
S	M	T	W	T	F	S
						1
2	3	4	5	6	7	8
9	10	11	12	13	14	15
16	17	18	19	20	21	22
23	24	25	26	27	28	29
30	31					

FEBRUARY
S	M	T	W	T	F	S
		1	2	3	4	5
6	7	8	9	10	11	12
13	14	15	16	17	18	19
20	21	22	23	24	25	26
27	28					

MARCH
S	M	T	W	T	F	S
		1	2	3	4	5
6	7	8	9	10	11	12
13	14	15	16	17	18	19
20	21	22	23	24	25	26
27	28	29	30	31		

APRIL
S	M	T	W	T	F	S
					1	2
3	4	5	6	7	8	9
10	11	12	13	14	15	16
17	18	19	20	21	22	23
24	25	26	27	28	29	30

MAY
S	M	T	W	T	F	S
1	2	3	4	5	6	7
8	9	10	11	12	13	14
15	16	17	18	19	20	21
22	23	24	25	26	27	28
29	30	31				

JUNE
S	M	T	W	T	F	S
			1	2	3	4
5	6	7	8	9	10	11
12	13	14	15	16	17	18
19	20	21	22	23	24	25
26	27	28	29	30		

JULY
S	M	T	W	T	F	S
					1	2
3	4	5	6	7	8	9
10	11	12	13	14	15	16
17	18	19	20	21	22	23
24	25	26	27	28	29	30
31						

AUGUST
S	M	T	W	T	F	S
	1	2	3	4	5	6
7	8	9	10	11	12	13
14	15	16	17	18	19	20
21	22	23	24	25	26	27
28	29	30	31			

SEPTEMBER
S	M	T	W	T	F	S
				1	2	3
4	5	6	7	8	9	10
11	12	13	14	15	16	17
18	19	20	21	22	23	24
25	26	27	28	29	30	

OCTOBER
S	M	T	W	T	F	S
						1
2	3	4	5	6	7	8
9	10	11	12	13	14	15
16	17	18	19	20	21	22
23	24	25	26	27	28	29
30	31					

NOVEMBER
S	M	T	W	T	F	S
		1	2	3	4	5
6	7	8	9	10	11	12
13	14	15	16	17	18	19
20	21	22	23	24	25	26
27	28	29	30			

DECEMBER
S	M	T	W	T	F	S
				1	2	3
4	5	6	7	8	9	10
11	12	13	14	15	16	17
18	19	20	21	22	23	24
25	26	27	28	29	30	31

2023

JANUARY
S	M	T	W	T	F	S
1	2	3	4	5	6	7
8	9	10	11	12	13	14
15	16	17	18	19	20	21
22	23	24	25	26	27	28
29	30	31				

FEBRUARY
S	M	T	W	T	F	S
			1	2	3	4
5	6	7	8	9	10	11
12	13	14	15	16	17	18
19	20	21	22	23	24	25
26	27	28				

MARCH
S	M	T	W	T	F	S
			1	2	3	4
5	6	7	8	9	10	11
12	13	14	15	16	17	18
19	20	21	22	23	24	25
26	27	28	29	30	31	

APRIL
S	M	T	W	T	F	S
						1
2	3	4	5	6	7	8
9	10	11	12	13	14	15
16	17	18	19	20	21	22
23	24	25	26	27	28	29
30						

MAY
S	M	T	W	T	F	S
	1	2	3	4	5	6
7	8	9	10	11	12	13
14	15	16	17	18	19	20
21	22	23	24	25	26	27
28	29	30	31			

JUNE
S	M	T	W	T	F	S
				1	2	3
4	5	6	7	8	9	10
11	12	13	14	15	16	17
18	19	20	21	22	23	24
25	26	27	28	29	30	

JULY
S	M	T	W	T	F	S
						1
2	3	4	5	6	7	8
9	10	11	12	13	14	15
16	17	18	19	20	21	22
23	24	25	26	27	28	29
30	31					

AUGUST
S	M	T	W	T	F	S
		1	2	3	4	5
6	7	8	9	10	11	12
13	14	15	16	17	18	19
20	21	22	23	24	25	26
27	28	29	30	31		

SEPTEMBER
S	M	T	W	T	F	S
					1	2
3	4	5	6	7	8	9
10	11	12	13	14	15	16
17	18	19	20	21	22	23
24	25	26	27	28	29	30

OCTOBER
S	M	T	W	T	F	S
1	2	3	4	5	6	7
8	9	10	11	12	13	14
15	16	17	18	19	20	21
22	23	24	25	26	27	28
29	30	31				

NOVEMBER
S	M	T	W	T	F	S
			1	2	3	4
5	6	7	8	9	10	11
12	13	14	15	16	17	18
19	20	21	22	23	24	25
26	27	28	29	30		

DECEMBER
S	M	T	W	T	F	S
					1	2
3	4	5	6	7	8	9
10	11	12	13	14	15	16
17	18	19	20	21	22	23
24	25	26	27	28	29	30
31						

Contents

Contents

Lammas

Mabon

Introduction

NEARLY EVERYONE HAS A favorite sabbat. There are numerous ways to observe any tradition. The 2023 edition of the *Sabbats Almanac* provides a wealth of lore, celebrations, creative projects, and recipes to enhance your holiday.

For this edition, a mix of writers—Melissa Tipton, Michael Furie, Susan Pesznecker, Mickie Mueller, Suzanne Ress, and more—share their ideas and wisdom. These include a variety of paths as well as the authors' personal approaches to each sabbat. Each chapter closes with an extended ritual, which may be adapted for both solitary practitioners and covens.

In addition to these insights and rituals, specialists in astrology, history, cooking, crafts, and spells impart their expertise throughout.

Daniel Pharr gives an overview of planetary influences most relevant for each sabbat season and provides details about the New and Full Moons, retrograde motion, planetary positions, and more. (Times and dates follow Eastern Standard Time and Eastern Daylight Time.)

Kate Freuler explores history, myths, and practices from around the world and how they connect to and sometimes influence each sabbat. From historical werewolves and vampires to the Norns of Norse mythology, this section is the place for celebration.

Gwion Raven conjures up a feast for each festival that features seasonal appetizers, entrées, desserts, and beverages.

Ivo Dominguez Jr. offers instructions on DIY crafts that will help you tap into each sabbats' energy and fill your home with magic and fun.

Charlie Rainbow Wolf provides color magic tips and spells to celebrate and utilize the unique forces in each season.

About the Authors

Kate Freuler lives in Ontario, Canada, and is the author of *Of Blood and Bones: Working with Shadow Magick & the Dark Moon*. She owns and operates White Moon Witchcraft, an online witchcraft boutique. When she isn't crafting spells and amulets for clients or herself, she loves to write, paint, read, draw, and create. Visit her at www.katefreuler.com.

Suzanne Ress has been practicing Wicca for about twelve years as the leader of a small coven, but she has been aware of having a special connection to nature and animal spirits since she was a young child. She has been writing creatively most of her life—short stories, novels, and nonfiction articles for a variety of publications—and finds it to be an important outlet for her considerable creative powers. Other outlets she regularly makes use of are metalsmithing, mosaic works, painting, and all kinds of dance. She is also a professional aromatic herb grower and beekeeper. Although she is an American of Welsh ancestry by birth, she has lived in northern Italy for nearly twenty years. She recently discovered that the small mountain in the pre-alpine hills that she inhabits with her family and animals was once the site of an ancient Insubrian Celtic sacred place. Not surprisingly, the top of the mountain has remained a fulcrum of sacredness throughout the millennia, and this grounding in blessedness makes Suzanne's everyday life especially magical.

Charlie Rainbow Wolf is happiest when she is creating something, especially if it can be made from items that others have cast aside. An artist, author, alchemist, and astrologer, Charlie immerses herself deep into the roots of living, but she happily confesses she's easily distracted, because life offers so many wonderful things to explore. She follows an herbal mystery path, is an advocate of organic gardening and cooking, and in her downtime relaxes with a bit of knitting. She lives in the Midwest with her husband and special-needs Great Danes. Visit her at www.charlierainbow.com.

Ivo Dominguez Jr. has been active in Wicca and the Pagan community since 1978. He is an Elder of the Assembly of the Sacred Wheel, a Wiccan syncretic tradition, and is one of its founders. He is a part of the core group that started and manages the New Alexandrian Library. Ivo is the author of *The Four Elements of the Wise: Working with the Magickal Powers of Earth, Air, Water, Fire*; *Keys to Perception*; *Practical Astrology for Witches and Pagans*; *Casting Sacred Space*; *Spirit Speak*; *Beneath the Skins*; and numerous shorter works. Ivo is also a professional astrologer who has studied astrology since 1980 and has been offering consultations and readings since 1988. Visit him at www.ivodominguezjr.com.

Gwion Raven is a tattooed Pagan, writer, traveler, musician, cook, kitchen witch, occult shop owner, and teacher. He is the author of *The Magick of Food: Rituals, Offerings & Why We Eat Together* and coauthor of *Life Ritualized: A Witch's Guide to Honoring Life's Important Moments*. Although initiated in three magickal traditions, Gwion describes his practice as virtually anything that celebrates the wild, sensuous, living, breathing, dancing, ecstatic, divine experiences of this lifetime. Born and raised in London, he now resides in Northern California and shares space with redwood trees, the Pacific Ocean, and his beloved partner. Visit Gwion at GwionRaven .com.

Lupa is an author, artist, and naturalist in the Pacific Northwest. She is the author of several books on nature-based Paganism, as well as the creator of the Tarot of Bones and Pocket Osteomancy divination sets. More information about Lupa and her works may be found at http://www.thegreenwolf.com.

Elizabeth Barrette has been involved with the Pagan community for more than thirty-one years. She served as managing editor of *PanGaia* for eight years and dean of studies at the Grey School of Wizardry for four years. She has written columns on beginning and intermediate Pagan practice, Pagan culture, and Pagan leadership. Her book *Composing Magic: How to Create Magical Spells, Rituals, Blessings, Chants, and Prayers* explains how to combine writing and spirituality. She lives in central Illinois where she has done much networking with Pagans in her area, such as coffeehouse meetings and open sabbats. Her other public activities feature Pagan picnics and science fiction conventions. She enjoys magical crafts, historic religions, and gardening for wildlife. Her other writing fields include speculative fiction, gender studies, and social and environmental issues. Visit her blog *The Wordsmith's Forge* (https://ysabet wordsmith.dreamwidth.org/) or website PenUltimate Productions (http://penultimateproductions.weebly.com). Her coven site with extensive Pagan materials is Greenhaven Tradition (http://green haventradition.weebly.com/).

Natalie Zaman is the author of the award-winning books *Color and Conjure* (with Wendy Martin) and *Magical Destinations of the Northeast* and is a regular contributor to various Llewellyn annual publications. Visit Natalie online at http://nataliezaman.blogspot .com.

Michael Furie (Northern California) is the author of *The Witch's Book of Potions, Supermarket Sabbats, Spellcasting for Beginners, Supermarket Magic, Spellcasting: Beyond the Basics*, and more, all from Llewellyn Worldwide. A practicing Witch for more than twenty-five years, he is a priest of the Cailleach. He can be found online at www.michaelfurie.com.

Mickie Mueller is a witch, author, illustrator, tarot creator, and YouTube content creator. She is the author/illustrator of multiple books, articles, and tarot decks for Llewellyn Worldwide, including *Mystical Cats Tarot, Magical Dogs Tarot, The Witch's Mirror*, and

Llewellyn's Little Book of Halloween. Her magical art is distributed internationally and has been seen as set dressing on SYFY's *The Magicians* and Bravo's *Girlfriends' Guide to Divorce.* She runs several Etsy shops with her husband and fellow author, Daniel Mueller, in their studio workshop. Her YouTube videos are shot in her studio where she creates art, writes on the subject of witchcraft and folklore, and manifests her own style of eclectic everyday magic. She's been a witch for over twenty years, and she loves to teach practical and innovative ways to work magic using items and ingredients in your home.

Susan (Sue) Pesznecker is a mother, grandmother, writer, nurse, and college English professor living in the beautiful green Pacific Northwest with her poodles. An initiated Druid, green magick devoteé, and amateur herbalist, Sue loves reading, writing, cooking, travel, and anything having to do with the outdoors. Previous works include *Crafting Magick with Pen and Ink*, *The Magickal Retreat*, and *Yule: Rituals, Recipes & Lore for the Winter Solstice.* She's a regular contributor to the Llewellyn annuals; follow her on Instagram as Susan Pesznecker.

Daniel Pharr writes from his home in the woods of the Pacific Northwest. Much of his Pagan training was at Our Lady of the Shining Star, a residential Pagan seminary in New Mexico. He held the station of High Priest at Our Lady of the Sacred Rose, under the auspices of the Aquarian Tabernacle Church in Washington, a Wiccan spiritual organization.

Melissa Tipton is a Jungian Witch, Structural Integrator, and founder of the Real Magic Mystery School, where she teaches online courses in Jungian Magic, a potent blend of ancient magical techniques and modern psychological insights. She's the author of *Living Reiki: Heal Yourself and Transform Your Life* and *Llewellyn's Complete Book of Reiki.* Learn more and take a free class at www.realmagic.school.

Samhain

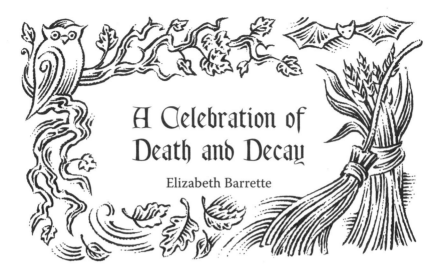

A Celebration of Death and Decay

Elizabeth Barrette

SAMHAIN CAN BE VIEWED as the end of the year or the beginning. It is sometimes called the Witches' New Year. It takes place in late autumn—the end of the growing season and the beginning of the dormant season. This holiday focuses on death and decay. Yet these things, too, exist in the liminal space between life and death, two sides of the same coin, two stages in the same process. To Pagans, they don't have to be unfamiliar and frightening. It's all one grand adventure.

Respecting Death

Part of Samhain tradition deals with the soul. The spark of spirit is eternal, undying. When it sheds the flesh, it continues to exist. It may take new form in the future, but for the time being, it is undeterred by having none. We appreciate life because it is fleeting and ephemeral. Even if we are reborn later, we know it will never be *this* life again—this time and place, these people, this home, these particular treasures. Those become memories when we die, but only things fade with time. Souls and their connections are forever.

This awareness of life, death, and rebirth spans many Pagan traditions. It offers a different perspective compared to religions that view life and death as separate and unbridgeable rather than part of a natural cycle. So some Pagan holidays celebrate death as a transition rather than an end. This encourages people to think about death—their own and that of others'—rather than pushing it out of mind. We can cultivate a relationship with death messengers and deities instead of shying away from them, so that when the time comes, we will be greeted by a friend and not a stranger. Familiarity makes the journey easier.

Another part of Samhain tradition deals with the flesh itself. This carries through all the holidays of death and decay that appear at this time of year. Look at all the imagery! Vampires, ghouls, zombies, skeletons—all kinds of dead things walk the night. Jack-o'-lanterns suggest the leering grin of a skull. Tattered costumes suggest the rot of the grave. They all belong to a category called *memento mori*, which is Latin for "Remember you must die."

These things remind us that life is ephemeral, and while souls are eternal, bodies are mortal. A body is just something a soul wears for a while. No matter how much you may relate to it, you are not your body. So it's better not to get too attached to something impermanent, lest we make painful mistakes at the end of days. Enjoy your body and those around you while you can, as we enjoy the fleeting flowers of spring or brilliant foliage of autumn. Someday you will die, as everything dies. It is better to approach this with grace and comfort than with resistance and fear.

One way to do this is through art. Many cultures have a tradition of macabre art that features images of death. Skulls and other bones have long been popular in still life paintings. They are complex and interesting to draw; they contrast well with live things, such as flowers. By reminding people of death, they encourage us to appreciate art. Sculptures sometimes feature death as well, and there are wall carvings of dancing skeletons.

Day of the Dead

Mexico has some particularly colorful examples. *Calaveras* are decorated skulls. They are most often made from sugar, but clay versions also exist. These can be labeled with the name of a deceased person, inviting them to come home for a visit during *Día de los Muertos*, the Day of the Dead. *Calacas* are skeletal figures customarily shown in fancy clothes and festive poses. These figures embody the idea that "life goes on" even after death, representing a happy and festive afterlife. The Day of the Dead encourages people to view death as a joyful occasion—after all, you are reuniting with your dead friends and relatives, who are excited to see you again.

Cemeteries

Another way of respecting death is through cemeteries. In some cultures, these are merely places to store the remains, but in others they are much more. They can contain beautiful sculptures of the ancestors or guardian spirits. Some tombs are miniature edifices. Often there are plentiful flowers, from bouquets in vases to those growing in flowerbeds. When crowds are expected, the cemetery usually has lawns or pavilions to accommodate them. Other cemeteries create quiet grottoes where people can grieve in private.

People visit cemeteries for many reasons. For some, it is about mourning those they have lost. For others, it is a happy occasion, spending time with the departed. Mexican families have picnics in cemeteries on the Day of the Dead for this reason. The Stoic tradition recommends meditating on your own death so you lose the fear of it. Samhain is just one of many death holidays clustered in late fall, so the cemetery activity is higher at this time of year.

There are multiple ways to show appreciation for cemeteries. Simply visiting the dead is a good start. Most people bring flowers or, occasionally, other offerings. Biodegradable ones are best. Another popular activity is tending graves. Brush off any dirt. Pull or trim weeds and grass around the headstone so they don't obscure it. In a vigorously tended cemetery, you won't need to do much, if anything, but in older or less-maintained ones, the grass can completely cover stones that are flat on the ground. Respect for a cemetery shows respect for death.

Exploring Decay

Yet death isn't always as dead as it seems. Dead things are actually teeming with life! This is the process of decay, which breaks down things so their material can be used again. Life and death are infinitely recyclable, and the biosphere doesn't believe in landfills. A human corpse, a dead deer, and a fallen log are all swarming with life that creates its own little ecosystem while the bounty lasts.

This is the world of the detritus food web, and it generates a whole swath of imagery appearing at Samhain and related holidays. They're all chthonic, or underworld, creatures. They break into groups. We have the amphibians like toads, frogs, and salamanders whose double life has long associated them with magic and transformations. They all lay their eggs in water. We have the creepy crawlers such as spiders, insects, and other arthropods, who wear their skeletons on the outside. They can move surprisingly fast. We have the little wrigglers like worms, larvae, and other soft slimy beings who ooze through the muck and make it fertile again. They are soft and slow, requiring a moist environment. We have the fungi and their kin in mushrooms, mold, and other growing things that directly break down dead matter. They often appear after a rain. There are many more things too small to see, but our decorations mostly focus on the visible ones.

This is the thriving ecosystem of the forest floor, the leaf litter, the compost pile, the wood chip mulch, the graveyard. Here, life and death are so intertwined that there is no separating them. It is important for decay to have its own places so that it doesn't encroach too much on the living, but often, the living walk right over the top and don't even notice what thrives and rots below their feet.

Sometimes things get really weird, especially when detritus dwellers feed on the living instead of the dead. *Ophiocordyceps sinensis* is a fungus that infects caterpillars, kills them, and then sprouts from the head like a unicorn horn. It is believed to have medicinal qualities. Other types of *Ophiocordyceps* attack ants, hijack their brains, and manipulate their behavior to spread the fungus. So yes, the zombie-brain connection is a real thing, although different in biology than in folklore.

You can see this reflected in the colors associated with Samhain. We have the white of bone and the black and gray of many fungi. We have the moldy blues and greens of plant and animal matter breaking down. There are pops of purple and orange like poison arrow frogs. Occasionally you might see the bright red of blood or the darker red of *Amanita* mushrooms. When we dress in the colors of decay, we honor this part of the cycle. Of course, fungi themselves appear as fun decorations for Samhain and Halloween. You can often find red-and-white *Amanita* printed on fabric or done up as knickknacks, and most people don't even know its mystical symbolism or shamanic history.

I love the detritus food web because it demonstrates that everything is connected, that life and death are literally part of the same cycle. Here in my yard, it is three days to apex, not three weeks or three months. We had a fallen tree ground into wood chips once, then it rained, and when I checked the pile on the third morning, a toad hopped out of it. Fungal threads already spread through the pile, and it was crawling with millipedes and pillbugs, who doubtless attracted the toad. I was delighted by the evidence of a thriving ecosystem.

We have a fallen log that started as a whole tree. It snapped off in a storm about fifteen feet above ground, and I decided to leave it because snags are good habitat. That snag lasted nine years before falling over to begin the next stage of its journey as a downed log. Fungi grow in it, bugs crawl through it, and it holds water through the dry summer.

We have another pile of old, rotten logs that started out as a fallen tree. Currently, I have a row of four log pots. I filled the rotten centers with potting soil and planted seeds there. Some of my flowerbeds, like the wildflower garden, are edged with logs or branches. So many things can be done with dead wood in the yard! Compost is another aspect of decay. The whole purpose of a compost pile is to take garbage you don't need and turn it into fertile earth. It's the perfect medium for entropic magic—any work meant to make things diminish, go away, break down, and decay. You don't have to worry about putting "bad energy" into the earth because the detritus food web is designed to handle waste. Negativity just gets chewed up and spit out as worm castings along with the potato peels and cowpats. We have done a number of rituals for banishing things using a compost pile as the focus. You don't even need to wait for the outgoing tide of a waning moon, because the compost is *always* rotting down. It's very gratifying to throw biodegradable symbols on the heap and then cover them with mulch.

Samhain is a time to give thanks for the messy, smelly, often unappreciated parts of the life-death cycle. It's a chance to embrace decay. We should all feel grateful for the detritivores, without whose hard work we would be buried in garbage. Imagine a world where nothing rots. Everything from fruit peels to manure, fallen logs to corpses, would all just *lie there*. Instead, entropy and decay ensure that these things break down to become new things. A compost pile shrinks dramatically as it cures, becoming humus. So rejoice in the rot. We need it to thrive.

Conclusion

These are just a few of the themes that people celebrate at Samhain. It can also be a "changing of the guard" holiday for deities, usually paired Beltane/Samhain or Midsummer/Midwinter depending on the chosen mythology. It can be the last of the three harvest festivals after Lammas and Mabon. In this case, it circles back to death again, because it is when animals are slaughtered and the last of the crops are brought in. This time, the ritual focuses on death and decay, so watch for those themes.

Cosmic Sway

Daniel Pharr

DECIDING WHAT DAY TO celebrate Samhain and honor the start of another year should be as simple as baking crescent cookies, but determining the actual dates for Samhain, Imbolc, Beltaine, and Lughnassadh can require a bit of math and an analysis of the Wheel of the Year. Three methods of determining the date for Samhain give three different sets of astrological influences.

Solar Samhain

The simplest date for Samhain is fixed on the solar calendar as October 31, and since night comes before day, Samhain begins at sundown on October 31 and ends at sundown on November 1, which this year will be under an Aquarius Moon. Easy. Simple. Crescent cookies.

The Aquarius Moon influences will underlie feelings, choices, and experiences throughout the Samhain celebration. Deep compassion coupled with deep thought may bring a solid understanding of the plights of the self and other people and circumstances, leading to assertive decisions driven by instinct and righteous indignation. The independent person under the Aquarius Moon will never back down, which could lead to a feisty Samhain gathering. If this energy can be used to enliven a person's natural characteristics, Samhain could become a gathering of superheroes.

Cross-Quarter Samhain

Then there is the analytical idea that the cross-quarter days are precisely the midpoint between solstices and equinoxes, meaning Samhain is exactly halfway between Mabon and Yule. The cross-quarter days are the beginning and ending of the seasons, while the solstices and equinoxes are the middle points of each season. This natural phenomenon is sometimes in contradiction with the dates on the solar calendar used by many—for example, Samhain on October 31 to November 1. First experiencing these seasonal starts and stops on dates different than we have become accustomed can feel premature, such as the first day of winter being Samhain instead of Yule; however, they make perfect sense, as nature starts and stops slowly.

The two solstices, midwinter and midsummer, and two equinoxes, mid-spring and mid-autumn, alternate every quarter and are usually thought of as being on the twenty-first of the appropriate month: December, March, June, or September. Actually though, the days vary between the twentieth and the twenty-third, causing the midpoint cross-quarter days to vary as well. This year, Samhain is exactly November 6 at 6:56 p.m. EST, halfway between Mabon on September 22, 2022, at 9:03 p.m. and Yule on December 21, 2022, at 4:48 p.m. Samhain begins at sundown on November 6 under an Aries Moon and will transition into Taurus at 12:15 a.m on November 7.

The fiery Aries "my way or the highway" energy will be present leading up to Samhain. A group of people blazing their own trail of preparations for Samhain might not work well, but if properly channeled, Samhain could be the most perfectly elaborate and impulsively quaint High-Holiday celebration in memory. The lunar energetic influences will begin to shift into Taurus, possibly earlier than 12:15 a.m. when the Moon is void-of-course beginning at 5:30 p.m.

The Taurus Moon brings emotional safety, stability, joy, physical affection, peace, and gentleness—all held together with stubbornness. The Aries Moon will get the party started; the Taurus Moon will soften the edges and bring happiness.

Pleiadean (Pleiades) Samhain

Many ancient cultures over many millennia tracked the Moon throughout its annual cycle, the Celts among them. Dark before light, winter before summer. The first day of the year and the first day of winter was Samhain and was celebrated on the first Full Moon of the year, which was sometimes also the last Full Moon of the previous year. The Full Moon that was considered to be the first Full Moon, and was sometimes also the thirteenth Full Moon like this year, came after the culmination of Pleiades, when Pleiades rested halfway across the night sky, straight up, at midnight—not 12:00 a.m., but actual midnight, halfway between sunset and sunrise. Actual midnight is generally closer to 1:00 a.m. or 1:30 a.m. Pleiades was considered a "calendar star," used to determine the beginning of the year and the first day of winter.

In very late winter, what we now refer to as spring, the appearance of Pleiades in the pre-dawn sky like a morning star foretold of the sea being once again safe to sail without the worry of winter storms. Pleiades also signaled the time to plant from seed and the coming of summer. Originally the ancients acknowledged only two seasons: winter, Samhain to Beltaine, and summer, Beltaine to Samhain. Applying this ancient dating method to this year, Samhain falls on the evening of November 6, actually the morning of November 7, at 12:15 a.m., and the Taurus Full Moon is eclipsed beginning early morning on November 8 at 3:02 a.m, peaking at 5:59 a.m.

Lunar Eclipse

The lunar eclipse on Samhain's Taurus Full Moon adds loads of energy to the new year. Abundance is forthcoming—abundance in a big way, and with great abundance comes the need for offering great gratitude and accepting great responsibility. Gratitude will be the mark left on the coming year. The responsibility to recognize the abundance received must be stubbornly observed. Stubbornness must be used for positive outcomes, especially of gratitude rather than indulgence, as the Taurus Moon is known to do.

Dark Moon

Leading up to the Dark Moon in Sagittarius on November 23 at 5:57 p.m., the Moon will be void-of-course in Scorpio beginning at 1:16 p.m. November 22 will be appropriate for a Dark Moon celebration. Scorpio will encourage the profound exploring of buried and hidden emotional issues. The Scorpio Moon specializes in the deep dive. If the Dark Moon rite happens on the twenty-third, the Moon will be in Sagittarius, and the rite may feel like a relief from the intense Scorpio Thanksgiving preparations.

Thanksgiving

Thanksgiving dinner should prove to be relaxed and social—a pleasant family holiday, which is not always the story with feasting holidays. The road to Thanksgiving may be paved with Scorpio Moon's hidden agendas, but once the Dark Moon and Thanksgiving arrive, the Sagittarius Moon will rule the tranquil preparations and relaxed celebration.

Full Moon

The second Full Moon of the year will be on December 7 at 11:08 p.m. in Gemini. Thanksgiving ended with the family, and Christmas is still to come. This Moon will help to feel the family dynamics: consider them, talk with friends about the issues, and make adjustments so Christmas doesn't repeat family turmoil that may have happened on Thanksgiving.

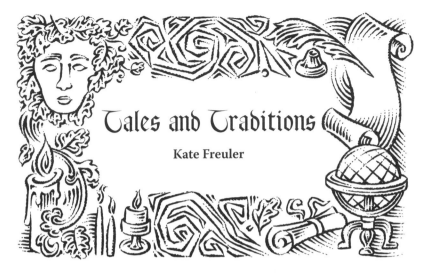

Tales and Traditions

Kate Freuler

FOR MANY OF US, Samhain is the night when we celebrate our ancestors and honor the dead. There are many well-known ways to do this, such as setting a place at the table for the deceased, building an altar to those who have passed, and dedicating October 31 and November 1 to communicating with them.

Along with these traditional things, some members of the magical community relish the modern-day joys of Halloween: trick or treating, ghost stories, and general spooky fun. One of the best parts of this holiday is, of course, the costumes, which give people an opportunity to get creative and transform themselves for the night.

While Halloween has undergone many changes over time, and you might see more superheroes and princesses traipsing about than monsters these days, there are a few classic costume choices that have consistently withstood generations. Most notably, vampires, werewolves, and witches. It's interesting how these figures never seem to go out of style and, at this point, are almost a traditional part of the season in their own right. They're consistently featured in movies, books, and comics, but they weren't always considered fodder for fiction. There was a time when people genuinely believed in their existence.

In searching for folklore about werewolves and vampires in an attempt to understand their staying power, I came across some unexpectedly disturbing historical information. These stories revealed that the truth is sometimes far scarier and ghoulish than fiction. In the spirit of scariness, here are two of the most unsettling.

The New England Vampire Panic

Most people know about the witch-hunting craze, and some have heard of the Satanic Panic of the '80s. But did you know there was a vampire panic in the eighteenth century? During this time, New England was plagued with tuberculosis, which at that time was called consumption. The misunderstood illness appeared to consume a person's life, spirit, and body until they wasted away. Consumption was highly contagious, especially within families. Due to the way that the illness appeared to suck the life out of a person, people mistook it for the work of vampires.

It was believed that when one family member died of tuberculosis, their body would leave the grave, return to their family, and feed upon them by sucking their blood and life force. When this happened, the victim became infected with the disease too, also becoming a vampire. Those who had lost people to the illness considered themselves at risk for vampirism and often had their relatives exhumed from the grave to ensure that they were, in fact, dead. The heart and organs would be examined for signs of fresh blood, the appearance of which meant they were not dead, but actively leaving the grave at night to feed upon the living.

To keep the rest of the family safe, the vampire needed to be destroyed by burning the deceased's heart to ashes. This not only stopped the vampire from feeding on others but created a cure for consumption. The ashes were made into a tincture said to heal the disease, and afflicted people would drink it in hopes of being cured.

As you can see, this tale is far more disturbing than our current image of sexy vampires, who are often characters in love stories.

The Werewolf of Bedburg

Another terrible tale of a true monster is that of Peter Stubbe, the werewolf of Bedburg. The story of this man-turned-wolf is as terrifying today as it was in 1589. In a small German farming community called Bedburg, there had been an alarming number of deaths among farm animals. These especially violent deaths appeared to be the work of wolves, which wasn't uncommon at that time. However, when human beings began getting murdered, the villagers were terrified and confounded. Rumors started circulating that these deaths were not from wolves at all, but a horrific half-man half-beast and that walking among them was a person who engaged with the community during the day and turned into a bloodthirsty wolf at night. There was no telling who it could be. Panic set in as the villagers realized the werewolf could be any of their neighbors or friends.

One day some townspeople set out, determined to catch the creature responsible for the horrors taking place. They hunted for days before finally coming upon a huge wolf. They gave chase but the wolf was fast and elusive, leading them deep into the woods. When they finally caught up to the monster in the thick underbrush, they discovered not a wolf at all, but a local man named Peter Stubbe. They dragged him back to town, where he was tortured into confessing. Stubbe said that at night he donned the pelt of a wolf (in some stories it is a belt or girdle), which gave him carnivorous hunger and supernatural strength. He admitted to committing the many violent, indescribable atrocities inflicted upon the village while in werewolf form, although it's unknown if this was sincere or because he feared being tortured. At the time, people believed the werewolf story, and he was executed.

In the end, while there was not truly a werewolf targeting the village, there *was* a monstrous human being who disguised himself as one, which is even worse.

What Really Makes a Monster?

Both of these stories are truly horrifying, but not in the way we might expect. They're not at all supernatural or paranormal like most monster stories, instead recounting very real circumstances that seem too awful to be genuine. They're scary because they're true.

Samhain isn't a frightening celebration for most Pagans. It's a night to honor the dead and welcome the dark months of the year. However, it's also a time to peer into the shadowy undertones of life and contemplate what we find there. Sometimes what we discover are monsters in the form of human conditions, such as fear, as in the vampire story, or unfathomable cruelty, as with Peter Stubbe.

Dressing up as monsters on Halloween was once meant to frighten away unwanted spirits and to protect against evil. When learning about historical horrors like these, it's no wonder vampires and werewolves are popular considering the fears they once represented.

Whatever you choose to dress up as this year, give it some thought. Why are you choosing that particular character, monster, or creature? Does it represent something to you that you're secretly afraid of? You might be surprised by what you learn about yourself.

References

Klein, Christopher. "The Last American Vampire." History. November 25, 2018. https://www.history.com/news/the-last-american-vampire.

Wagner, Stephen. "The Werewolf of Bedburg: The True Story of a Monster That Terrorized a German Village." LiveAbout. Updated July 15, 2018. https://www.liveabout.com/the-werewolf-of-bedburg-2597445.

Feasts and Treats

Gwion Raven

IT SEEMS THAT SAMHAIN lasts much longer than just one day. It's really a whole season from just after the Autumn Equinox right up through the beginning of Yule. Our thoughts turn to long, dark nights and the cold, bleak days of the oncoming winter.

All these recipes come from my family, handed down from grandparents, aunts, and uncles. When we come together and share food, we honour those who have come before us, taught us, nurtured us, challenged us, frustrated us, annoyed us, and loved us. When we tell their stories and say their names, we keep their memories alive. We see ourselves in them and, if we're very lucky, we will learn from their wisdom and from their mistakes.

It's time to nourish our bodies and our souls and tell stories of our ancestors.

Simple Roasted Chicken (GF)

A perennial favourite with just four ingredients. The smell of a chicken roasting makes the whole house seem more inviting. Trussing the chicken, tying the legs and wings close to the breasts, makes for a more even cook, but it's not 100 percent necessary. I recommend using a meat thermometer just to be sure. You'll want the chicken's internal temperature to be 165°F.

Prep time: 10 minutes
Cooking time: 1 hour 10 minutes
Servings: 4

1 3-pound whole chicken
1 tablespoon salt
1 handful fresh parsley
4 sprigs fresh thyme

Preheat the oven to 450°F. Remove the giblets from inside the chicken. Rinse thoroughly inside and out. Pat dry with paper towels. Season the cavity with half the salt. Put the parsley inside the chicken. This is when you'll want to truss the chicken if you're going to.

Season the outside of the chicken with the remaining salt. Salt makes the skin crispy.

Place the chicken in a roasting pan and cook for 1 hour or until the internal temperature reaches 165°F. Take the chicken out of the oven. Using heat-resistant mitts, tilt the pan so the juices run to one end. Add the thyme sprigs to the juices and baste the chicken. You can use a baster or a spoon. Remove the chicken from the pan and put it on a cutting board to rest for 10 minutes.

When you're ready to serve, remove the twine (if you trussed the bird). Carve the chicken at the table or remove the legs, cutting into drumsticks and thighs. Cut away the wings. Slicing right down the middle, carefully remove each breast and arrange all the bits on a platter. After the meal, consider making chicken stock with the bones, skin, and carcass.

Serve with Oven-Roasted Potatoes and Maple-Glazed Carrots or your favourite veggies.

Oven-Roasted Potatoes (GF)

I have distinct memories of my grandmothers standing at their kitchen counter, wearing pinnies, and wielding sharp little knives. I can still hear the plopping sounds of quartered potatoes hitting the water in a big pot.

Potatoes. What's not to like? Diced and roasted, this recipe highlights the potato at its finest. Deep golden brown and salty, they're an incredible complement to almost any dish. And, let's be honest, they are kind of great just by themselves!

Prep time: 15 minutes

Cooking time: 60 minutes

Servings: 4

6 Yukon Gold potatoes, peeled and quartered

1½ tablespoons salt

4 tablespoons beef tallow (bacon fat, goose fat, duck fat, or vegetable oil all work too)

Preheat oven to 400°F. Peel and quarter the potatoes. Grab a big saucepan, fill ¾ of the way with water, add potatoes and 1 tablespoon salt. Bring to a boil, then simmer for 5 more minutes. Drain the potatoes with a colander and shake them up a bit to rough up the edges of the potatoes. Set aside for 2 minutes.

If you're not familiar with cooking fats, I highly recommend duck fat for this recipe. The taste is simply sublime. Scoop the fat, whichever fat you're using, onto a rimmed baking pan large enough to accommodate all the potatoes without crowding them. Put the pan into the hot oven for 3 minutes. Carefully remove the hot pan and add the potatoes and remaining salt. Pop the pan back in the oven for 40 minutes. At 20 minutes, baste the potatoes. Once golden brown, remove to a plate lined with paper towels.

Serve in a large bowl with salt and pepper to taste.

Maple-Glazed Carrots (GF)

Pumpkins get all the glory at Samhaintide, but the lowly carrot is such an incredibly versatile vegetable. And it's orange too! Maple syrup enhances the natural sweetness in carrots. Whole carrots chopped up or baby carrots work equally as well.

Prep time: 15 minutes
Cooking time: 60 minutes
Servings: 4

2 pounds carrots, scrubbed and cut into 1-inch chunks
¼ cup light brown sugar
⅓ cup maple syrup (pure maple syrup is best)
6 tablespoons unsalted butter

Preheat oven to 400°F. Get a rimmed baking pan and cover it with two layers of aluminium foil. In a large bowl, add the carrots, sugar, and syrup. Mix with a spoon so everything is evenly coated. Spread the carrots out on the baking pan. Dot the carrots with butter and pop them in the oven for 60 minutes. After 20 minutes, shake the pan and turn the carrots over. After another 20 minutes, shake the pan again.

To serve, remove the carrots to a large bowl or platter with a slotted spoon. Then pour over any pan juices (which is lava-hot syrup and butter). Add a pinch of salt and pepper to taste and dig in! They're better than candy corn!

Bread and Butter Pudding (Vegetarian)

This is my great-grandmother's recipe. I only know her as Nanny Pink, but I was lucky enough to meet her a handful of times. She lived in a farmhouse in Kent, England. I remember three things about her: She was scared of the telephone and refused to use it. She had two teeth. And she made bread and butter pudding every Sunday with leftover bread.

Bread pudding, made with whiskey and cream and leftover bread, is extremely easy to make and even easier to eat. Trust me. You'll have seconds or thirds or forget to tell anyone you made it and eat it all!

Prep time: 10 minutes
Cooking time: 45 minutes
Servings: 6

Bread Pudding

2 cups milk
¼ cup butter
2 eggs
2 tablespoons of vanilla extract
½ cup sugar
1 teaspoon cinnamon
1 teaspoon nutmeg
¼ teaspoon salt
6 cups bread, torn into rough cubes
½ cup raisins

Whiskey Sauce

½ cup butter
¼ cup granulated sugar
½ cup heavy cream
¼ cup whiskey

Preheat your oven to 350°F. Pour the milk into a large saucepan over medium heat. Add the butter and stir until the butter is melted. You want the milk to be hot, but don't let it boil. In a separate bowl, mix the eggs, vanilla extract, sugar, cinnamon, nutmeg, and salt. Tear the bread into rough cubes and place it in a lightly greased 9 × 13-inch pan. A quick note about the bread: I'll pretty much use any bread for my bread pudding. My preference is brioche, but French bread is great, and so is plain ol' sliced bread.

Sprinkle the raisins over the bread, then pour the milk mixture over the bread, making sure to soak all the bread. Pop the pan in the oven for approximately 45 minutes. You'll know your bread pudding is done when you can insert a knife in the middle of the bread pudding and pull it out clean. Just before the bread pudding is done, combine the butter, sugar, cream, and whiskey in a saucepan over low heat. Keep stirring until the sauce is just boiling. Pour it over the bread pudding and serve.

This is a dense, sumptuous dessert, so I recommend eating smaller portions… Who am I kidding? Sometimes my bread pudding never makes it out of the pan and into a dish. Enjoy it however it makes you feel good!

Crafty Crafts

Ivo Dominguez Jr.

WHEN I BEGIN TO feel Samhain in the air, usually around the middle of October, my thoughts turn to those who have departed to the world beyond this one. Although I know the beloved dead can be present at any time of the year, there are times when it is easier to experience their presence. The breeze carries whispers from my relatives by blood or marriage and my spiritual relatives that are from my families of choice. Samhain is about all who have died who are meaningful to you, not just those in your family tree.

Communication is more satisfying when you can speak as well as listen. This craft project gives you a way to send messages to the dead that carry your feelings and your thoughts more clearly.

Illuminated Letters to the Dead

There are many rituals where brief notes to the dead are written on slips of paper, which are then offered to a fire to deliver the messages. This craft project expands upon that ritual practice with inspiration from collage, mixed media art, and illuminated manuscripts. The first step is to decide what you want to do with the finished product. Will you be using it on an ancestor altar? Will you hang it on a wall as a lasting declaration to one of your dead? Is this letter meant as an offering that you will burn or bury? Is this an individual project or a family effort? There are many more possibilities, so make sure you take time to brainstorm and decide on what you want to create.

Materials

Paper, whatever you like
Colored pencils or other media
Adhesives, glue or strings and such
Miscellaneous trinkets and mementoes
Optional: picture frame

> *Cost:* $0–$20
> *Time spent:* 2 hours, plus drying time

Design Ideas

First, pick the paper that you will use. This can be copy paper, parchment, color paper, handmade paper, newsprint, or whatever feels right to you. The type of paper you choose will have an impact on whether you can frame it, roll it like a scroll, burn it easily, and so on. Do you want a rectangle or square, or do you have a shape in mind that is meaningful and becomes part of the message? Do you want the edges of the paper to have clean, straight lines, or do you want to scallop it, cut a softly curving line, or tear it gently to give it a ragged edge?

Second, think about people, places, and things that you associate with the person you've chosen for your message. These images can be almost anything, but they need to have a strong emotional link to the target of the letter. I like to create a border or images around the edge of the paper. If you like to draw and trust your ability, then consider illustrating the border by hand with colored pencils or whatever media you prefer. Another option is to copy family photos, postcards, etc. to make a glued collage of cut-out images along the border. In addition to images, you can also use single words, phrases, song lyrics, and so on for the border. When I create

one of these, it is a mix of inspiration from illuminated manuscripts, tarot cards, vision boards, scrapbooks, and magick scrolls.

Third, select and collect materials that have a special link to the person you will be sending this spiritual letter. For example, if there was a beverage they loved in life, you may wish to dip a cotton swab or small brush in it and paint your paper with dots or flourishes, or dab it for an aged and mottled look. Perhaps there is a fragrance they loved that you could add a few drops of at the corners of the paper. Plan on enough time for the paper to be fully dry before constructing the letter.

Are there any objects that you want to include? Maybe you have some dried flowers, a swatch of cloth, a pinch of soil from their garden in a vial, some costume jewelry, or something else that belonged to them or reminds you of them. These could be glued, tied, stitched, or affixed in some way to the paper or the frame if you are using one.

Fourth, compose what you want to say to them. You can mix prose with poetry and change up your tone and mix your metaphors. The only real rule and guideline is to be fully yourself and speak your truth to them. Once you've written and polished your message, then you can place it on the paper you've selected. You may wish to write your message by hand if that makes it feel more personal. (Don't worry about your handwriting, as the spirits can read it.) You may wish to print it out so you can use fancy fonts that fit the style of the whole piece.

Assembling the Letter

This is a spiritual and magickal act, so take a moment to breathe and prepare yourself to assemble the letter. If you like, you may burn incense, listen to music your beloved dead liked, etc. to set the mood. Collect all the pieces and lay them out loose and dry atop the paper so you can move them and rearrange the pieces until it looks and feels right. Consider taking a picture with your phone to have a guide when you start gluing things down. What you use to glue or attach the pieces will vary according to your choices. I find that a glue stick, white glue, or rubber cement works for most things. If you are familiar with decoupage or other techniques, you may use them.

Once everything is affixed to the letter and dry, you have one more opportunity to embellish your work. Bring out your colored pencils, pastels, markers, watercolors, or other art supplies, and let your instinct guide you in adding details, highlights, and pops of color to your letter.

Putting the Letter to Work

Before you put the letter in its intended location, read the letter out loud if you can or silently if you must. Then take a breath and blow on the letter three times. Be assured that the message will be received by the spirit. It is time to put the letter on your altar, hang it on the wall, roll it up to offer to the earth or a fire, and so on.

Reference

Ellwood, Taylor. *The Magic of Writing: How to Use Writing and Practical Magic to Get Consistent Results.* Portland, OR: Independently published, 2020.

Color Magic

Charlie Rainbow Wolf

IN MY TRADITION, SAMHAIN marks both the end of the old year and the beginning of the new one. It's marked on the calendar as the modern-day Halloween festival. Here at The Keep—our name for our little smallholding—we celebrate Samhain over three days: All Hallows' Eve on the thirty-first of October, All Saints' Day on the first of November, and All Souls' Day on the second of November. The deities associated with Samhain are those which deal with the underworld, such as Persephone and Cernunnos.

Samhain is the festival where many believe the space between our reality and those of other dimensions is the thinnest, making those other realms more easily accessible. The colors of Samhain reflect the autumnal colors in many ways with the pumpkin orange and the muted greens, but black and white also feature. To an artist, black is the blending of all colors, while white is the perceived absence of color.

The Colors of Samhain

Many of the traditions associated with Samhain reflect the colors of the festival. For example, the specters from other realities are often depicted as white ghosts. I see this as being twofold: for one, white is the absence of color, and two, spirit has no form or shape. White is also seen by many as the color of purity, depicting the departed ancestors as having transcended into the afterlife in a pure and unsullied way. Another side of white is something that is sterile, void, or a blank canvas waiting for something to fill it. It's usually associated with good things, things that are helpful or benign—things that are soothing. All of these meanings—and more—might be applied to various aspects of the Samhain season.

Another popular Halloween color is black. Black cats, black witches' costumes, black cauldrons, and more fill the seasonal decor aisles of the department stores and online shops. Black is often seen as the opposite of white; where white is perceived to be light and good, black is sometimes thought to be dark and mysterious, or even evil. It's a strong and intimidating color, one that often brings uneasiness or apprehension. Many folks are fearful—or at least wary—of what cannot be seen, and black tends to keep things secretive or hidden. Black is enigmatic, it is seductive, and it often surrounds sadness and distress, such as when people are in mourning. Others see it as a color of integrity and a rite of passage. It's the powerful, secretive, and seductive side of black that draws it deep into Samhain traditions.

More modern colors associated with this time of year are orange, purple, and green. Orange is possibly the more familiar, because it is the color of many of the ripening harvest fruits: pumpkins, persimmons, squash, some types of apple, and others. It's the color associated with the sacral chakra, with wants and desires; how life unfolds is very much associated with the connection to this energy center.

Orange is associated with warmth, ambience, and concern for others. It's a blend of red and yellow and is reflected in the glow of the Samhain flames and the Bonfire Night blazes. Just as Samhain is a bridge between this world and other realms, and between the old year and the new, orange is also a bridge between the past and the future. It keeps a strong foothold in the here and now, yet it pays homage to what is past and peeks into what is yet to come. I see this as another aspect of the harvest fruits: their seeds were sown in the past, they can be enjoyed now, but they can also be preserved to be savored in the coming winter.

Purple and green are more perplexing to me. I don't necessarily associate them with Samhain, yet the shops are full of Halloween decorations of these colors. I see Frankenstein's monster with green skin wearing purple and black clothing. I see lime green and "black" (which glows a shade of purple) fairy lights adorning the aisles. Purple—or, more accurately, violet—is associated with spirituality and the crown when it comes to chakra colors, though, so it could be incorporated into Samhain rituals with that in mind.

Green is a conundrum because I associate green with spring festivals, not autumnal ones. Granted, the green that is hawked in the shops around Samhain is rather a dull or more muted green than I see in the vernal season, but I cannot get my head around the fact that it's *still* green! I suppose it is the color of some pumpkin stalks, and it is the witch in *The Wizard of Oz*—which sticks in my mind because as a child I was fascinated that parts of it were in color and parts of it were still in black and white.

More recently, a shade of green is apparent in the Teal Pumpkin Project. This venture began in 2012 as a way of letting those who were out trick-or-treating know that the household was giving out nonfood treats so that children with allergies might partake in nonfood goodies such as glow sticks or simple toys. It's a good idea, and teal "pumpkins" are quite popular in fall decor.

Celebrating Samhain

One of my favorite ways to bring color into Samhain is with candles. Candle magic has many uses, and it seems even more appropriate at this time of year as the seasons march toward the longest night. My beloved medicine elder was convinced that the ancestral spirits were drawn to flame, and used firelight and candles regularly in ceremony.

At The Keep, we mark this time of year with a three-day vigil: All Hallows' Eve, All Saints' Day, and All Souls' Day. I have a black candle burning on the thirty-first of October, representing the end of the year. I have a white candle burning on the first of November, representing the dawn of the new year. On the second of November, I burn an orange candle for warmth and light as we head into winter and the shortest days of the year.

When it comes to stones for Samhain, my go-to stone is quartz, which comes in clear and milky varieties (as well as others). I have a large crystal point, which I use for divination, and it seems particularly appropriate for this time of year. According to Katrina Raphaell, it is both an Isis crystal and a phantom, and it does seem to help with deep meditations (Raphaell, 1989, 153; Raphaell, 1991, 75). Samhain is traditionally a time of scrying and divining, of contacting the other realms, and any clear stone can be used as a scrying stone.

Using these colors for Samhain is easy because there are so many choices, and they are readily available everywhere. Stay traditional or go wild! There's no hard-and-fast rule when it comes to what color says Samhain to you.

Reference

"Teal Pumpkin Project." Food Allergy & Research Education. Accessed July 27, 2021. https://www.foodallergy.org/our -initiatives/awareness-campaigns/living-teal/teal-pumpkin -project.

Raphaell, Katrina. *Crystal Enlightenment: The Transforming Properties of Crystals and Healing Stones.* Crystal Trilogy, vol. 1. New York: Aurora Press, 1991.

———. *The Crystalline Transmission: A Synthesis of Light.* Illustrated ed. Crystal Trilogy, vol. 3. Santa Fe, NM: Aurora Press, 1989.

Samhain Ritual

Elizabeth Barrette

THIS RITUAL HONORS the power of entropy through the detritus food web, which turns bothersome garbage into valuable compost. So, too, negative energy can be poured into a compost pile, which will recycle it into positive energy through the same natural process of decay.

Honoring Compost

The ritual is modular so that you can perform it alone or with a coven, indoors or outdoors. If you have multiple participants, you can give each person a complete copy or just their lines.

Materials
Copy of the ritual text
Altar table
Dark altar cloth
Vase of dead flowers
Bowl of finished compost
Chthonic incense (kyphi, myrrh, or patchouli)
Incense burner
Lighter or matches

Moldy-green candle for Phthisis
Brown candle for Sterquilinus
Black candle for Tlazolteotl
Light-blue candle for Shiva
Candleholders for the four candles
Garden tool for casting circle
Paper and pencil
Compost, or representation of compost
Dirt cakes and ale

For this ritual, you need a small altar table. If you don't have a dedicated altar, then a card table or end table will do fine. Choose a dark altar cloth for this ritual. It can be plain, or you can look for one with Samhain imagery such as skeletons, spiderwebs, or mushrooms printed on it.

Set up the altar with a dark cloth, a vase of dead flowers, a bowl of finished compost, chthonic incense, an incense burner, and a lighter. Place the four candles at the corners.

Circlecasting

Chthonic incense like kyphi, myrrh, or patchouli is associated with earth and the underworld. Light it and say, "The spark of life unites spirit and flesh. As it burns out, the spirit rises up like smoke while the flesh falls down like ash."

Carry a pitchfork or other garden tool with its business end down. As you walk, say, "Iron and wood come from the earth and work the earth, pushing the compost into the soil. Let nothing from above, below, or beyond cross this circle."

Light the moldy-green candle, then say,

Phthisis, goddess of rot, join this ritual.
All that lives must someday waste away,
Fall and die, rot into soil once more.
Everything your withered hand touches
Is yours to claim and turn to earth.
Hail and well met!

Light the brown candle, then say,

Sterquilinus, god of manure, join this ritual.
All that lives must eat and excrete.
Yours is the fertilizer that makes
The earth fecund, from which
Humble beginning comes all food.
Hail and well met!

Light the black candle, then say,

Tlazolteotl, goddess of compost, join this ritual.
All that lives sometimes suffers from impurities
And must be cleansed of the contamination.
You eat the black dirt and swallow the sins,
Passing them forth as clean earth again.
Hail and well met!

Light the light-blue candle, then say,

Shiva, god of destruction, join this ritual.
All that lives must be destroyed in time
To make way for new life yet to come.
You dance the death of the world and
Turn the Wheel of Time with your feet.
Hail and well met!

Statement of Intent: Lift the bowl of compost in one hand and the vase of dead flowers in the other. Then say,

Tonight is Samhain, the holiday of death and decay. Everything alive comes from the earth, dies and decays, returns to the earth that it may bring forth new life. Entropy is the power that unmakes so that fresh things can be made. Rot is the process by which garbage and manure become humus to enrich the earth. In the same way, they take in bad energy and turn it good again. Tonight we honor the forces of decay, without which we would drown in our own filth.

We worship the deities of death and decay: Phthisis, goddess of rot; Sterquilinus, god of manure; Tlazolteotl, goddess of compost; Shiva, god of destruction. We revere the creatures of the detritus food web: the two-lived amphibians, the creepy crawlers who eat of the dead, the little wrigglers who live in slime, the fungi and their kin who bind the web with their fibers. We give honor to all those who work unseen and unappreciated in darkness and in dirt, that the world may be reborn in the new year. So mote it be!

Return the bowl and the vase to their places on the altar.

For this ritual, you need a representation of compost. If you are working outside, a compost pile or composting bin is ideal. If you are working inside, you have several options. You can fill a clear glass jar with finished compost. You can make a compost jar by putting a layer of wood chips or twigs, then soil or compost, then a "green" material like vegetable scraps or grass clippings, then a "brown" material like leaves or sawdust. Continue alternating the layers as needed to fill the jar, ending with soil or compost. Another option is to use a large, disposable picture of a compost pile.

Hold one hand over this representation of compost and reach the other to each colored candle in turn as you recite the blessings for each deity.

Phthisis, goddess of rot, bless this compost.
Let it seethe and thrive with the beings of decay,
Breaking down organic matter into clean humus,
So good things can grow from it. So mote it be!

Sterquilinus, god of manure, bless this compost.
May it embrace the leavings of cows and sheep,
Horses and rabbits and hens. Let waste become
Fertilizer through your magic. So mote it be!

Tlazolteotl, goddess of compost, bless this compost.
Send the creepy crawlers and all your worm children

To devour the garbage and swallow the dirt, leaving
Their rich castings behind. So mote it be!

Shiva, god of destruction, bless this compost.
Destroy what was, tear it apart, and make way
For new things to emerge from the ruins of the old,
As the lotus rises from the muck. So mote it be!

On the paper, write things you want to banish. Say, "I give these problems to the power of entropy, that they may rot away and be-gone!" Place a pinch of compost on the paper. Fold the paper so it stays closed. Bury it in the compost pile or jar. If you're using a picture of compost, set the paper on the picture and fold the image around the paper.

Speak about your feelings for compost. Nobody likes doing a thankless job, so give thanks to the deities and creatures who do this important work in the world.

Raise power with dancing, music, and singing. If you are outside with a compost pile or composting bin, dance around or beside it. If you are inside, dance around or beside your altar table. Play drums or other musical instruments. If possible, choose instruments up-cycled from discarded items or things otherwise associated with refuse. (Our coven has a bunch of drums made from PVC pipe and clear packing tape.) Here is a song to sing while you dance:

Come, coffee grounds and veggie peels,
Bad memories and nasty feels.
Bring all the dead things, large and small,
To rot away in compost's thrall.

Decay, decay, and go away!
Let life spring forth another day!

Bring stable sweepings from the barn
And wool too bad to spin in yarn.
Manure brown and also green
Will turn to compost, still unseen.

> *Decay, decay, and go away!*
> *Let life spring forth another day!*
>
> *Destroy the things left past their prime*
> *And wash them down the river Time.*
> *Come dance the rubble down to dust*
> *And place in Entropy your trust.*
>
> *Decay, decay, and go away!*
> *Let life spring forth another day!*

When you finish the song and dance, hold your hands over the compost to direct the energy there. Stomp your feet to make sure that you are well grounded again.

Dirt Cakes and Ale

Dirt cake is chocolate cake crumbled to look like dirt, with gummyworms in it. Say, "Eat of the rich earth." The ale can be any fermented beverage like beer, kombucha, or yogurt drink. Say, "Drink from the cup of transformation." Leave some of each to add to your compost.

Closing

Release each of the deities invoked for this ritual.

Put out the light-blue candle, then say,

> *Shiva, god of destruction, thank you*
> *For joining this ritual. We honor your work*
> *In bringing death that new life may rise.*
> *Stay if you will, go if you must.*
> *Hail and farewell!*

Put out the black candle, then say,

> *Tlazolteotl, goddess of compost, thank you*
> *For joining this ritual. We honor your work in*
> *Consuming impurities and making them clean.*

Stay if you will, go if you must.
Hail and farewell!

Put out the brown candle, then say,

Sterquilinus, god of manure, thank you
For joining this ritual. We honor your work
In turning manure into good fertilizer.
Stay if you will, go if you must.
Hail and farewell!

Put out the moldy-green candle, then say,

Phthisis, goddess of rot, thank you
For joining this ritual. We honor your work
In ensuring that the refuse decays.
Stay if you will, go if you must.
Hail and farewell!

Release the circle by carrying the garden tool business end up, widdershins (counterclockwise), saying, "The earth is one, and all may now cross at will."

End with, "The circle is open but unbroken. Merry meet, merry part, and merry meet again!"

Notes

Notes

Notes

Yule

Your Whole Self and the Magic of Krampus

Melissa Tipton

My first Krampus encounter came courtesy of my fascination with weird vintage postcards. I was scrolling through Christmas cards from the late 1800s, lingering on particularly strange ones, like a demonic clown slicing into a pie, casting the viewer a leering smirk (so cheery!) and a mouse riding a lobster (where to even begin with that one?), when I came upon Krampus stuffing an unfortunate child into a sack, his red tongue curled like a snake. What I didn't know at the time was that Krampus would become a welcome Yuletide figure in my practice, one who urges me to let go of unhealthy tethers to the past and integrate my inner "demons." But who is Krampus, and what's with the antagonistic relationship to kids? To begin our explorations, we need to look at another festive figure: good ol' St. Nick, because Krampus is usually depicted as Nick's unruly sidekick.

History

Nicholas was a bishop living during the time of the Roman Empire, but his legend swells far beyond the scant historical record. Among his many good deeds, he was said to have rescued three sisters from sex work, which their father planned to force them into to save his finances. St. Nick threw sacks of gold coins through the father's window during the night, solving his money woes and freeing the sisters from his scheme. In another story, a greedy innkeeper and his wife murdered a group of schoolboys who were overnighting in the inn. They hid the bodies in barrels, but St. Nick came to the rescue and brought the boys back to life. You can find illustrations of St. Nick with three boys in a pickling tub, depicting this reanimated miracle. Perhaps here is where we see the beginnings of St. Nick as the patron saint of children and the giver of gifts.

Krampus's origins are even more heavily shrouded by the mists of time. We know that he originated in the Alpine region of Germany and Austria, but local variations prevent a clear-cut tracing of his lineage. Even his name is tricky to pin down, with Kramperl being the usual title in the Bavarian foothills and Salzburg, Klaubauf in East Tyrol, or Tuifl or Toifi ("devil") in other regions. It wasn't until the introduction of holiday cards in the late nineteenth and early twentieth centuries that the name "Krampus" gained wide usage.

His connection to St. Nick stems most likely from the saint's "dark companions" known in a number of traditions, such as Knecht Ruprecht ("Servant Ruprecht") or Zwarte Piet ("Black Peter"), both of whom accompanied St. Nick on his gift-giving rounds, punishing naughty children or handing parents a switch to carry out the discipline themselves. Interestingly, these companions didn't necessarily look like what we associate with Krampus now—cloven hooves, lascivious tongue, and goat horns. They were often quite human-looking, wearing a dark cloak or, more controversially, blackface. In predominantly Catholic lands, Krampus became associated with the devil, the imagery of which, in turn, has been heavily influenced by the Pagan god Pan. And then, shortly after the advent of postcard delivery in Austria in the late 1800s, the first Krampuskarten (Krampus cards) appeared, solidifying the hairy, hooved, and red-tongued imagery we associate with him today.

Krampus and the Shadow

We could view Krampus's role simplistically: he carries out St. Nick's dirty work, punishing misbehaving children with a switch or, worse, stuffing them into a sack and either eating them or dumping them in a fiery hell pit. On the surface, this seems like a clear-cut morality tale: Be good, kids! But for the modern witch, is there more to the story? In working with Krampus myself, I've found another angle, that of identifying my own "misbehaving children," i.e., inner parts that are clinging to a less mature state of being, resistant to learning new skills, operating under an outdated self-image, or remaining loyal to relationship patterns that simply don't work anymore. And as opposed to whipping those parts into shape or obliterating them, Krampus has inspired me to offer those less-developed parts to my internal fire of transformation, which ushers in change and growth.

The first step in this process is recognizing that we all have a shadow side—that we contain aspects of both St. Nick and Krampus, but the latter is often shoved into the unconscious through self-judgment, social pressure, and striving for perfection. When this shadow side remains unrecognized and unintegrated, it can cause chaos in our inner system, which then manifests as unwanted external circumstances, but when we learn how to bring these undervalued aspects of self into consciousness, what was once harmfully destructive instead helps us dissolve what no longer serves our evolution.

Let's look more closely at the concept of the shadow, because the duality of light and dark is vital in magic, especially at a time like Yule when we're poised at the brink of the longest night, ready to shift into increasing light. During these transition times, the liminal aspects of our psyche are more accessible, meaning that it's easier to draw unconscious contents into our awareness, so we'll be using this to our advantage in the Yule ritual to follow. The psychological shadow is a component of your personal unconscious. It contains energies and psychic contents (images, thoughts, aspects of the self, etc.) that have been deemed incompatible with your ego. We might view the ego and shadow as two sides of the same coin, much like St. Nick and Krampus. And just as Krampus has been cast mythologically as the "bad one," the ego assigns badness to the shadow.

Qualities end up in the shadow usually for one of two reasons: either we can't imagine expressing these qualities because they don't align with our chosen self-image (e.g., "I can't say no when people ask for help because I'm a giving person!") or because when we did express them, other people reacted negatively (e.g., Dad shamed you when you praised your own accomplishments, so now you keep that stuff to yourself). Often, it's a bit of both, because people's negative reactions to something will shape our belief that if we want to see ourselves as good, then this "bad" quality can't possibly be a part of who we are.

Because the shadow has been rejected by the ego and is now unconscious, you aren't aware that its contents belong to you. Instead, they make themselves visible through your dreams and something called "projection." Projection is an automatic process that happens within all of us, and it's not something we do intentionally. Projection occurs when we perceive something rightfully belonging to our own unconscious as existing in someone else instead. Let's look at a simple example: You meet someone new, and they seem incredibly charming and fascinating—you just can't get enough! Everything they say is dashingly clever, and you feel more charming when you're around them. While this person might actually be charming, to some extent, the flames of your fascination are likely fanned even higher by projection. This person demonstrates qualities that match up with your shadow content, qualities that aren't being allowed expression in your own life.

On an unconscious level, you're yearning to embody these qualities, but the ego won't allow it (remember, the ego has rejected whatever is in our shadow—that's how it got there in the first place). And now, those qualities are being projected onto the other person, making them seem especially charming and interesting. This same process happens with undesirable shadow qualities too. While in the previous example you projected qualities that you want to embody but that feel unattainable according to the ego, you can also project qualities that you can't stand to see in yourself. For instance, we might refuse to acknowledge that we're even a little bit selfish, but then we mysteriously find ourselves in relationships with a bunch of selfish people.

To continue this example, projection sets up a wonky dynamic, not only by upping the chances that we'll perceive other people as being selfish, but we're also more likely to attract people who actually are behaving selfishly. That's the thing with unconscious contents: they possess a certain magnetic quality, drawing us toward things that share their resonance and, in turn, drawing those things toward us. Why? Well, it's not simply to drive us nuts, much as it might appear at first glance. In truth, projection and the ability of the unconscious to pull matching energies into our sphere is the psyche's attempt to remind us of our wholeness. Remember, the ego believes those qualities don't belong to us, but in reality, they're very much a part of who we are. As long as they remain unconscious, we'll always have a nagging sense that something's missing, in addition to falling prey to the pitfalls of projection we've just outlined: misperceiving others and drawing unwanted circumstances into our life. But when we learn how to recognize what we've projected onto someone else, we can call back those misplaced qualities, and our sense of self and wholeness expands. In this way, our projections serve as a mirror of what within us is seeking expression.

How do we do this? We're going to approach it in two simple parts: The first is doing a gentle self-inventory when you notice yourself experiencing a strong emotional reaction, positive or negative, to a person or situation. These reactions frequently point to projections in action. And the second is a ritual in which you'll call on Krampus to help you retrieve those projected energies and transform them into self-awareness.

A Self-Inventory to Remember Your Wholeness

Grab your magical journal or a piece of paper. For the next week, keep a log of things that trigger heightened emotions. Remember, these can feel pleasant, such as discovering someone inspiring on social media and being flooded with awe and the desire to absorb everything they have on offer, or unpleasant, such as feeling like your coworker is trying to undermine you in front of your boss again and spinning out mental stories of what a turd they are. Capture the following in your log:

- Brief description of the situation
- How you felt
- Why you think the other person or people behaved the way they did (if applicable)

For the latter, don't worry about whether or not you're correct; for now, simply capture what you think their motivation was. At the end of the week, spend some time going over your notes, noticing if there are any common themes in how you felt or the stories you've attributed to other people's actions, such as frustration attached to "If I don't do things myself, they won't get done" or resentment around "My coworker always wants to hog all the credit." During the ritual, you'll be opening to alternatives beyond the ego's favorite narratives, and something that I've found helpful in softening my ego's resistance is exploring a common misunderstanding around projections: the fear that, when you call them back, you'll be confronted with the uncomfortable realization that other people are actually blameless angels and the problem is all in your head. Not so! For instance, if you feel like your friend tends to dominate conversations with her issues, always needing support but rarely offering any in return, it's unlikely that, after calling back your projections, you'll suddenly see that she's consistently supportive and you're simply being too sensitive.

And the reason for this is that we don't project qualities onto just anyone. Remember when I explained how unconscious contents magnetize similar energies into your life? Well, the unconscious is very skilled at scanning your surroundings, picking up on subtle cues to assess what does and doesn't match, and when it finds a resonance, this becomes a likely target for your projections.

In other words, while projections do inflate and distort what we're seeing, rarely are they entirely off base, because our unconscious predisposes us to project qualities onto people who are, to some degree, expressing those very qualities. So while you might be seeing your friend in exaggerated terms due to your projection, it's also quite possible that there truly is an imbalance in the friendship dynamic.

Reference

Ridenour, Al. *The Krampus and the Old, Dark Christmas: Roots and Rebirth of the Folkloric Devil.* Port Townsend, WA: Feral House, 2016.

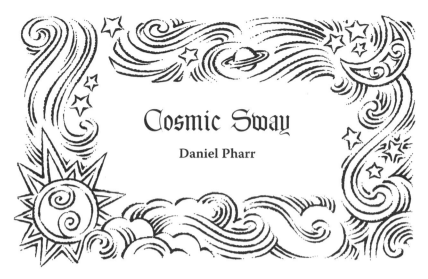

Cosmic Sway

Daniel Pharr

THE YULE RITE CAN begin at sundown on December 20, but the moment of Yule will be December 21 at 4:48 p.m. Considering the sun will set about 5:34 p.m., a night celebration on the twenty-first would be appropriate. Yule is the winter solstice, also known as midwinter, halfway between Samhain, which is the start of winter, and Imbolc, the end of winter.

Scorpio cradles the Moon until 2:12 a.m. on December 21, when it enters Sagittarius, but will be void-of-course starting on December 20 at 9:45 p.m. The Scorpio Moon will also square Saturn. This astrological arrangement foretells of the Moon asking for deep dives into and the exposing of emotional turmoil. Saturn's energy will be merciless in the pursuit of meaning and in teaching the stringent lessons of truth brought into focus through emotional pain.

A better option might be to hold a late-night celebration beginning after the Moon enters Sagittarius. A fun, enthusiastically relaxed, well-attended celebration can be expected. Spontaneity will be important to keep the energy moving. Light a balefire or any fire; dance around it. Wishes for the year are energized by tossing written desires into the flames with a good helping of positive intentions, especially intentions spoken aloud to witnesses.

Vocalizing an intention, or any thought for that matter—be it a spell, a curse, a helping phrase, a promise, or a dire warning— transforms what was an image in the mind into a sound in the world, a sound that travels on waves and impacts bodies and eardrums and objects of all types. Verbalizing thought forms breathes life into them. Vibration manifests in all sorts of ways. Think of a singer's voice shattering a wine glass or soothing a baby to sleep. Things said can have a powerful influence on the globe and the people on it. Magical workers learn to discipline their thoughts and speech. They reserve their words and focus their thoughts, knowing things said or thought create reality. If a terrible thought arises, like crashing a car, falling off a ladder, or any negative omen, immediately say, "No, it won't happen," aloud. The word is stronger than the image. Take care in this Moon. Scorpio will be trying to bring up painful memories, and in times of stress, words of malice are an easy hex.

To manifest the maximum benefit of this Moon, set some goals for the coming solar year or focus on a quest, something that requires a search for meaning and an understanding that will only come from the safety of personal dogma.

Super Dark Moon

Capricorn lunar energies will rule the night of December 23, having moved into Capricorn at 2:49 a.m. The Dark Moon comes about two-and-half hours later at 5:17 a.m. Before nightfall on December 22, the Moon will be void-of-course in Sagittarius, beginning at 3:16 p.m., so the Dark Moon ritual would best be celebrated at the moment of the Dark Moon instead of earlier. Capricorn will ask that the quest committed to on Yule benefits society. Connecting the quest to personal history will help to feel secure. These feelings may last until the Moon enters Aquarius at 2:14 a.m. on Christmas morning.

Christmas

Aquarian Christmas may arrive with childhood angst, fears, jealousies, and other negative feelings on Christmas Eve, when the moon is void and might otherwise stalk Christmas. On Christmas Day, be thankful and joyful, and avoid giving advice to others around family members. Release concern over their feelings and emotional life situations. Show empathy, of course, but avoid giving advice based on being an empath or clairsentient. Listening is best.

Boxing Day

The Aquarius Moon will still be hanging around all day after Christmas, not transitioning to Pisces until 2:34 a.m. on December 27; however, the Moon will be void-of-course after 1:19 p.m. Practice safe gift-giving. Keep it light. Sit for tea, discuss the weather, Christmas dinner, upcoming vacation plans. Stay away from politics and feelings.

New Year's Eve

The Taurus Moon takes over on New Year's Eve at 12:08 p.m. and carries through New Year's Day and the observed holiday on January 2, 2023, until 9:44 p.m., when Gemini steps in. Even though many will have a three-day holiday from work, practicality may well put a damper on party plans—a damper that may seem unwarranted but will come to be appreciated late on the second when the Moon enters Gemini. The material aspects of life may rise up to be noticed. Stress is not a good look in the Taurus Moon, so stay grounded regardless of the stressors that may arrive. Accept the changes that seem inevitable.

Full Moon

The Full Moon in Cancer occurs on January 6 at 6:08 p.m. This will be the third Full Moon of the yearly lunation cycle. Nothing special about this Cancer Full Moon: tears, emotional vacillations, and feelings of instability—the usual. Stock the pantry during the Gemini

Moon; cooking therapy will be in order. Gardening, rearranging the furniture, or cleaning the junk drawer are all homebound restorative Cancerian activities. Full Moons are always intense, but the Cancer Moon can illuminate even the darkest of psychic corners. Gatherings are often essential for Full Moon celebrations, but many may feel a solitary lunar evening will better suit the moment. Watch for traumas to surface.

Martin Luther King Jr. Day

January 16 will be influenced by the Scorpio Moon. Shallowness in relationships and even conversations will not satisfy the needs of this Moon. Deep dives into the meaning and feelings of this holiday, and the recognition and action that is summoned forth, will likely be expressive, demonstrative, and passionate.

Dark Moon

The Dark Moon will be in Aquarius. This Moon is not a Supermoon, but a fine Dark Moon nonetheless. Be prepared on January 21 for the Dark Moon to arrive at 3:53 p.m. This Moon could be celebrated on January 20, which changes the Moon sign to Capricorn. The Moon will also conjunct Mercury, adding another big energy around communication and intellectual pursuits to spread across the Dark Moon proceedings. If it all seems too heavy, remember this day is also National Hugging Day. Another option is an Aquarian Moon rite after the Dark Moon on January 21. The Aquarian influence may bring up excuses for not following through on goals of personal freedom and creativity.

Tales and Traditions

Kate Freuler

YULE, OR THE winter solstice, is perhaps the sabbat that has maintained most of its Pagan elements over the years. Wreaths and garlands of vibrant evergreens are brought into the home to symbolize hope and cheer, their bright colors a reminder that the earth is still thriving beneath the snow and ice. Customs such as the Yule log, gift-giving, and adorning a pine tree with lights and trinkets are all traditions that are still going strong today. While the big man in the red suit is a newer addition to the seasonal imagery, there are quite a few symbols that have stood the test of time. While some symbols' meanings are obvious, like candles or religious iconography, others are a little more curious. For example, I always wondered why and how bells became associated with Yule. Bells are included in holiday decorations almost as often as Santa Claus and candy canes. They are nestled into wreaths, hung on the tree, and grace the front of Christmas cards. They're mentioned in many carols, and Santa's reindeer are known for their jingling sleigh bells in the sky. So do bells have Pagan origins, or are they new to the party?

The Power of Bells

Yule marks the longest night of the year and is a celebration of the rebirth of the sun god. After this long night, the sun begins its gradual return. In pagan times, bells were rung on the solstice to drive out the evil spirits of darkness and welcome the coming light. The jingling was also meant to scare off storms and disease during the harshest time of year on the longest night of all. Perhaps it is this act that led to bells being a symbol of the season.

Historically speaking, bells are much more than just your average noisemaker. The earliest bells were made from pottery in Asia and are thought to be around 3,000 years old. Like anything dating back thousands of years, bells have played many roles and represented many conflicting things all around the world. They've been used to drive out evil, as mentioned, but also fulfilled many practical purposes like summoning a community together for an announcement or to warn of imminent danger. They were rung to signify birth and to announce a death. Bells signify both beginnings and endings, joy and grief. They were rung to welcome some spirits and ward off others. They were often included in religious ceremonies, lending them mystical and spiritual aspects.

Although bells have been around for a long time, most of the folklore that survives about them is associated with the church. It was believed that the devil found the music of church bells unbearable, so their ringing would protect a town from his clutches. Handheld bells, rung to fend off the devil, were sometimes referred to as "devil drivers," acting as purifying and protective tools. It's interesting to note that it's said faeries also can't stand church bells and will flee at the sound of them.

As early as the ninth century in England, church bells were inscribed with the names of saints and blessed with holy water when installed, which made people believe further that they had special powers to bless and protect. People could pay the church to ring the bells during the birth of a baby to ensure a healthy delivery. When someone died, the bell-ringing could be purchased to drive away any evil spirits awaiting the soul of the deceased in the afterlife. The more money paid, the louder the bells would toll. The louder their peals, the stronger their powers.

The Duality of Bells

The truth is, bells weren't originally associated with the joys of flying reindeer and sleigh rides. They were often considered foreboding, as they so often announced a death or warned of impending misfortune. They even played an important role in funerals and burials. In the 1800s, something called the "coffin alarm" was invented, its main component being a bell. In the past, people were terrified of being buried alive due to a few alleged incidents of this exact thing occurring, the accounts of which were spread with nightmarish detail. A solution was designed to protect against this problem: A bell was installed upon the grave with a rope hanging from its flapper. The rope was threaded through a hole in the ground, into the coffin of the deceased. This ensured that if a person were to awake in their tomb, they could ring the bell, alerting the graveyard worker to come and dig them out.

While on the surface this morbid tale certainly doesn't seem very fitting for the season of joy, it does reflect a meaningful metaphor of the larger picture: Yule is when the sun god is reborn and comes back to life, much like the poor soul ringing the coffin bell seemingly rose from the dead. The coffin bell's story of resurrection and rebirth makes an undeniable parallel with the meaning of the solstice, albeit a rather strange one.

While it appears that, over time, bells became a symbol seemingly belonging to the church, that doesn't render them irrelevant to Pagan celebration; after all, there are many parallels to be made between the holiday and bells for us too. Many Pagan practices and rituals include them. They're used as a means of cleansing an area, to signify the beginning and end of a ritual, and even to dispel evil spirits, just like in the old days.

In looking at all the uses of bells throughout history, it can be concluded that their association with Yule stems from a mix of practical and spiritual aspects. As bells ring on the winter solstice, they signify the death of darkness and the birth of the sun. In Yule rituals, bells can be sounded to banish the past and the darkness, while heralding in a bright new beginning. The pealing of bells inspires feelings of hope, announcing the return of the sun with their celebratory voices.

References

Masaro, Daniela, and Jacob Lopez. "Traditions and Symbols of Yule." Sacred Earth Journeys. Updated December 2020. https://www.sacredearthjourneys.ca/blog/traditions-and-symbols-of-yule/.

Warren, Melanie. "The Folklore of Bells." #FolkloreThursday. May 18, 2017. https://folklorethursday.com/folklife/the-folklore-of-bells/.

Tarazano, Lawrence. "People Feared Being Buried Alive so Much They Invented These Special Safety Coffins." *Smithsonian* magazine. Accessed January 2, 2022. https://www.smithsonianmag.com/sponsored/people-feared-being-buried-alive-so-much-they-invented-these-special-safety-coffins-180970627/.

Feasts and Treats

Gwion Raven

Whether your household celebrates Yule or honours the winter solstice or opens presents on Christmas morning or has created your own way to mark the season, one thing is for sure: there will be plenty of food to share. One of the best things about the winter holidays is enjoying food we don't always prepare all year long.

You'll notice these dishes are a bit lighter, less formal, and easy to prepare. Enjoy them with friends and family, or treat yourself to a scrumptious feast for one. Like any good meal, the spices and flavours match the season, with hints of pine and clove and peppermint.

Salmon with Berries (GF)

If you want to serve something other than a big roast beast meal that takes hours to cook, this should be your go-to recipe. It's ready in under 30 minutes and looks as festive as your Yule tree. Juniper berries provide a touch of spruce flavour to the salmon. If you choose to cook the salmon over an open fire or grill, add pine needles to the charcoal or wood as you cook the salmon.

Prep time: 10 minutes
Cooking time: 30 minutes
Servings: 4

1 cup fresh raspberries (frozen works too)
1 cup fresh blueberries (frozen works too)
¼ cup honey
1 teaspoon dried juniper berries (fresh works too, but they are harder to find)
1 teaspoon whole black peppercorns
2 teaspoons salt
2-pound salmon fillet (or 4 individual fillets)

Preheat the oven to 400°F. Feel along the salmon fillet and remove any small bones.

Grab a small saucepan. Add the raspberries, blueberries, and honey along with 2 tablespoons of water. Cook over medium heat for 4 minutes. Reduce heat and simmer for 8 more minutes or until the fruit is very soft and thick. Remove from the heat and set aside.

Using a mortar and pestle (or a spice grinder), grind the juniper berries, peppercorns, and salt to a powder. Rub the spice mix all over the salmon. Place salmon on a rimmed baking pan, spoon on half of the fruit mixture, and put it on the top rack of the oven for 12 minutes.

Get your biggest wooden cutting board or plank and serve the salmon right on it. Top the fish with the remaining fruit compote. Dispense with plates and just give everyone a fork so they can tuck right in.

Potatoes with Horseradish Crème (GF & Vegetarian)

Potatoes were served at every winter holiday meal I ate when I was growing up. And while I love, love, love roasted potatoes, it's nice to have something a bit different every now and again. Horseradish is most often associated with roast beef dinners, but it's excellent on potatoes, and it pairs really well with salmon too. You can serve this dish hot or cold, which means you can make it a day in advance and keep it in the fridge ready to go.

Prep time: 10 minutes, plus 2 hours to chill
Cooking time: 30 minutes
Servings: 4

½ cup sour cream
2 tablespoons fresh horseradish, grated
½ tablespoon Dijon mustard
½ teaspoon white wine vinegar
¼ teaspoon kosher salt
¼ teaspoon freshly ground black pepper
20 small red bliss potatoes, unpeeled
1 tablespoon salt
1 tablespoon fresh parsley, chopped

In a large mixing bowl, combine the first 6 ingredients. Whisk until smooth. Cover with plastic wrap and refrigerate for 2 hours.

Fill a large saucepan ¾ full with water. Add the whole, unpeeled potatoes and bring to a boil. Once boiling, reduce the heat to medium-high and cook at a rapid simmer for 15 minutes or until you can pierce a potato with a knife easily. Drain the potatoes and sprinkle with salt.

To serve, pour the potatoes into a large mixing bowl and spoon in the horseradish sauce. Top with the chopped parsley. If you're making the Salmon with Berries dish, just mix the potatoes and horseradish together in a bowl and arrange them around the salmon.

Mince Pies (GF & Vegetarian)

I make mince pies every Yuletide, and I have to confess something to you here: my immediate family doesn't like them very much, so I usually end up sharing one or two with guests and eating the rest myself. It's like a Yuletide present from myself to myself!

These are gluten free, but you'd never know! I use store-bought mincemeat, because as much as I like being in the kitchen, I want these on my plate as soon as I can. There's a story from the Middle Ages that says if you eat a mince pie from Christmas Day to Twelfth Night, you'll have good luck all year. Who am I to mess with tradition?

Prep time: 30 minutes, plus 30 minutes to chill
Cooking time: 20 minutes
Servings: 12

2½ cups gluten-free 1-to-1 flour
1⅓ cups cold unsalted butter
3 tablespoons superfine sugar
2 large eggs
1 jar mincemeat
1 extra egg

Preheat the oven to 350°F. Get a big mixing bowl and add the flour. Cut the butter into cubes directly over the flour. Using your hands, rub the flour and butter together until it looks like breadcrumbs. Add in the sugar and stir.

In a separate bowl, beat 2 eggs. Slowly pour them into the flour mix and combine with a fork. You'll end up with a ball of sticky dough. Wrap the dough in plastic wrap and refrigerate for 30 minutes.

Remove dough from the fridge and roll it out on a well-floured surface until it's about ⅛-inch thin. Using a 4-inch round biscuit cutter, cut out 12 discs. These are the bottoms of your pies. Lightly grease a 12-cup muffin pan and place a disc in each hole and gently press them into place. Fill each muffin cup with 2 teaspoons of mincemeat.

Reroll the remaining dough and cut out 12 lids with a 3-inch cutter. Place the lids on top and sprinkle a little more superfine sugar on each lid. Pop the muffin tray in the oven for 20 minutes or until the pies are golden brown. Let them cool for 10 minutes. Gently remove from the muffin pan.

Serve with a dollop of fresh cream or a little condensed milk, or eat them just as they are—or hide them and tell your friends you forgot to make them.

Candy Cane Cocktail (GF)

Ever wonder what to do with leftover candy canes? It's time for a winter solstice cocktail. This is just a bit of festive frivolity in a glass. For a special touch, put candy canes or peppermint candies in a plastic bag and crush them up with a rolling pin. Spread the crushed candies onto a wooden cutting board and rim the glasses with the candy.

Prep time: 5 minutes
Servings: 4

3 ounces vodka (berry vodka is good here too)
3 ounces peppermint schnapps
3 ounces white crème de cacao
1 ounce grenadine
3 ounces half-and-half
Crushed candy canes
4 mint sprigs

Mix the first five ingredients in an ice-filled cocktail shaker. Shake it up really well so all the ingredients are fully combined. Rim a glass with crushed candy canes and pour in the cocktail. Add a sprig of mint to each glass and enjoy!

Crafty Crafts

Ivo Dominguez Jr.

AS A PART OF the celebration of the returning light and the longest night, the image of a Yule fire burning in a fireplace or on a bonfire is often called to mind. However, this classic version of a Yule fire isn't always an option, and there are other ways of having one. The flames of Yule remind us of the home, hearth, family, and community. They remind us of the promise of longer days and the return of the sun's warmth. In my tradition, the flames are also symbolic of the spark of Spirit making the choice to come to the earth by incarnating. The Yule fire represents the steadfastness of life to always turn the wheel toward rebirth. This craft project lets you create a smaller Yule fire that is large in meaning.

Yule Sun Candle and Tray

We will be creating a decorated candle and tray (or holder) that will symbolize the Yule fire and its setting in the holiday or a ritual. Think of it as if it were a scale model of a ritual space, a fanciful diorama, or an altar the size of the candle and tray. This can serve as your Yule fire to celebrate the holiday or the special candle used to light your fire if you have a bonfire or fireplace. You may wish to invest the time to create one that you will put away and reuse every year, or you may enjoy the process of making it so much you'd rather make a fresh one every year. Whenever I create ephemeral ritual pieces, I try to use up craft supplies I already have, found objects, and gifts collected from nature.

Materials

Wooden plate, or metal platter or tray, diameter 9–12 inches
Candle in glass, 7-day or 15-hour votive
Coaster, small and nonflammable
Paints, acrylic paints or enamel markers
Paper, depends on your choices
Glue, hot glue or white glue
Other decorations, such as ribbons, pine cones, holly leaves
   Cost: $0–$25
   Time spent: 2 hours, plus drying time

Plate Design Ideas

Get out a pencil and some paper so you can make simple sketches to plan your design that will go on the plate. You may want to use a water glass to trace several circles on the paper to help you come up with something that works as a circular design. Remember to leave a spot in the center for the candle. Think about what aspects of Yule you're trying to capture. Find the balance you want between the symbolic and the representational. Here are some examples of what you might paint on the plate:

- A blazing sun on a night sky with stars.
- An eight-spoked wheel to represent the Wheel of the Year. (This is easier to do if you use blue painter's tape to mask off the spokes.)
- Logs arranged around the center on a mottled background of white and pale blue-gray to signify a Yule fire in a snowy field.

If you don't want to freehand paint, then here are some other options:

- Take holly and ivy leaves and put paint on them. Use them like stamps to create a mandala on the plate.
- Use stencils with winter themes to create a design. Don't be afraid to overlap them.
- Take some pinecones and pull off the scales. Paint the scales gold or red and use white glue to attach them to the plate in a sunburst pattern. Hot glue is an option, especially if it is a metal plate or tray.

If you have a plate or tray that you like the color of or want to show the beauty of the material, such as wood grain, you may wish to not paint a background. You may wish to decorate the plate first so that you can put the blank candle on it to see what kinds of decorations will make the two pieces look good together.

Candle Design Ideas

Decorating the candle will, in part, be determined by the size of the glass that holds it. Think about what you want the candle to say as a part of your overall design. For example:

- To emphasize the fire idea, you may want to give the impression of flames rising from a bonfire. Take a strip of paper about half as tall as the glass and big enough to go around it with a small overlap. Draw or paint flames onto the paper or find a printed image of flames. Then wrap the paper around the bottom of the glass like a label. You can affix it with a few dots of hot glue, superglue, or double-sided tape.
- Another way to create symbolic flames is with red- or gold-wired ribbons. Cut four pieces at different lengths long enough to go around the candle three or four times. Wrap them around two fingers to give them a curl. Cut or fold the end of the ribbon to make a pointed flame shape. Then wrap them around the base of the candle, one at a time, and twist them in place. Pull the tips upward and use a spot of hot glue or super glue to tack some of the points onto the glass. Adjust the ribbons until it looks like rising flames.

- To emphasize the winter theme, cut out small paper snow-flakes or holly leaves and affix them to the candle in a design that pleases you.

- To remind you of the importance of community at Yule, you could cut paper doll chains to wrap around the candle. This looks a bit like people holding hands around a Yule fire.

Construction Tips

For painting the plate, acrylic or enamel paints are best for this project. Make sure the plate has been cleaned well so the paint will stick. If you are decorating the candle with paper embellishments, use paper that is thin and flexible enough to follow the curve of the glass. It is easier to glue to the glass if you wash it, dry it, and then wipe it with alcohol cleaning wipes and let it dry again. Glue sticks or hot glue are your best bet.

Safety

Do not add herbs, oils, or other things as decorations in the candle, as they increase the risk of the glass cracking because of uneven flames. The coaster should be between the candle and the plate. Be mindful of the candle and snuff it out if you are leaving it alone for long.

Reference

Pesznecker, Susan. *Yule: Rituals, Recipes & Lore for the Winter Solstice.* Woodbury, MN: Llewellyn Publications, 2015.

Color Magic

Charlie Rainbow Wolf

YULE FOLLOWS SAMHAIN IN the Wheel of the Year, and it marks the time when the nights are the longest in the Northern Hemisphere (and shortest in the south). It's marked by the sun moving into the astrological sign of Capricorn. Although it falls roughly around the same date in December, because of the natural ebb and flow of the sun signs, its exact time will vary from year to year. The deities of this festival include the Holly King, Hodr, and—my favorite—Frau Holle.

I always find Yule to be a multifaceted festival, with many cultures and religions having some kind of a sacred day in December. In the Wheel of the Year, Yule is the first festival of the new year; yet in the Gregorian calendar, it is the last holiday of the old year! It's a time of bustling and business, a time of sharing and giving, a time of gathering and feasting. It's when the Holly King gives way to the Oak King, and when Demeter starts to anticipate the return of her daughter, Persephone, again.

The Colors of Yule

It's easy to recognize the familiar colors of the season. The green of the wreath, Father Christmas's red and white robes (or Santa's jolly red and white suit), the white of the snow, the gold of the star, the dark blue of the midwinter sky... There are so many colors that symbolize Yule, you could take your pick of nearly anything!

When I think of Yule, I automatically go to green—not the bright spring green, but rather the dark and mysterious green of the forest and of growth and balance. The seasonal tree we put in our home to decorate is green—although nowadays there are artificial trees readily available in any and every color. Green is the color of life, so abundant in nature as the flora grows. The evergreen trees, garlands, and wreaths give hope that, in the midst of the long, dark nights, there is promise; there is life.

Shades of green are usually quite easy on the eye. I remember the waiting room of the hospital in Blackpool being painted in a muted green, complete with green upholstered furniture. It's little wonder that institutions use the color green in abundance; it's believed that it calms and refreshes. It's a color that does need to be used with another complementary color, though, or it might promote lethargy and laziness. I do not remember a single room in my school being painted any shade of green!

Green is the heart chakra color. It's the color of love and acceptance, but it is also said to be the color of ambition and fertility. It's the dominant color in many natural settings, which is one reason why it is easy on the eye. Being associated with the heart chakra, it builds a bridge between the lower chakras and the higher ones—between the physical needs and the spiritual ones.

There's a charming story about why the evergreens keep their leaves in the winter written by Florence Holbrook (1860–1932), which tells the tale of evergreen trees being kind to a broken-winged bird who could not fly south for the winter, so when the North Wind came to take the leaves from the trees, the Frost King would not let him take the leaves of the evergreens. This seems similar in some ways to an even older story I once heard at a folk festival in England, about the sun taking a sabbatical and only the evergreen trees staying true and not giving up hope that it would return. Both stories feature the trees holding fast throughout the winter.

Ivy and holly have been the traditional garlands in my family and, of course, there's the traditional song about the holly and the ivy, with the holly representing many aspects of the birth of the Christ child. The holly used in many Yuletide decorations embodies both green and red—red being another popular seasonal color. It complements green very well; it's directly opposite green on the color wheel, with red being a primary color and green being a secondary color—a mix of yellow and blue.

Holly is said to be the evergreen counterpart of the oak tree. Holly rules the winter months, and the oak rules the summer months. I have heard tales from my elders that holly used to be brought inside before the popularity of the Christmas tree, with mistletoe attached to make a kissing bunch. My Aunt Joan always made sure that the holly she used to decorate the sideboard had smooth-edged leaves—not the prickly ones. She said the prickly leaves were male, and she wanted the smooth leaves (representing the female energy) so that she and her sister would govern the household for the next year. She always made sure that the holly had berries too so that the year would be fruitful—besides, it made for a much more colorful garland!

Red seems to be everywhere at this time of year. Not only does it adorn the holly and the jolly old man's garb, but many other decorations feature different hues of crimson and scarlet. The seasonal poinsettias are a natural mixture of green leaves and red bracts with gold centers. (There are also poinsettias with white bracts, but they do not seem to be quite as popular as the red version.) Red baubles and garlands embellish much of the seasonal greenery, and with good reason: they stand out so well against the boughs and branches. Stockings hung by the chimney with care are frequently depicted as red. Red is the base chakra color, one that represents the very life force of the blood that courses through the veins of most living creatures (the exception being some sea life). It is the color of passion and emotion—something that tends to run high with the excitement of the season. These red stockings are often decorated with white tops, or white heels and toes, and this goes back to the purity that white represents. White snow is featured in many of the seasonal songs and images. Gold also comes into Yule with its heavenly or spiritual symbolism; it's often seen as boot and belt buckle or among the angelic decorations and tree-topping stars. Gold is reputedly one of the gifts brought to the manger by the wise men: a color of royalty and high spirituality. I see it as a sign of the sun returning to the skies and a promise that the days are starting to lengthen—but then, I *am* an astrologer, after all!

Another less-popular color, but one that is still well represented, is blue. The Mother Mary, angels, and some gods and goddesses are often illustrated as wearing blue—from the richest cobalt to the palest sky and everything in between! The winter sky is midnight blue, the moonlight on the snow shines a glistening ice blue, even the snow itself sometimes looks blue in the light of day. Blue is said to represent trust, faithfulness, and fidelity and is believed to promote peace and keep negative energy at bay.

Celebrating Yule

Bringing the colors of Yule inside is perhaps the easiest way to embody them in seasonal festivities. Availability goes without question—some well-known hobby and craft shops start putting out their winter decorations before the middle of July! We still bring in a tree to decorate—something we have done ever since I can remember. On it are white lights and multicolored ornaments that have been collected by the family since before I was born. Green, white, and red are the most prominent colors in our household at this time of year, permeating everything from our "ugly sweaters" (which even the dogs wear) to the table decorations. Some years we've gone big, with a huge tree dominating the living room; other years we've gone small with just a simple table centerpiece—a lighted ceramic tree that my mother made when I was still in grade school. In more recent years, we've had great fun with the aforementioned ugly sweaters. Usually garish combinations of red, green, and other seasonal colors, we've dressed up outlandishly for our Yule feast. Part of that feast has involved traditional fare: we often make a Yule log and decorate it with holly sprigs and icing sugar "snow," while I bake ugly sweater cookies or gingerbread people in similar designs as our attire. The fun that we create invokes a wonderfully optimistic vibe, one that will take us into the new year on a high note. As with everything else when it comes to magic, intention is the greatest ingredient of all.

I add bloodstone to my incense altar at this time of year because it embodies so many of the seasonal colors. It is a form of jasper— which in itself is usually a "feel-good" stone—and has a green base with flecks of red and gold. Bloodstone is also known as *heliotrope*, from the Greek words for "sun" and "turn," which to me is most fitting as the sun turns in the sky to bring back the light.

Reference
Holbrook, Florence. "Why the Evergreen Trees Keep Their Leaves in Winter." Lit2Go. Accessed July 28, 2021. https://etc.usf.edu /lit2go/68/fairy-tales-and-other-traditional-stories/5109/why -the-evergreen-trees-keep-their-leaves-in-winter/.

Yule Ritual

Melissa Tipton

THIS RITUAL CALLS UPON the wisdom of Krampus to help you perceive yourself and situations more clearly, particularly recurring situations or dynamics that feel difficult to disengage from, such as finding yourself dating partners with similar issues or ending up in chronically frustrating work environments. During the ritual, you'll access liberating insights and call back your energy, freeing yourself from any patterns that aren't in alignment with your highest self.

Calling in Clarity and Energy with Krampus

This ritual is largely unfolding in your psyche, so you don't need much in the way of tools, but you're welcome to use any enhancements you'd like, such as festive incense or a picture of Krampus. The only necessary supplies are a black and a white candle, a safe place to burn them, and your magical journal or some paper to jot down insights.

Start by casting a magic circle. Use the method of your choice, or stand in the center of your space, close your eyes, and take a moment to connect to the energy of the earth below you and the sky above you. Draw the energies of earth and sky into your body, feeling them condense at your heart, and then send the energy out through your dominant hand's index finger as you draw a clockwise circle to enclose your space. Envision the protective circle around you and say, "This circle draws in energies most harmonious for this working and blocks out all other energies. So mote it be!"

If it's part of your practice, you can call the quarters and any deities or spirit guides you work with. Then, prepare to call on Krampus. Notice without judgment what you're feeling in your body and any thoughts that arise, such as fear, excitement, or curiosity. When you're ready, use the following evocation:

Krampus, I now call on thee!
Show me what 'tis hard to see:
The parts within that hold me back,
Reflecting Self through eyes of lack.

I see my nature, full and true
And accept myself, through and through.
In wholeness here I do reside
And projections shall no longer hide.

Light the black candle and say, "I see the projections that are most relevant for me right now." Close your eyes and come into a meditative state by focusing on your breathing for a few rounds as your body and mind soften. Notice if your thoughts are drawn to a particular situation or person, and watch your thoughts like a detached observer, allowing different perspectives to float into your awareness. Now, focus your attention a bit more. Ask, "What's important for me to see right now about [person or situation]?" Allow any insights to arise.

Then ask, "What part am I playing in this situation?" If, at any point, the guidance feels unclear, gently refocus with the following intention: "Guidance is arriving in a form I can easily understand." Finally, home in on your projections with the question, "What in this situation rightfully belongs to me?" These insights can appear in numerous ways. For me, I see an image of the situation in my mind and part of the scene will light up or grab my attention.

Then, when I focus on this aspect, my claircognizance kicks in, and I'll suddenly "know" what I've projected and need to call back to myself. Once you've identified at least one quality that you've projected, it's time to call this energy back. Imagine your aura is a magnet, and it naturally draws to you any energies that rightfully belong to you—those parts of yourself that have been projected onto others. See and feel the energy returning, passing through your aura, where it's cleansed of any potentially harmful additions before being reabsorbed by your system. It's at this stage that I often feel Krampus's presence most strongly, and I've seen him aiding in the process of gathering this wayward energy in his sack and handing it back to me, where it belongs.

Once you've retrieved this projected energy, spend a few minutes focusing inward, imagining an inner fire in your belly. See the called-back energy entering the fire, where it's further purified and transformed in accordance with your highest good. When this process feels complete, see the fire imagery fade from view and sense the purified energy flowing to wherever it naturally belongs in your system. Notice if you feel more whole, more complete now that you've welcomed back this cast-off energy. Take a moment to thank Krampus:

Krampus of the wintry night
Your guidance has enhanced my sight.
I see myself through eyes most true
And embody my wholeness, thanks to you.
Hail and farewell, Krampus!

Open your eyes and use the flame of the black candle to light the white one as you say, "I usher this new awareness into my consciousness fully and in accordance with my highest good." Capture any insights in your journal, including any pointers on specific actions you're being called to take in the coming days and weeks to further the work you've done in this ritual. If you called on other guides, deities, or elements, thank them and give your farewells, then release your magic circle.

You're free to snuff the candles out now with thanks, and they can be used in the future when you need another dose of clarity. If you find yourself getting wrapped up in an emotionally heightened situation, light the black candle first, asking to be shown what you're not seeing, what you might be projecting. Then, after those insights have come through, use the black candle to light the white, fully welcoming this new awareness into your being.

After doing this ritual and calling back projected energy from a situation, you'll likely find that you're less drawn to similar situations in the future because you no longer need them to remind you of your wholeness. But if they do continue to present a subtle draw, don't panic. It's common for us to project multiple aspects onto a single situation, so use the black and white candles to identify another projection that needs to be peeled off and welcomed home. Once you've retrieved them all, this situation will feel much more neutral to you, leaving you with the clarity and energy to make wise decisions that are truly in alignment with your total Self.

This ritual is incredibly potent during Yule, when we have increased access to the in-between spaces, which includes the liminal zone between conscious and unconscious, light and dark, which is what this ritual taps into. On a magical level, being able to loosen our attachments to energy in one form so that it can transform into another is part and parcel of effective magic. Often, we reach for magic when we're no longer happy with a particular energetic arrangement, but we can derail our magical efforts by harboring unconscious attachments to the comfort of the same old, same old. This ritual frees you from those limitations, allowing you to tap into the full range of your witchy powers. Blessed Yule!

Notes

Notes

Notes

Imbolc

Celebrating Imbolc: Me, Myself, and I

Susan Pesznecker

HELLO, DEAR READER! WE'RE about to plunge into ideas for celebrating Imbolc. But before we go there, you need to know that I'm more or less a solo practitioner, and this impacts my personal view of all types of magical and spiritual practice. Now to be clear, I'm writing this during the COVID-19 pandemic, and because of medically fragile family members, my family and I have been strictly quarantined: masking, distancing, vaccinating... all of it.

Thus, I'm even less likely than ever to engage in group ritual or activities. But in truth, that's not much different from my usual status quo. Although I'm happy to take part in group ritual or magical workings with others when the chance arises, I'm much more in tune with my own individual practices, developed and honed over several decades. Most of my magical workings happen with just me, myself, and I—pandemic or not. By gearing ritual to my own needs and preferences, I find it becomes deeply personal, leaving me with an afterglow of satisfaction and, typically, a sense of pondering what will come next.

That said, over the years, I've found that most rituals in books or on websites are geared toward groups, or at least several people. People gather, everyone has a specific role, there are rules and time frames and sometimes special garb or props, the ritual happens, everyone eats and chats, and then they go home. The experience may be lovely, but many are left feeling unfulfilled. "Okay. That was Imbolc. Done. I guess I'll go home." Further, there's often an under-the-radar feeling in the magical community that if one is working solo rather than with a group it's "not enough." Like, "Oh. You did your own Samhain ritual? How nice."

Speaking of ritual: the word "ritual" comes from a Latin word meaning "rite," namely a solemn ceremony or observance. The word is also related to the concept of "rite of passage," during which one marks a personal passage or event. How do we magnify these ideas, creating a ritual that doesn't simply go through the motions, worrying more about where a person is standing or whether they follow a set script than about the meaning in the ceremony? One that honors both solemnity and joy? One that doesn't just mark a moment in time but leaves us looking into the future? One that leaves participants feeling satisfied and challenged to move forward?

I argue that individualized ritual answers many of those questions. In this essay, I'll propose something different: namely, a *day-long*, individual-focused, intentional celebration of the Imbolc sabbat for one person: *you*. Instead of using pre-written, canned rituals, I'm going to encourage you to go rogue and DIY, creating rites that have unique meaning for you. By focusing a complete intention-inspired day on your Imbolc experience, the work will take on special value and give you ideas for further practices, inspiring you with the beauty and benefits of solitary work.

First: What Is Imbolc?

Imbolc (also spelled Imbolg), pronounced like *EE-melk*, is one of the eight "Wheel of the Year" celebrations and falls on February 1, about halfway between the winter and summer solstices. Along with Beltane, Lughnasadh, and Samhain, Imbolc is known as one of the four seasonal festivals—sometimes called fire festivals. In some traditions, it marks the summer half of the year, while Lughnasadh marks the start of the winter half. Imbolc is also known as Candlemas (a Christianized, February 2 celebration) and as St. Brigid's Day or the Feast of St. Brigid. Brigid-focused celebrations may include Brigid's (pronounced *Breed*) crosses, the Brigid bed, and various types of blessings.

For me, Imbolc marks the ebbing of winter and the earliest signs of spring. Snows begin to melt, temperatures moderate, the first flowers appear, the days lengthen, and winter constellations wheel over the horizon and are replaced by summer stars. This is also the time baby animals are born, and lambing is a traditional touchstone of Imbolc. Thinking about the Wheel of the Year and the rotation of the natural seasons puts us deeply in touch with the here and now and with our place in the cosmos. This is where our focus will be for this day-long ritual retreat. Why am I calling it a retreat? Because this day-long celebration is for you. Think of it as a dedicated time to retreat into your real or metaphorical cave, celebrate Imbolc's passage, and do personal work. And you'll have fun as well!

Start with Intention

Begin by considering the purpose for your retreat:

- Who are you? What do you need right now? How could you benefit most from a period of time focused on you and your magics? Consider that Imbolc is the start of spring—a stirring of life and a gentle awakening, a wonderful time for initiations and new beginnings. How can you link these energies to your own ideas?

- The very nature of a retreat is solitude. Be somewhat selfish in carving out space for your ritual retreat. People have sought private time and space to accomplish personal goals, and you're no different. Think of a setting where you will not be disturbed and can focus on your ritual goals. Given that, where will you spend your retreat time? At home? In a local park? At a special farther location?

Think About Focus Topics

We'll talk in a bit about the specifically ritualized components of the day. But what else would you like to focus on during your ritual retreat? Given the day-long time frame, you'll have plenty of time to explore other subjects or ideas. Here are some examples for filling the hours:

- Begin or continue a path toward initiation
- Focus on spellwork or other magical practice
- Work with herbs: collecting, preparing, using
- Research a craft topic of interest
- Work with or create magical tools
- Harness the written word: journaling, story writing, ritual, or prayer craft
- Focus on handwork or arts and crafts
- Practice one or more forms of divination, or create and use a new divinatory tool
- Use a late-night retreat to practice star study and moon scrying
- Hone your kitchen magic
- Catch up on your magical reading, sinking deeply into one or more texts
- Work with meditation, yoga, or other types of enforced mindfulness
- Spend the time in nature: hiking, collecting, nature journaling
- Create magical garb or jewelry: robes, a bag, a prayer shawl, a bead string
- Go on a field trip to local occult, spiritual, herb, gem, or art supply shops

Those are only a few ideas to get you thinking. As you do, consider how each choice might exemplify Imbolc's energies. Be sure to choose activities you enjoy!

Correspondences

This ritual retreat is about Imbolc and celebrating the first signs of spring as we emerge from the dark winter. The days begin to lengthen, the temperatures warm, and we see the first signs of spring's seasonal changes. All that has slept through winter now awakens and stretches, gathering energy in the first rays of a warm sun. It's a time of fresh energy and new beginnings.

Throughout your day, interweaving these Imbolc-relevant correspondences will add to your intentions and enrich the inherent magic of your actions.

- **Foods:** anything seasonal in your area or anything you've preserved, plus alliums (onions, shallots, garlic); breads, seeds, and grains; dried fruits; herbal teas; hot chocolate and spiced cider; stored vegetables like potatoes, onions, and squashes; wine and mulled wine
- **Herbs, soaps, and oils:** chamomile, lemon balm, and rosemary (cleansing); frankincense (purification); lavender (relaxation); bay and rosemary (incense or brazier use)
- **Stones and crystals:** amethyst, bloodstone, obsidian, onyx, salt (purification, circlecasting)
- **Trees and wood:** resinous woods (cedar, juniper, pine); dried leaves and cones
- **Colors (altar cloths, candles, etc.):** dark blues and purples for the winter night; white for winter snow; gold and yellow for the glimmers of sun
- **Symbolic elements:** baby animal statuary; candles or a small brazier; small pots of herbs or bulbs; snowflakes; leafless deciduous trees
- And, of course, **anything relating to Brigid**, if you want to go that route: Brigid's cross, corn doll, chalice (symbolizing well blessing), small hammer (goddess of the forge), colors of red and white, and more

Also:

- For magic with a powerful grounding force: work with soil, sand, crystals, and stones.
- For magic that is to rise into the heavens, use fire: candles, flash paper, small fires (outdoors or in a fireplace), or lights. (Practice safety!)
- For magic intended to change or transform, work with water.
- For the magic of movement or transition, work with air: ribbons, pinwheels, and wind chimes.

The "Simples"

Including small ritualized activities throughout the day makes a retreat more meaningful simply via intention. In other words, every part of your day should be special. Ideas:

- **Awakening:** gentle stretching and awareness of every part of the body; deep breathing; prayers of gratitude; meditation; yoga sun salutation; self-blessing
- **Garb:** putting on clean clothes and visualizing a protective cloak; wearing magical garb or jewelry
- **Cleansing:** showering or bathing (purifying, washing away negativity) with herbal soaps, bath bombs, or oils; bathing as ritual immersion and cleansing; anointing with lotions
- **Meals:** washing hands and face before dining as cleansing and preparation; table settings to add beauty; blessings or prayers of thanks before and after dining; use of simple, seasonal, sustainable, local foods
- **Bedtime prep:** washing hands and face; gentle stretching and appreciation for the body; reflection on the day's experience; prayer

The "Formals"

Creating your own prayers, blessings, invocations, and rituals adds great meaning to any magical activity. There's no pressure or judgment: after all, this is a solo event. You may want to begin by looking up readings, rituals, and prayers in books like this one. Get the feel of how these work, jotting down any initial ideas you might have.

Prayer or beseechment follows a three-part structure:

1. Call upon a deity or force: St. Brigid, Mother Nature, the forces of the universe, the tides of Imbolc, etc.
2. Make your request, using proper humility
3. Offer gratitude

Example:

Powers of Earth and Sun, I call on you at this time of Imbolc.

As energy and light return to the world and winter loosens its grip, I feel reverence toward the turning of the seasons. May I be filled with gratitude and respect for these natural processes.

I am grateful for your constancy. You are the Infinite.

Blessings, which are favorable and focus on bestowing abundance or protection, can be simple or formal in tone. Consider favorite authors, poets, or philosophers for inspiration.

A simple blessing over food:

I am grateful for this gift of food.
May it nourish me throughout this day.

(See how easy that was? It didn't even need to rhyme!)

And one of my own created blessings:

Not above you, not below you, but within you.

Invocation is the act of calling upon someone or something for assistance.

St. Brigid, I ask for your presence here tonight as we honor the turning of the great wheel and the advent of Imbolc. May you be here now and always.

Structured ritual is typically complicated and often quite long. Here are some of the more common steps in a full-blown ritual. Use any combination of these to create your own rite:

1. Gathering
2. Procession to the ritual space, often with music, singing, drums, etc.
3. Draw and close the circle, open the cardinal points or elements (earth, air, water, fire)
4. Offer a welcome and a statement of purpose
5. Light central fire, activate central space, etc.
6. Call upon deities or natural forces
7. Raise energy (dancing, singing, circling, drumming)
8. Conduct ritual actions: initiations, charges, spellwork, invocations or appeals, prayers, and such. Specific actions for Imbolc might include seed blessings (for the spring garden), spells for land fertility, a request for safe passage through the remaining winter, and so forth.
9. Make offerings
10. Carry out a divinatory "read" (Were the actions and offerings successful?)
11. Bring down energy (soft singing, drumming)
12. Close central altar space and activities
13. Release cardinal points or elements; open circle
14. Offer a blessing to participants
15. Process away from ritual site
16. Enjoy "cakes and wine" (Communal snacks and chatter!)

Cosmic Sway

Daniel Pharr

GROUNDHOG DAY! THE traditional day of Christian Candlemas was affixed in the solar calendar to February 2 by the church. On this day, the priesthood of the European church encouraged people to bring candles to be blessed. Candles were needed to brave the cold, dark weather, and were claimed to ward off storms. According to the meteorological belief, if the Sun shone on this day, winter would keep its grip until the spring equinox. Likewise, if the day was cloudy or foul, winter was near over and spring was soon to follow. Burning a candle blessed by priests, for light and protection every night of winter, provided a constant reminder of the power of the Christian God.

The first report of a groundhog prognosticating the weather was celebrated in Punxsutawney and printed in 1887. For decades before coming to America, Germans had been consulting a hedgehog about the weather. In America they adopted the plentiful groundhog, also known as a woodchuck or a whistle pig, because it whistles when it's frightened.

The Christianized solar calendar places Imbolc (pronounced *em-bowl-ck*) on February 2 year after year. However, night before day, Imbolc would begin at sundown on February 1 and end at sundown on February 2.

Cross-Quarter Imbolc

As was discussed in Samhain, Imbolc and all other cross-quarter days are actually midpoints between solstices and equinoxes, and this High Holiday is midpoint between the winter solstice and the spring equinox, both seasonal midpoints, making Imbolc the first day of spring, as priests, groundhogs, and hedgehogs have known for decades (unless the weather was nice).

Where previously only two seasons had been considered— summer from Beltaine to Samhain, and winter from Samhain to Beltaine—Imbolc was actually midwinter. But, when quarterly seasons were delineated, Imbolc became the first day of spring and Lughnassadh the first day of autumn.

This year, the actual cross-quarter date and time when calculated between solstice and equinox is February 4 at 5:06 a.m. in Cancer. If honoring the natural cycle on this calculation of Imbolc, the High Holiday begins at sundown on the third. Even though the Moon is shining from Cancer, there will be a strong Leo-like influence since the Moon is in the tenth house and is void-of-course. Participants will be drawn to hearth and home, baking and decorating, and preparing the perfect indoor celebration or after-celebration. The Leo influences will mean that these same folks will expect compliments and raves about the effort expended and the quality of outcome. Recognition will be a driving force around both the balefire and the mead barrel.

Full Moon and Pleiadean Imbolc

The Leo Full Moon will arrive on February 5 at 1:29 p.m. After sunset on the fourth, the Moon will appear full. This is the fourth Full Moon in the annual cycle, and the evening would have been considered the night of Imbolc based on the ancients' Moon-counting method that began with Pleiades at Samhain.

Leo will bring its usual desire for the spotlight and admiration. However, this time around, receiving praise may feel awkward and difficult in finding a perfect response. Seeking recognition is one aspect, but receiving recognition is on a different emotional plane. Positive or negative, accepting feedback is important and educational. Poise in accepting feedback is essential—no excuses, no reasons, just expressions of genuine thankfulness.

Valentine's Day

Thank the goddess for a Sagittarius Moon Valentine's evening. Spontaneity will be key to fun on the Valentine's date—more precisely, planned spontaneity. That phrase might sound quixotic or in juxtaposition, but a Valentine's date or any arranged meeting cannot be purely spontaneous. Make plans of when and where, have a backup plan in case things go badly, and then stop planning. Allow the date to unfold as it will. Sagittarius lunar energies are that of romance and fun and hilarious freedom.

Dark Moon

Nonconformist Aquarian lunar energies will be the influencer leading up to the Dark Moon, but the Moon moves into perceptive Pisces at 11:56 p.m. on February 19 and becomes new at 2:06 a.m, two hours later, on the twentieth. This unseen Moon and dark sky may be the most productive time for divination this year. Venus is also in Pisces, and the Sun and Moon are together in the fifth house. These aspects will bring great sensitivity, imagination, and creativity. Opening the mind to possibilities unseen by others will yield huge benefits. This is a wonderful Moon to hone the craft of the mystic.

Presidents' Day

Monday, February 20 is Presidents' Day, and for some, the end of a three-day weekend. The Pisces Moon will be displaying its graciousness and awareness for most of the day until it goes void-of-course at 11:06 p.m. on February 21, quickly making its way into Aries at 12:14 a.m. on the twenty-second. Feminine and masculine energies will be in balance with the Moon and Sun both in Pisces. However, Mars is in Gemini and, given the holiday is political, there will likely be plenty of arguing, with all sides of any argument trying to win and have their way. Under the Pisces Moon, some folks may find themselves too sensitive to handle such shenanigans.

Mardi Gras

Figuring out the day of Mardi Gras is slightly more complicated than figuring the date for Easter. For now, Fat Tuesday is forty-seven days before Easter Sunday, which accounts for forty days of Lent plus seven Sundays, and is the day and night that Pope Gregory XIII proclaimed for partaking of all the indulgences that would be fasted during Lent. This year, Mardi Gras begins on February 21 under a Pisces Moon until just after midnight, at 12:14 a.m. the twenty-second, when the Moon moves into Aries and gets the party started. Aries will bring plenty of fire to the party and could boil over.

Full Moon

The fifth Full Moon in the annual cycle will be in Virgo on March 7 at 7:40 a.m. Night before day, the Moon will be in Virgo all of March 6 and early morning March 7, so no worries about shifting energies during the Full Moon rite. Don't let the need for perfection outweigh the good that will be experienced during the rite. This Moon will support showing the personal dark side.

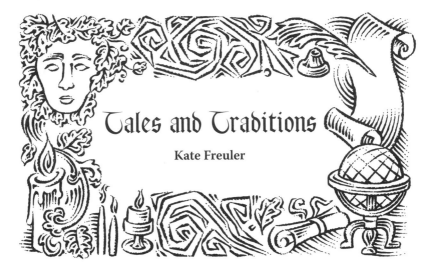

Tales and Traditions

Kate Freuler

IN SOME CLIMATES, FEBRUARY is the coldest, most difficult time of year. The celebration of Imbolc originated as a ritual meant to lure the sun back to the earth, bringing warmth and springtime with it. Many traditions included candle rituals and sacred fires, acting as beacons to attract gentler weather. A well-known feature of Imbolc is a circular ring of eight candles, one for each of the sabbats; when the candles are lit, they represent the warming of the earth. Another familiar symbol of the day is the sun wheel, or Brigid's cross. This is woven from straw, vines, or wheat and represents the sun.

In any fire-based ritual, it's important to consider what the spirit of fire brings to the meaning of the day. It is associated with passion, transformation, and action, but also with warmth and security, which presents an interesting dichotomy. A controlled fire can be a gentle nurturer providing heat and nourishment, but in a split second can become a devastatingly destructive force, demolishing everything in its path. This duality gives the spirit of fire some very intense traits.

The Elemental Spirit of Fire

You may have heard of "elemental spirits." These beings encompass the power or soul within each of the four elements of earth, air, fire, and water. In the spirit of Imbolc, we're going to look into the elemental spirit that resides within fire.

The idea of elemental spirits (also called "elementals" or "nature spirits"), was first presented by a Swiss alchemist and physician named Paracelsus in the sixteenth century. He theorized that each of the elements contained an otherworldly creature within it. He believed that these elementals possessed both a physical body and an invisible spirit. Earth elementals were called gnomes, undines were of the water, sylphs were the spirit of air, and salamanders embodied fire.

Each of these beings is believed to possess varying temperaments and appearances and can be invoked in magical ritual, although some caution against it. There are many conflicting beliefs about elementals, and opinions about their inclusion in magic run the gamut. Some say they're dangerous and should be left alone, claiming they're unpredictable tricksters who cause unexpected trouble, much like some of the mischievous Fae. Others insist they're benign and helpful.

Elementals can enter the human world but not vice versa. While generally hidden from view, every so often it's rumored that elemental spirits have been glimpsed in their physical form by especially spiritual people or those who are in a heightened psychic state. Some say that only children can see them. Some tales say that elementals keep treasures hidden in their realm and that they'll share these gifts with a few very lucky people. Elementals are known for striking a deal with humans, helping them with magic in exchange for a deed or object. However, if you don't keep your end of the bargain, you're likely to find yourself in a lot of trouble.

Amphibian or Spirit?

If you're like me, when you hear the word "salamander," you probably picture a slimy amphibian and wonder how it came to symbolize fire. Well, there is a surprisingly logical explanation. Salamanders, being amphibians who favor dark, damp places, often take up residence in rotting logs. In days past, when someone threw a log onto the fire, salamanders would come jumping out of the hearth, appearing to emerge directly from the flames. Pliny the Elder, a Roman philosopher and naturalist, popularized some of the salamander's more fantastical traits. He and others before him claimed that salamanders were born of fire itself, were flame-proof, and could even extinguish large blazes. Interestingly enough, the flame-resistant, highly toxic material known as asbestos was once referred to as "salamander wool" because of its non-flammability.

In the context of elemental spirits, however, a salamander is a very different thing than an amphibian. A salamander in the form of an elemental spirit is said to be the embodiment of the energy that creates fire itself. They are the power that causes a struck match to burst into flame or the life within the spark that forms when flint is struck. A salamander is difficult to include in magic because everything they come in contact with turns to ash. If you touch a flame, you're going to get burned. The same can be said of getting too close to fire elementals. Like fire, salamanders are considered especially unpredictable and should be handled with caution, if at all.

Salamander spirits inhabit places like the hearth and fire pits and are present in every single candle flame. They are also the driving spirit within a terrible forest fire. Salamanders are quick, destructive, and unpredictable. They can keep you warm, or they can burn your life to ashes. Salamanders are generally considered the most dangerous of the four elementals and the least likely to interact with humans. However, some practitioners leave them offerings in hopes of appeasing them and even include them in divination practices. The safest way to connect or communicate with a salamander is through smoke.

On Imbolc, it was tradition to divine how much longer winter would last, similar to what some of us do on Groundhog Day. One technique was to throw a handful of grain into a fire: If it was quick to burn, then spring would come soon. If it smoldered slowly, that meant winter was going to last a while longer. Even though salamanders are sometimes considered dangerous, you can still include them in your Imbolc celebration without getting too close. Consider burning some fragrant herbs in your Imbolc fire as an offering to them or incorporating smoke divination into your ritual. Ask a yes or no question and then throw some grain into the fire. If it burns fast, the answer to your question is yes. If it smolders sluggishly or doesn't burn at all, the answer is no. Also, pay attention to the smoke that forms from your offering and divine any symbols or shapes that appear. You can even add green wood to the flames and listen closely to the popping and hissing sounds that emerge. If your green wood squeaks as it burns, it might be a salamander trying to tell you something!

References

Hall, Manly P. "The Elements and Their Inhabitants." In *The Secret Teachings of All Ages*. n.p. San Francisco: H. S. Crocker, 1928. https://www.sacred-texts.com/eso/sta/sta25.htm.

McCoy, Edain. *The Sabbats: A New Approach to Living the Old Ways*. St. Paul, MN: Llewellyn; Enfield, 2001.

Szeintuch, Yechiel, Daniella Tourgeman, and MaayanZigdon. "The Myth of the Salamander in the Work of Ka-Tzetnik." *Partial Answers: Journal of Literature and the History of Ideas* 3, no. 1 (January 2005): 101–32. https://doi.org/10.1353/pan.0.0122.

Feasts and Treats

Gwion Raven

ALMOST EVERY IMBOLC RITUAL I've been to calls upon Celtic deities. Food offerings are frequently bread and milk and lamb and associated with the goddess Brigid. So often when we hear the word "Celt" we think of Ireland and Britain, but the Celtic peoples were spread all over what is now modern-day Europe.

These four recipes are heavily influenced by traditional Spanish foods and are best described as heartwarming and belly filling. Each dish can be made on its own or as one big feast. I always recommend the feast option!

Spanish Lamb Casserole (*Caldereta de Cordero*)

This dish harkens back to the Celtiberian shepherding practices of Andalusia and Aragon, with hints of North African spices. I cook this in a cast-iron Dutch oven on my stove, but if you're feeling adventurous, cook it over an open fire in a *caldereta* (cauldron) for an authentic experience.

Prep time: 10 minutes
Cooking time: 1 hour 15 minutes
Servings: 4

1½ lbs lamb stew meat
1 teaspoon salt
1 teaspoon black pepper
2 tablespoons olive oil
1 slice bread, cubed
4 cloves garlic
2 cups red onion, chopped
1 cup red bell pepper, chopped
2 teaspoons smoked paprika
½ cup tomato, diced
¾ cup red wine
3 cups water
2 bay leaves
8 sprigs fresh thyme
2 sprigs rosemary
12 peppercorns
3 cloves (or ⅛ teaspoon ground cloves)
½ cup parsley, roughly torn

Grab a big bowl. Add the lamb chunks. Toss in the salt and pepper and give it a good mix. Set aside.

Heat the oil in Dutch oven. Fry bread until crisp. Remove to a paper towel.

Crush the garlic with the back of a knife. Add peeled garlic cloves and lamb to the Dutch oven. Sauté meat on medium-high heat until browned, about 8 minutes. Set lamb aside. Add garlic cloves to the paper towel with the bread.

Add onions and red peppers to the Dutch oven. Cook over medium heat for 8 minutes. Add paprika. Cook for 1 minute, stirring frequently. Stir in tomato. Add wine. Cook for 4 minutes. Return lamb and any juices to the Dutch oven. Pour in water, just enough to mostly cover the meat. Add the bay leaves, thyme, and rosemary. Cover and simmer for 15 minutes. Remove bay leaves, thyme, and rosemary. Cook the lamb until tender, about 30 minutes.

Add bread, garlic, peppercorns, and cloves to a blender with 4 tablespoons of water. When the lamb is tender, add the paste to the stew and cook for 10 minutes.

Serve hot in bowls with a garnish of fresh parsley.

Roasted Spiced Potatoes (GF & Vegan)

Caldereta de Cordero is often served with these piping hot, spicy potatoes, and I can't resist a big bowl of potatoes! It's such an easy recipe to make. Perfect as a small-plate dish with a dollop of sour cream and fresh parsley. You can add them right in the bowl with the *Caldereta de Cordero*, which is more traditional. The aroma of smoked paprika always reminds me of sitting in a warm kitchen around an old farm table, with plenty of fresh bread and wooden spoons.

Prep time: 10 minutes
Cooking time: 12 minutes
Servings: 4

4 medium Yukon Gold potatoes, unpeeled, cubed
1 teaspoon salt
1 teaspoon smoked paprika
2½ tablespoons olive oil

In a large bowl, combine potatoes, salt, paprika, and ½ tablespoon olive oil. Heat a large skillet over medium-high heat for 1 minute. Add remaining oil. Heat for 1 minute. Add potatoes and sauté, stirring frequently, until golden brown, about 10 minutes. You may have to cook the potatoes in batches depending on the size of your skillet. Remove to a paper towel.

Roasted Whole Chickpeas with Warm Spices and Mint (GF & Vegan)

Chickpeas (or garbanzo beans) have been part of Mediterranean cuisine for more than 8,000 years. This simple dish is as delicious as it is ancient. Imagine people from thousands of years ago gathered together, sharing these crunchy, spicy legumes. Better yet, make them part of your Imbolc feast and share them with your beloveds. Roasted chickpeas are a fantastic table food, especially when served warm. Put a bowl or two out, and your guests will soon gobble them up. You can also use them in soups and salads, like croutons.

Prep time: 5 minutes
Cooking time: 40 minutes
Servings: 4

1 15-ounce can chickpeas, drained and rinsed
3 teaspoons olive oil
½ teaspoon salt
2 teaspoons ras el hanout spice
Zest of 1 lemon
Juice of 1 lemon
¼ cup fresh mint, chopped

Preheat the oven to 350°F. Pat the chickpeas really dry with a paper towel.

In a mixing bowl, combine the chickpeas, olive oil, and salt. Make sure the chickpeas are evenly coated. Spread onto an unlined baking sheet (no foil or parchment paper). Roast them for 20 minutes and pour into a bowl. Add the ras el hanout and mix. Put the chickpeas back on the baking sheet and cook for 20 minutes more or until they are crispy. Carefully pour the chickpeas into a mixing bowl. Add the lemon zest and juice. Mix well with a spoon.

Serve in small bowls with a garnish of fresh mint. Then start looking in your cupboard for more chickpeas, because you'll want to make more.

Hot Sangria

Sangria is often thought of as a summer drink: cool, fruity, and refreshing. Served warm, sangria is the perfect antidote for cold winter evenings. Spanish Sangria dates back at least 3,000 years and is likely inspired by Greek *hippocras*, or mulled wine. The taste is lovely, for sure, but just holding a warm mug, cozied up in a blanket in my favourite chair, somehow makes the cold winter's evenings more bearable.

Prep time: 5 minutes
Cooking time: 8 minutes
Servings: 4

¼ cup sugar
½ cup orange juice, pulp free
½ cup water
1 bottle red wine (Syrah is great, but anything will do)
¼ cup orange-flavoured liqueur
¼ teaspoon ground cloves
¼ teaspoon ground nutmeg
3 orange slices, cut in half
3 lemon slices, cut in half

Grab a saucepan. Combine sugar, juice, and water. Simmer for 5 minutes, stirring occasionally. Don't let it boil. Add the remaining ingredients and heat until hot, about 3 minutes. Remove the orange and lemon pieces.

Serve in mugs and enjoy. Remember to toast each other's health and happiness.

Crafty Crafts

Ivo Dominguez Jr.

THE SPARK OF LIFE and light that began to grow, to journey toward manifestation at Yule, is beginning to push through and become visible. The days are noticeably longer, and the green life of the earth is starting to awaken. Many of the celebrations and observances for Imbolc center on those changes. However, it is also a time for purification—to welcome in the new cycle of growth in a fresh and clean environment. This is one of the best times to do spring cleaning and clear away any stale energy that is lingering in your home or life.

A Besom for Cleansing Your Home

The witches' broom, which is also called a besom, can be leapt over to mark the joining of a couple in a handfasting. It can be used to clear a space to prepare it for a ritual. It can be used to sweep misfortune and bad luck out of a home. I have used a besom by moving it gently through the edges of someone's aura to remove emotional and energetic clutter. A besom can also be placed or hung near doors or windows to protect the home as well. Imbolc is a great time to create, decorate, and bless a besom to be used at Imbolc and for the rest of the year. The tide of energy that comes with Imbolc will be embedded in the besom that you craft.

Materials
Besom

Ribbons, colored raffia, beads, etc.

Dried flowers, feathers, and such

Adhesives

Acrylic paints and sealers

Floral wire

Carving or rotary tool

    Cost: $0–$25

    Time spent: 2 hours, plus drying time

Design Ideas
I suggest you buy a broom that is close to what you need rather than making one from scratch. Also, do you ever intend for it to be used to physically sweep a floor, or will it be used for symbolic actions like sweeping the air of stale energies? Your planned uses have an impact on choosing the proper size for the besom. The besom must be sturdier and larger if it will be used like its more mundane cousin, the kitchen broom. If you find a broom that you like that is too long, you can saw off the handle to the length that you need and sand the end.

Take some time to research and think on what colors, scents, symbols, herbs, etc. represent cleansing and symbolize Imbolc. Since you can use this besom year-round, not just at Imbolc, try to find the right balance.

There are four areas on the besom that you can embellish and ornament. They are the handle, shaft, band that attaches the bristles to the shaft, and bristles. Depending on your aesthetic, you may decorate as many or as few of these areas as you like. Go through your collection of craft supplies, notions, and bits of beauty that you've saved for reuse to help you brainstorm. (Recycling, upcycling, and reuse are good things, but do not use any greens, such as holly, that you brought into the house to celebrate Yule.

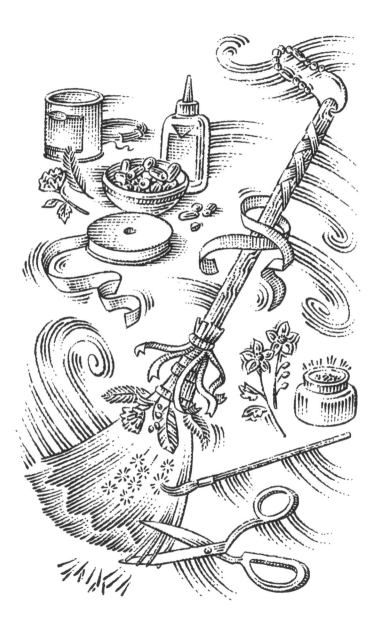

Those holiday decorations need to be out of your home before Imbolc lest you attract unwanted spirits.)

I like to drill a hole near the top of the handle and add a loop so I can hang the besom on the wall. This is also a prompt to start thinking about how you'll embellish it. You may wish to add wooden or gemstone beads or small charms to the cord that you loop through the top of the handle. You could also braid and tie off ribbons on the handle. A single ribbon or cord glued or hot glued down the shaft of the broom in a spiral can also look good and convey a sense of energy in motion. Another option is to draw a pattern of sparks, stars, or streaks down the shaft with a pencil. Then whittle or carve on the wood, or use a rotary tool (like a Dremel) or a woodburning tool to give texture to the pattern. You can add color with paint where you have carved or leave the carvings natural. You can also produce a lovely effect by putting gloss medium or gloss polyurethane on the carved areas.

The band and the bristles are perhaps the best places to focus your artistry. For example, you could create a skirt or a tier of feathers, dried lavender spikes, ribbons, colored raffia, or anything else you like. It is better if the materials are an inch or more away from the end of the bristles so they don't catch on things when you use the besom. To liven up the bristles, you can consider using a brush and some acrylic paints to add streaks of color to some of the bristles. If you like a bit of sparkle, I suggest using metallic paints rather than glitter, as the glitter will get everywhere when you use the besom. Another way to add a design element is to take shears and shape the edge of the bristles. They could come to a point, a zigzag, a slant, a crescent, and so on.

Construction Tips

Arrange and group your craft supplies in the order that you will use them. If you are sanding any wooden parts, be sure to clean the sawdust off away from your work area before starting with the rest. Floral wire, a heavy-duty hand needle or upholstery needle and thread, or simply knotting and braiding are good alternatives to gluing in this project. If you've drilled a hole in the handle, use it to hang the besom on a shower pole or another reasonable spot to dry if you've used glues or paints. After that, shake it gently, and if anything seems loose, attach it more solidly. Should you choose to anoint the besom with some fragrance, make that your last step.

Using the Besom

The besom is a tool for cleansing your space, but you need to start the flow with some of your energy. Look at the besom and think about the meaning of all the changes that you added to it. Feel energy flow through your hands and all the way down to the bristles. As you move the besom, continue to feel the energy moving through it. Use it to dissipate stale energy and to brush things out your windows and doors as needed.

Reference
Blake, Deborah. *The Witch's Broom: The Craft, Lore & Magick of Broomsticks*. Woodbury, MN: Llewellyn Publications, 2014.

Color Magic

Charlie Rainbow Wolf

IMBOLC FOLLOWS YULE ON the Wheel of the Year and falls around the beginning of February. It's one of the quarter turns, as my medicine elder would have phrased it, falling between a solstice and an equinox. This is when Brigid is honored, and here at The Keep, we can see the days lengthening quite quickly, even though we may still be knee deep in snow!

Imbolc is the first festival on the Gregorian calendar, and many believe that it is the first festival of spring. I tend to resonate with this, not just because of the Wheel of the Year, but because of my time spent on the Lincolnshire farm, when lambing season started and snowdrops began to peep through the frosty soil. There's a bit of speculation as to what the word "Imbolc" actually means, but I was always told that it meant "ewe's milk," which fits in nicely with the spring lambing that I witnessed.

The Colors of Imbolc

It might not be so easy to see the colors of Imbolc as with some of the other festivals. Mention Samhain and thoughts automatically turn to black cauldrons and orange pumpkins, but what about this first of the spring festivals? For me, the color that immediately springs to mind is white: mornings white with frost, the white of the sheep's wool, the white of the seasonal snowfall.

In the Samhain section I talked a bit about the purity of white, and it fits in with Imbolc too. Imbolc marks the start of the new season of growth, a new beginning, a new chance to start something fresh with new hopes to succeed. In his collection of Celtic hymns and incantations, Alexander Carmichael describes Imbolc as Bride breathing life into Winter to awaken him to the springtime (Carmichael, 1992, 172).

White is quite enigmatic. Even though it is perceived to be the absence of color, I was taught in art class it is actually a mixture of all colors; it's seen as white because that is what is reflected back and what the eye picks up and translates. White is a positive color—or lack of it—and is linked with illumination (white light) and understanding.

The next color I link to Imbolc is silver. This may not be one of the more popular colors, but bear with me. Think of the way the moonlight glistens on the February snow or the way that the frost gleams in the first light of morning. Silver is cool, refined, regal. It is one of the precious metals and—on its own—is quite soft, having a hardness of only 2.5 on the Mohs scale. To me, this reflects the duality of this festival: it has the hard coldness of winter within but gives glimpses of the softer spring season ahead.

Silver is also quite a sovereign color, which brings to mind Brigid, the goddess associated with this sabbat. In gemstone magic, silver is said to represent hope, motherhood, the moon, and intuition. I have no issue aligning all of these qualities and more with the festival of Imbolc.

The traditional colors of Imbolc are white, red, and black. Red is the color of blood and the life force, while black is the mixture of all colors—or as I was taught in art school, the absence of color. It brings the same complexity and air of sophistication and mystery to Imbolc as it does with Samhain, but in a slightly different way. At Samhain, black represents going into the darkness of winter, while at Imbolc, it mirrors leaving the darkness as the days lengthen.

Red echoes life returning to the land. The blood of the trees—their sap—is starting to rise in preparation for their leaves. It's a determined color, assertive and strong-willed. As mentioned in Yule, red is a root chakra color, the color of survival and material gain. This aligns it with Imbolc nicely, for survival in the harshness of winter can be earnest work for some, and the promise of the coming lambs is the livelihood of the farmer. Red also echoes the color of the placenta, shielding new life as it grows in readiness to be born.

Most wild animals and even some humans eat the placenta after the birthing has finished. I was told that animals in the wild did it to try to "clean up" the birthing site, making it harder for predators to find them. The placenta is full of nutrients, but I'm not going to suggest this as an Imbolc activity! It's possible to represent this in other, more mundane edibles.

Celebrating Imbolc

In the past, we have had a variation on the Yule log to mark our Imbolc feast. This seemed very appropriate, as Imbolc is halfway between Yule and Ostara. We took a dark chocolate cake (representing the darkness—it wasn't quite black) and filled it with raspberry jam (red) and fresh whipped cream (white, and linking with the ewes coming into milk as their lambs were waiting to be born). The top of this culinary delight was then decorated with chocolate ganache, more whipped cream, and topped with a fresh raspberry. It made a very welcome sweet treat as we celebrated the earth awakening from her slumber here in central Illinois.

Milky quartz is definitely my choice of crystal for Imbolc—the reference to milk is even in its name! Sometimes called snow quartz, this stone brings the qualities of innocence and clarity. It helps to get rid of preconceived ideas so that things as they truly are can be experienced.

Reference

Carmichael, Alexander. *Carmina Gadelica: Hymns & Incantations*. 1st ed., Edinburgh: Lindisfarne, 1992.

Imbolc Ritual

Susan Pesznecker

IN THE SECTION ABOVE, we considered what goes into good ritual: understanding, intention, focus, select correspondences, and ritualized actions or activities. Now it's time to give these ideas shape by planning your ritual retreat. You'll focus on the earliest stirrings of spring and, likewise, on the stirrings of your own ideas and how to move them from seed through fruition.

A Ritual of Retreat and Contemplation

What is it you want or need? What do you want more of in your life? What would you like to begin or perhaps get better at? How could your days be richer or full of meaning? What would help you quiet yourself and feel the joys of this life more deeply? Sit quietly and spend time asking yourself these questions before you go any further. And then ... Begin!

Make a Plan

Whether you're a detailed-outline or seat-of-your-pants planner, I suggest you create a basic framework for your ritual retreat. You'll probably want to do your ritual on February 1 or as close to it as possible. Are you an early bird or a night owl? Do you want to be up for sunrise? Will you use the entire day or just a few hours? Is it meaningful to you to watch the sunset or work during the evening? You can always change this later, but right now, ballpark the timeline for your retreat. Consider that sunrise is a fabulous time to announce one's intentions or for any kind of beginning. Midday is a powerful moment of balance, while sunset and early evening are especially good for completions, closures, and bindings. And midnight? The witching hour, of course!

Here's an example of how you might set up a schedule for a daylong ritual retreat, and you can shape it according to the time you have available as well as adding your own ideas, switching ideas around, or removing anything that won't work for you. My goal here is simply showing you how this might look.

Time	Activity	Notes and Materials
7:30 a.m.	Wake up, stretch, greet the day (spontaneous). Get dressed, wash face, brush hair and teeth.	"MAGIC AF" T-shirt.
8:00 a.m.	Breakfast, focusing on seasonal foods. Blessing over the food. Clear all dishes after.	Prepare a food blessing. Charge phone for later music.
8:30 a.m.	Morning walk with awareness of seasonal change. Watch for potential wand wood and any signs of natural augury.	
9:00 a.m.	Set up Imbolc altar. Light candle and pray for guidance and discovery. Turn a tarot card to get a reading, write goals on a piece of paper and leave it on the altar. Meditate on the goals, then extinguish the candle.	Prepare a prayer. Altar materials: dark blue altar cloth, yellow or gold candle, matches, extinguisher, paper, pencil, other materials TBA. Tarot deck.
9:20 a.m.	Morning activity: tarot study (goal: deep learning of two cards), practice with different layouts, create an Imbolc spread, color blank cards, always considering relationships to Imbolc.	Tarot decks and guide books. Tarot coloring deck and colored pencils.

Time	Activity	Notes and Materials
11:45 a.m.	Journal about the morning, energy, goals, etc. Add sketches, altar layout.	Journal, pens, and colored pencils.
12:00 p.m.	Lunch, same process as breakfast. Contemplate midday magic and changing light.	Repeat food blessing.
12:30 p.m.	Relaxation: reading, meditation.	Choose a book.
1:00 p.m.	Afternoon activity: wand craft. Imbolc's gathering energy is a good time to create magical tools.	Wand wood, sandpaper, copper wire, small drills, pocketknife, beeswax. Background music? Or watch *Practical Magic*.
3:00 p.m.	Afternoon tea, journaling. Review evening ritual and make any changes.	Prepare treats in advance. Tea bags, teacup, small plate. Journal, etc. Ritual outline printed out.
4:00 p.m.	Outdoor activities: another walk, nature study, sit in the sun with a book, ride a bike. Whatever sounds good. Contemplate earth's magic, watch for special objects.	Book? Bike?
5:00 p.m.	Simple dinner: outdoors if weather permits. Notice ebbing light and long shadows, aware that winter still holds sway.	Repeat food blessing.
5:45 p.m.	Relaxation: read, meditate, journal, contemplate what I've accomplished.	Journal, etc. Book.
6:45 p.m.	Prepare for Imbolc ritual. Gather materials, lay a small fire in the fireplace or firepit (outdoors if weather permits). Wash hands and face, don ritual garb.	Ritual materials, notes, scripts, etc. Firewood and kindling; matches. Fire safety materials. Robes and jewelry.
7:00 p.m.	Start background music.	Phone.

Time	Activity	Notes and Materials
7:05 p.m.	Formal ritual begins with procession to site. Carry out the ritual, including fire lighting.	
7:45 p.m.	"Cakes and wine," extinguish fire.	Cookies, tea.
8:00 p.m.	Tidy up after ritual, staying in ritual garb.	
8:30 p.m.	Return to morning altar space; put the altar to sleep, saving the paper from this morning.	Black altar cloth cover.
8:45 p.m.	Relax, read the paper from my altar. Goals realized? Maybe pull another tarot card. Journal about the day, including the ritual. Reflect on what comes next. Set goals! Prayer or self-blessing. (Next morning, when the fire is cold-out, I'll collect some of the ashes. I'll use these to kindle my next fire, then save and add those ashes, and so forth.)	Journal. Tarot deck. Closing prayer or blessing. Container for ashes.
9:15 p.m.	Cleansing bath, focusing on clearing my mind and being at peace. Clean, soft PJs after.	Lavender bath bomb. Clean PJs.
And then...	Bed! Happiness! Success!	A good book!

Reflection

However you design your day, complete it with some reflection. Reflection—a kind of evaluation—is a key part of any undertaking, designed to help you hone and develop your practices. It's simple; just ask yourself the following and record in your journal:

- What did you accomplish during the retreat?
- What parts did you like best or find most satisfying?
- Was there anything you didn't enjoy? Or anything that was clunky?
- If crafting another day-long ritual retreat, what would you keep the same? What would you change?

- What did you find out about yourself during the retreat?
- What's next?

Make It So!

You can do this. Decide what you want to do, take notes, and watch it come together. Plan it and make it happen. And remember: this is win-win. Whatever you do, it'll be fabulous.

And now, in the words of the immortal Elle Woods: "Congratulations … we did it!"

Resources

Henes, Donna. *Celestially Auspicious Occasions: Seasons, Cycles, and Celebrations*. New York: Perigee, 1996.

Pesznecker, Susan. *Crafting Magick with Pen and Ink. Learn to Write Stories, Spells, and Other Magickal Works*. Woodbury, MN: Lewellyn Publications, 2009.

———. *The Magickal Retreat: Making Time for Solitude, Intention, & Rejuvenation*. Woodbury, MN: Lewellyn Publications, 2012.

Robert, Elizabeth, and Elias Amidon. *Earth Prayers From Around the World, 365 Prayers, Poems, and Invocations for Honoring the Earth*. HarperOne, 2009.

Reference

Witherspoon, Reese, Luke Wilson, and Selma Blair. *Legally Blonde*. Directed by Robert Luketic. MGM, Marc Platt Productions: 2001.

Notes

Notes

Notes

Ostara

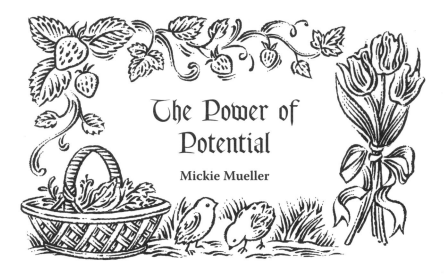

The Power of Potential

Mickie Mueller

OSTARA, ALSO KNOWN AS the spring equinox, has always seemed like a magical time of the year to me. Both the spring and autumn equinoxes are astrological moments in time when it seems that the natural world holds a deep breath just before exhaling into oncoming change. In spring that means the earth warms, insects begin to stir as buds burst forth, and animals come out from hibernation or migrate back as they prepare for the summer ahead.

The spring equinox in the Northern Hemisphere happens in March, and in the Southern Hemisphere it arrives in August and is the result of axial tilt. On the equinoxes, the sun sits right over the equator, resulting in the day and night being as close to equal as they will be all year. The tilt of the earth on its axis as it rotates around the sun causes the changing seasons. These are the yearly cycles that those of us who work with the energies of magic use to great effect as we manifest our goals. During the spring equinox the energies of balance, new beginnings, and rebirth swirl all around us.

Most of all, I see the spring equinox as a time of potential. The symbols that we associate with the spring, including flowers, eggs, and seeds, are all symbols of potential. In them we discover the mysteries that allow us to work magically with the cycles of the season to help us find our own potential within in order to accomplish our goals.

The Flowering of Life

Flowers are all about potential. They burst forth with their bright colors and sweet scents so that they can become something altogether different. Some will become fruit, berries, or vegetables, while others eventually grow into nuts or seed pods of various kinds. Every flower is full of transformative energy and possibilities.

In my area, we usually see nature heralding the season in with some flowers around the spring equinox. Some of the first of the wildflowers are known as "spring ephemerals." They bloom only briefly as they pop up across the forest floors, painting the area with splashes of their unique colors. Just as suddenly, they disappear, becoming dormant again under the ground. Spring beauties, toothwort, and bluebells are amongst the ones I've seen in the woods in my area. I wonder which ones bloom where you live? Many Pagan and witchcraft altars are decorated with spring buds and flowers. This not only brings beauty but also symbolism of overcoming winter and filling your magical space with the power of potential.

Some blossoming trees and shrubs are filling the world with their colors around the spring equinox as well. Forsythia, some varieties of cherry, and magnolias are among the first to burst into color where I live. Domestic bulbs like tulips, daffodils, and hyacinths have begun to emerge from the earth in a show of color. These are flowers that come from a very plain-looking bulb that must be planted deep in the ground and weather the cold winter in order to bloom in the spring. They remind me of the fact that growing into yourself isn't always a pretty process, and that's okay. I look at bulb flowers as a metaphor to point out that sometimes we become strong, beautiful, and vibrant from being surrounded by mud and facing the cold with grace and steadfastness. It also reminds me that internal work might not always look like much from the outside, but the end result is always worth it.

I also love to notice the swelling buds that are on trees and flowering plants just before they burst into color. The liminality of buds has always fascinated me. I think of them as snuggling under warm blankets all winter and hitting the snooze button a couple times until they're finally about to rise to greet the day and get to work in the business of life, growth, and reproducing more plants.

Exploring your local woodland areas or walking through your neighborhood can be a very inspiring activity on or around the spring equinox. Seeing the power in delicate buds and blooms as they break inertia warms the heart and reminds us that even what may seem like small efforts can launch big possibilities into our own lives.

Sometimes We Must Crack an Egg

Eggs are a very old symbol of life and rebirth, and once again the theme of potential is represented in the egg. Depending on where you live, there might be birds hatching in your area. My husband and I usually keep an eye out for nests and fallen eggshells on our walks in Missouri, but we don't usually see them quite yet by the equinox. Occasionally that's when birds in my area begin to build nests. It can be fun to see if you notice nest building or nests with eggs in them this time of the year.

There is some folklore that revolves around eggs and the spring equinox. One belief is that you can balance an egg on its end at this time; in a similar myth, a broom may also be balanced on its bristles on this day. Neither of these is based on fact, however. There is no difference in gravity or the ability to balance physical items on the equinoxes versus any other day of the year, and this is probably a simplified interpretation of the balancing energy, although it is fun to try. Incidentally, many people have successfully balanced eggs, and you can easily spin an egg on its end any day of the year if it's hard boiled. You can also balance a broom anytime if you have a very flat-bristled broom and a lot of patience. It's definitely fun to post these photos or video clips online during the spring equinox!

Many animals lay eggs, but bird eggs specifically have become a representation of the spring equinox, and especially chicken eggs. This may be because the sabbats were inspired by the agricultural cycles of Western Europe, and there is a long history of domestication of chickens, making them the eggs that we are the most familiar with and that are most readily available to us. It's also important to note that chickens can lay eggs pretty much daily through spring, summer, and fall, making chicken eggs a particularly important symbol of fertility. The eggs that are fertilized will, of course, bring new life abundant, so the egg has a powerful association with potential; in other words, what *will* be. Chicken eggs are often used in modern spells and rituals to usher in something new. We also see the shells used in magic for protection and purification since the shell guards growing life and relinquishes its form to usher new life into the material world.

Perhaps the egg also reminds us that a state of peace might seem great but sometimes we need to break something apart to reach our full potential. For the baby chick growing within it, the peace and protection an egg provides is necessary for the chick's very life during most of its development. When the chick is fully developed, that same egg that protected it must be broken for the chick to survive. Peace can't remain in this instance; the chick must peck and fight to free itself. Some bust right out, while others take a break or two, even napping in between pecking. This can remind us that reaching our potential doesn't look the same for everyone, and we shouldn't judge each other or ourselves as we progress through life.

Many witches, Pagans, and other magic users enjoy decorating eggs with magical symbols using either store-bought kits or natural dyes. Eggs are often blessed before eating them on the equinox. This is a practice that brings the energy of the day inside of us to become one with our own bodies, consumed by our very cells. Aside from eating whole eggs, it's also popular among kitchen witches to incorporate eggs as an ingredient in a dish to be eaten on the day, such as a cakes, quiche, or cookies. For people who don't include eggs in their diet, seeds such as flax or chia can produce a great substitute in baked goods and still harness the energy of potential. Exactly in the way that an egg houses the potential for a whole living being, so does the seed house the potential for a whole plant.

Seeds for Thought

The spring equinox is also a wonderful time of the year to plant a garden and bless your seeds. Blessing seeds for flowers or vegetables on your Ostara altar is a lovely way to bring the energy of the day into your garden. A seed is a perfect representation of potential because it contains the code for an entire plant within itself. In the turning of the year, we see the cycle of the seed, sprout, stem, leaves, buds, flowers, and seed pods of autumn that begin the cycle all over again. Even those of us who don't have room for a big garden can work with the energy of seeds in their spring equinox celebrations. Some people choose to plant herbs in small pots to be grown on a kitchen windowsill, flowers or vegetables on an apartment balcony, or protective plants in pots by the front door. I've known many witches who plant these seeds with the intention of another project tied to their growth by including a petition or simply uttering words when planting the seeds. Intentions for things like a new career, creative project, or even growing your bank account can germinate in the soil along with the seeds and be grown into their full potential in this way. As the seed grows, so does the attached intention.

Not all magical practitioners have a green thumb, though, and that's perfectly okay; there are other ways to work with seeds on the spring equinox by using them in our spells, rituals, and feasts. Culinary seeds, such as poppy, sesame, and sunflower seeds, can be added to baked items, spring salads, or other recipes for the celebration. This brings the correspondences of that particular plant, plus harnesses the potential of the growing earth around you, into your food. Candles can also be dressed with a few seeds, sending the energy of potential into the ether along with your spell intentions.

Another lovely practice is to fill a handful of birdseed with your intention for any goal you wish to achieve. Leave those seeds out to feed birds, who are full of that feisty spring energy. They'll be grateful for the gift, and as they thrive and prosper, so do your intentions. In this case, the seed's potential is as food; it's full of energy much like a battery that just sits there ready to bring something to life. The energy of the seeds will power the life force of birds and will, in turn, fuel their flight, songs, mating, nest building, egg laying, and protecting their young. In this, we can see how just a bit of potential can lead to big things! When seeds are eaten instead of grown, the concept of potential remains just the same. Seeds can also be used in your Ostara magic by adding them to charm bags. If I want to work with a specific plant's energy and I don't have that plant, I'll sometimes use seeds from that plant instead. Since the seed basically holds the whole plant within, I've found this to be a powerful method for working with plant magic to power your spells.

The power of potential is everywhere we look in the spring, and bringing that power into your spring equinox spells, rituals, and celebrations is natural. I wonder if these ideas will inspire you to come up with ways to work your own magic. Blessings to you this spring when change and possibilities are so palpably in the air!

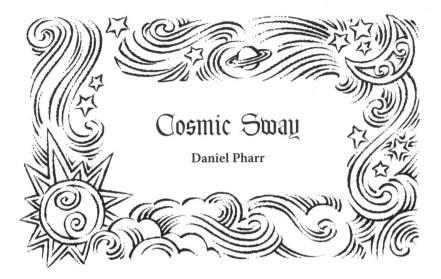

Cosmic Sway

Daniel Pharr

THE SPRING EQUINOX ARRIVES on a different date every year. The date is a product of celestial motion, as are all solstices and equinoxes. The vernal equinox lands between March 20 and 21 in the Northern Hemisphere. This year, Ostara is on March 20 at 5:24 p.m. under a sympathetic Pisces Moon.

The length of night equals that of day on the equinox, and day lengths are imperceptibly close the week before and after, leaving night and day, darkness and light, in balance. This is a day of equilibrium, the midpoint of spring, when winter has loosened her grip on the countryside and summer beckons.

The Pisces Moon encourages perception of the ethereal, which will provide better insight into the mundane. Use the Moon's energy to divine the coming summer months; plan a vacation and a plethora of weekend activities. Spend plenty of time with friends. The honoring of the equinox could be a fanciful foray into the many forms of divination, even something different like reading jelly beans.

Dark Moon

The Moon moves into Aries on March 21 at 12:01 p.m. The Dark Moon honoring will likely happen the night before on March 20 under a Pisces Moon. The Dark Moon is all about incubation and renewal. Use the Dark Moon to decide and prepare to move forward with the next generation of the quest set upon at Yule. The resistance from work, life, family, and everything that gets in the way of pursuing the quest goals softens with another iteration. Sleep. Repeat the last few steps that don't feel right and launch into the next phase. Pisces is the healer for the pineal gland, which controls some wonderful functions like sleep. Eat dark, chlorophyll-rich, leafy greens and raw cacao for dessert to support pineal health.

Standing Eggs

Eggs and hares are associated with spring. Spring hares were snagged for meat and eggs collected for, well, eggs. Easy to see why Easter celebrations co-opted the chocolate bunny and eggs. The dining room table is an excellent place to stand eggs on end, starting around a half hour before the equinox. Some say the idea of eggs standing best on Ostara is scientifically unfounded, while others like the ritual of it. Opinions vary; you be the judge. Allowing the eggs to warm to room temperature will facilitate the eggs to stand more quickly. Chilled eggs straight from the refrigerator move more slowly internally, and having the yoke move to the end of the egg helps it stay balanced, like a tightrope walker holding a long pole. Once the eggs are standing and the equinox has arrived, take photos and leave the eggs standing just to see how much time passes before they roll over. If the table experiences vibration, the eggs will stand for a shorter time. A good idea would be to surround the eggs with rolled or folded towels so a fallen egg will not roll off the table and crash Humpty-Dumpty style.

April Fools' Day

A Leo Moon will shine upon this April Fools' Day. This prankster Moon could turn up the heat. The desire for recognition under this Moon may make April's fools more vulnerable and April's pranksters more daring.

Full Moon

The diplomatic Libra Full Moon will arrive on April 6 at 12:34 a.m. She will be the sixth Full Moon in the cycle. Libra is a lovely place for the Moon to hang out, sending its balanced, fair, and idealistic energies to all, and especially enjoyed by those open to receiving the energy. Comfort and security will abound. Libra so appreciates balanced energy and harmony that chancing the loss of it prompts Libra to indecision, both for the self and in groups. The indecisive aspect of the Libra Moon wants everyone to have a say and then negotiate the result in a nonconfrontational way until everyone is happy enough to agree. Communal agreement is a great way to approach group dynamics, but try ordering a pizza! Once the negotiated logistical concerns are put to bed, enjoy the clever flirtations that are the Libra influence.

Easter

Easter's date varies with the equinox. Easter is celebrated on the first Sunday after the first Full Moon, after the vernal equinox. Easter is on Sunday, April 9, after the Full Moon on April 6, which is the first Full Moon after Ostara on March 20. Forty-seven days before Easter is Fat Tuesday, followed by Ash Wednesday. Easter this year will be under a Sagittarius Moon beginning at 8:57 a.m. Games are always fun in the Sagittarius Moon. Egg hunts, egg and spoon races, and all the rest should be a happy time.

Tax Day

Tax day is on April 17. The Moon will be in Pisces most of the day, moving to Aries at 9:09 p.m. Waiting until the Pisces Moon to file taxes may not be the best course of action. Pisces is altruistic and concerned with helping others. Getting down the "counting coppers" of tax preparation will be a slog. Taxes would be better done between April 11 and 13 under a Capricorn Moon. The hardened, practical approach to the calculation of taxation will serve the taxpayer, as Capricorn's detail-minded methodology will gather the deductions and find the applicable tax breaks and loopholes.

Dark Moon

This Dark Moon will arrive on April 20 at 12:13 a.m. and will be void-of-course in Aries for seventeen minutes; entering Taurus at 12:30 a.m. Dark and void-of-course is not conducive to stability; however, drive and directness will not be in short supply. The void-of-course aspect of the Aries Moon will struggle to display the coming Taurus characteristics while holding on to the Aries aspects. The late-night Dark Moon celebrations should be ready for the Taurus-provided stability and structure, and add a splash of overindulgence to give a nod to the Taurus need for beauty. If an earlier event is preferred, the night of April 21 works before the Moon is void-of-course at 11:41 p.m.

Earth Day

Earth Day arrives on April 22, the same day every year; however, the Moon sign changes each time. This year, a Gemini Moon will inspire the day, and good inspirations they shall be. Enthusiasm should be plentiful. Talking with folks about Earth Day—the mission and the need—will be easier than might be normally expected, plus Taurus will add a big dose of charm while conveying the urgency and asking for donations of time and money.

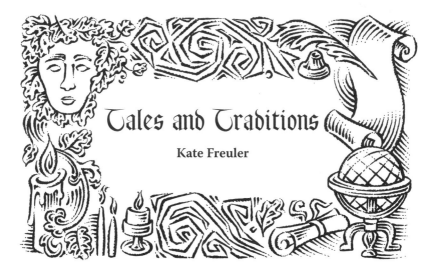

Tales and Traditions

Kate Freuler

OSTARA MARKS A CELEBRATION of new beginnings as the Wheel of the Year turns toward the season of hope, growth, and renewal. Many Ostara myths involve gods or goddesses making some kind of pilgrimage to the land of the dead to later return with renewed life and power, mirroring the seasonal change. This sabbat focuses on progress and fertility. Depending on where you live, you might begin catching glimpses of green through the snow or even early flowers. These things inspire a feeling of lightheartedness and excitement for the coming days. The earth is waking up from its long winter sleep and maybe your spirit is too.

Spring Cleaning for the Soul

A popular feature of the season is spring cleaning. The snow is melting into cleansing water that washes away all the debris of the last year, making it the perfect time to do the same in your own life. Doing a big cleanup of your space and scrubbing every nook and cranny is satisfying on its own but is even better if you follow it up with some form of energetic or spiritual cleansing to mark the equinox.

While Ostara is mostly a celebration of growth, part of growth is shedding that which is no longer useful, like leaves falling off of a tree to make room for new buds or a snake outgrowing its skin. While Ostara certainly focuses on the future far more than the past, sweeping away the old stuff is still a necessary progression. Cleansing and renewal go hand in hand.

Ostara bids a cheerful goodbye to the cold and darkness, allowing you to fully embrace the new season. This concept is demonstrated in an old Slavic tradition performed on the spring equinox. An effigy of Marzanna, a goddess of death, plagues, and winter, was constructed out of straw and cloth. The witchlike figure of death was featured in celebrations throughout the day. In the evening, Marzanna was set on fire and thrown into a river, symbolically "killing" the spirit of winter, death, and the cold. Afterward, the remains of the effigy were pulled from the water and paraded back into town, perhaps to illustrate the cyclical nature of death and renewal. In some cases, the effigy was left in the water, not to be looked at again, symbolizing leaving the past behind. Another way to think about this ritual is from a cleansing perspective: past hardships, represented by the effigy, are purged and washed away, thoroughly destroying them to allow for a new beginning to take hold. When you do a ritual cleansing on your home or your body, this is essentially what takes place.

Cleansing with Smoke and Water

Spiritual cleansing of spaces and the body has had a spike in popularity in recent years. Most people are familiar with burning herbs to purify their home or taking long, luxurious baths dappled with flower petals and fragrant oils to renew their spirit. However, the practice of ritual cleansing is far older than the self-care movement.

Currently, in the Western world, the most well-known way to bless or purify a space is by performing a smoke ceremony, which involves burning a bundle of herbs such as sage leaves. While this practice is embraced by many people, it's important to defer to the culture it belongs to and make sure you're respecting any living traditions, while taking care to use ethically sourced plant materials. Ritual purification is an ancient, worldwide practice. Different civilizations have various ways of doing it, but a frequent theme is the use of smoke or water.

Spiritual cleansing with smoke or water has many purposes. There is the cleansing of physical space to ward off negative or stagnant energy. There is symbolic cleansing meant to mark a rite of passage or new beginning. Some rituals are meant to banish illness or evil spirits, while others are for clarity and heightening consciousness.

Consider the word "fumigation." What comes to mind? Perhaps it's a vision of billowing fumes permeating every inch of an apartment building to rid it of insects, fungus, or some other unhealthy thing. Fumigation is actually a very old cleansing technique; the only modern feature is the addition of poison.

Hundreds of years ago in France, rosemary and thyme were burned in hospitals to ward off disease. This isn't as metaphysical as it sounds, as the smoke of certain herbs has been proven to possess antimicrobial qualities. Lavender, sage, and others do, in fact, rid the air of harmful bacteria when burned. Some herbs are also known for repelling mosquitoes and other insects when smoldered.

Spiritual cleansing with smoke is similar to fumigation, only instead of casting out critters or sickness, you're clearing out invisible energy. Some smoke cleansings are performed to freshen a space filled with stagnant energy, some to banish evil spirits, and others to drive out chaotic energy after an upsetting event.

Cleansing as a Ritual

Many religions around the world have some kind of cleansing practice. The washing of hands, face, or feet before entering temples or sacred spaces is common, as is dabbing the head or body with blessed water. Washing one's hands prior to prayer is sometimes an expression of respect. Immersing a person in a lake or river to cleanse away the past is often a rite of passage, as in the Christian baptism, when being dunked in water can symbolize being "born again." There's no denying that immersing yourself in a natural body of water has a renewing, invigorating effect. It can certainly refresh your body and soul, washing away stress and bringing clarity of mind.

Many magical practitioners will take a ritual bath before ceremonies or workings. Sometimes this is to purify themselves of all outside energy, and other times it's part of the working itself. Herbs and oils are chosen specifically for their magical properties and added to the hot water.

Some cleansing practices use both smoke and water. In ancient Egypt, those who tended the temples kept herbs burning at all times. To maintain spiritual purity, they kept their heads and body hair shaved and washed themselves twice a day. In Scotland, a ritual called "saining" was performed using blessed water and the smoke of rowan and juniper to cleanse and bless an area.

Ostara is the perfect time to say goodbye to the old stagnant energy of the winter, letting it trickle away with the melting snow. In addition to your traditional rituals, consider doing a good, intense house cleansing or taking a special ritual bath to mark the sabbat. Clear out your closets and cupboards, as well as your mind and soul, so you can focus on the wonderful new beginnings that are coming your way.

References

"Egyptian Civilization—Religion—Priests." Canadian Museum of History. Accessed July 29, 2021. https://www.historymuseum .ca/cmc/exhibitions/civil/egypt/egcr07e.html#:~:text=In%20 mortuary%20temples%2C%20priests%20conducted.

"Drowning Marzanna—Winter's Witch." Warsaw in Your Pocket. March 19, 2021. https://www.inyourpocket.com/warsaw /drowning-marzanna-winters-witch_72571f.

Feasts and Treats

Gwion Raven

THE SPRING EQUINOX BRINGS to mind fairy tea parties, decorating Ostara eggs, and the promise of warmer days to come. Words like "burgeoning" and "verdant" and "renewal" appear like so many spring flowers popping up in meadows and hedgerows everywhere.

There are two words I dread though: egg salad. Now, I like a good egg salad sandwich as much as the next person, but there's more to a good Spring Equinox brunch than egg salad. Look at the colours in these meals too. There are reds and yellows and shades of green, just like a springtime posey.

Each of these dishes can be enjoyed separately or as one meal.

Hard-Boiled Eggs with Tahini and Sumac (GF & Vegetarian)

Here's a play on egg salad that's a little lighter and packed with flavour. If you're super fancy, you can pipe the tahini mix into little flower designs on top of the hard-boiled eggs. I typically drizzle the eggs liberally so the sauce runs down the sides, and then I lick the spoon. If you're not familiar with tahini, it's ground-up sesame seeds. Sumac is made by grinding the berries of the wild sumac flower. Sumac is slightly acidic and tastes like lemons.

Prep time: 5 minutes
Cooking time: 25 minutes
Servings: 4

6 large eggs
¾ cup plain Greek yogurt
¼ cup tahini
1 tablespoon lemon juice
2 tablespoons olive oil
1 garlic clove, finely chopped
¼ teaspoon sumac

Hard boil eggs. Run under cold water and refrigerate for 15 minutes. While the eggs are cooling, mix the remaining ingredients in a bowl until they are smooth and incorporated.

Peel the eggs and halve them lengthwise. Arrange them on a plate, like a flower petal design, with bigger ends toward the middle and the yolks facing up. Drizzle or pipe the tahini mixture over the eggs. Sprinkle with a little more sumac.

Spring Peas, Leeks, Lettuce, and Mint in a Bowl (GF & Vegetarian)

If you could take spring and magically distill it down to one meal, this would be that meal for me. Fresh peas, the subtle flavour of leeks, and sweet lettuce are the stars of this incredibly simple recipe. I've eaten this meal for breakfast, lunch, and dinner. I don't mean I've served it at each of these times; I literally mean I've eaten this three times in one day! By the way, did you know lettuces are part of the daisy family and have been cultivated for over 6,000 years? Lettuces appear in Sumerian and Egyptian mythology.

Prep time: 5 minutes
Cooking time: 15 minutes
Servings: 4

4 tablespoons unsalted butter
1 leek, white and pale green parts, sliced into rounds
¼ teaspoon salt
2 cups fresh peas (frozen peas work too)
1 head of butter lettuce, torn into pieces
1 tablespoon fresh mint, chopped
Black pepper to taste

Heat a skillet over medium heat for 1 minute. Add 2 tablespoons of butter and let it melt. Add the leeks and salt and cook over low heat for 3 minutes, making sure the leeks are well-coated in the butter. Add the peas to the leeks and cook for 5 more minutes, stirring frequently. Grab the torn lettuce leaves, stir them into the leeks and peas, adding the remaining butter. You may need to add up to a tablespoon of water if the mixture looks a bit dry. Pull the sauté pan off the heat and continue to gently stir until the butter is melted and the lettuce has wilted.

Serve in four bowls with fresh ground black pepper and mint. I love this by itself, and it's scrumptious with rustic bread too.

Rhubarb and Strawberry Fool

No one is quite sure why stewed fruit desserts are called "fools," although if the alternative is to name them just "stewed fruit," then "fool" does sound much more appetizing! The word "fool," when referring to a dessert, is found in the late 1500s and appears in cookbooks from seventeenth-century England onward. There's something so very springlike and celebratory about fruit fools.

Prep time: 10 minutes
Cooking time: 25 minutes
Servings: 4

½ pound rhubarb, chopped
½ pound strawberries, sliced
½ cup sugar

Juice of one small orange
2 cups plain Greek yogurt
Zest of 1 orange
2 tablespoons honey
4 vanilla cookies, cut in half
4 sprigs of mint, no stems

Get a big saucepan and add the first four ingredients. Bring just to a boil and then simmer for 5 more minutes or until the fruit mixture is thick. Let cool for 15 minutes. While the fruit compote is cooling, mix the next three ingredients together in a bowl and refrigerate.

I like to serve this dessert in large wine glasses or sundae flutes, but any bowl will do just as well. Add a couple of tablespoons of compote to the bottom of the glass. Then 2 tablespoons of yogurt. Keep layering until the glass is full. Tuck 2 vanilla cookie halves into the glass (or crumble them) and add the mint.

Spring Tea with Mint and Lemon (GF & Vegan)

Depending on what the temperature is outside for your Spring Equinox brunch, you can serve this tea hot or iced. It's super satisfying either way. If you want to make this an iced adult beverage, add 1 ounce of citrus-infused vodka.

Prep time: 1 minutes
Cooking time: 15 minutes
Servings: 4

4 cups boiling water
4 green tea bags
1 small bunch fresh mint leaves
4 tablespoons honey
4 tablespoons lemon juice (1 large lemon)

Boil the water in a deep saucepan. Remove from the heat. Add the tea bags. Cover with a lid and steep for 5 minutes. Stir in the mint, put the lid back on, and leave it alone for another 5 minutes. Pour the contents through a sieve into a pitcher or large teapot. Stir in the honey and lemon juice. If you are serving warm, you're done; just pour the tea into your favourite cups. If you want this chilled, refrigerate for 1 hour. Add ice to four glasses and serve with a sprig of fresh mint.

Crafty Crafts

Ivo Dominguez Jr.

THE GLORIOUS BEAUTY OF the green life of the world bursting forth is a great gift that comes with the Spring Equinox. The craft projects for this holiday center upon magickal objects—gardening implements—that help plants grow and flourish.

Watering Can and Garden Stakes

If you have a garden to use these enchanted objects in, that is lovely but not necessary. If you have a window box, houseplants, a tree on your sidewalk, or a nearby bit of park that you love, you'll have a use for these projects. In these times of increasingly unpredictable or harsh weather, these two craft projects will help what grows near you. You'll be making a watering can that blesses the water and one or more enchanted stakes to support the growth of plants.

Materials
Watering can
Stakes
Paints, acrylic, enamel markers, spray paint
Florist supplies, wires, willow twigs, and such
Miscellaneous trinkets and ribbons

Cost: $0–$25

Time spent: 3 hours, plus drying time

Watering Can Design Ideas

For the watering can, I suggest that you buy a plain metal watering can that is of a size you can manage when it is full. Metal will conduct the energy more easily than plastic and will last for many years. If you find a used one, make sure it doesn't leak and be sure to sand away any corrosion.

Watering cans come in all styles and shapes, so study the one you select so that you can come up with a design that fits it well. Here are some ideas to get you started:

- Place four moons around the base of the can to call on the lunar cycle. A full moon, a dark moon, and two half-moons. Above each of the half-moons, add a sun to represent the sun at the Spring and Fall Equinoxes.
- Using stencils or freehand painting, do a border of leaves and flowers at the base and top of the can. In the space between

the borders, arrange spirals and triquetras of different sizes and colors.

• Select some symbols for the four elements or runes, glyphs, or sigils that mean health and growth. Then paint them in different sizes—some free-floating, some overlapping—in a swirling pattern around the can.

• Paint or decoupage figures of plant spirits, water spirits, or goddesses like Pomona or Flora.

• For the handle, consider flowers, twining vines, or a celestial motif of moons and suns.

Stake Design Ideas

To design your enchanted plant stake, first decide how it will be used. Will it be used to support a plant like a tomato, or will it be strung with lines to trellis peas? Or is it just for focusing vitality and growth into the soil and plants? Its size, shape, and purpose will determine some of your design choices. If used as a physical support, it must be a few feet tall and sturdy. Purely magickal ones can be whatever size matches your design ideas. You can certainly buy wooden garden stakes, hefty dowel rods, bamboo, perhaps lumber like two-by-fours or one-by-fours, and the like as your starting points. I always start by looking through scraps and junk first. A broken mop or broom can be just right for this project. The heavy-duty wooden paint stirrers you can get at hardware stores are perfect for small stakes.

Three-dimensional elements can add interest and help act as physical supports. Look in the floral supplies section of a craft shop for bundles of curly willow branches, spiral or wavy whimsies of bamboo or wood, etc. These can be bound to the main stake with knotted cords or thicker floral wire. Pierced capiz shells (windowpane oysters), ribbons, bits of old suncatchers or chandelier crystals, oversize ornate buttons, and other odds and ends can be hung, wired, or tied on to shine and move in the wind. You could also use metal hoops that they sell in craft stores to hang the ornaments like charms on a bracelet.

If you've decided to paint some sigils or decorations, or print words or phrases onto the stake, consider using enamel paint pens for the smaller details. These pens come in many colors, including metallics, and will hold up better outside in the weather. I am especially fond of using sigils to add the magick of desired intentions and actions to objects. The stakes or watering can are a perfect place to draw sigils that decorate and empower them. Think of sigils as abbreviations, acronyms, or zip files that contain lots of ritual power in a small amount of space.

Construction Tips

Before starting work on your watering can, you may wish to add a coat of spray paint that is suitable for metal. If you want the look of metal showing through your design, a clear coat spray is a good idea. You can mask off areas with painter's tape if you want specific areas left bare. An undercoat will make it easier for decorative paint to adhere, and it will last longer.

Check your measurements before cutting the wood for your stakes and be mindful of how much of the stake will be in the ground. In general, the heftier the stake, the sharper the angle of the point you will need to cut at the end to push it into the soil. If you leave the wood of the stakes bare, they will decay, which may be exactly what you wish. If you want them to last longer, you can apply some exterior paint or clear coat sealer. A compromise is to only paint the lower eight inches or so that will be in the soil and the top inch where the rain will get into the grain.

Making Things Grow

When you fill the watering can, bless the water with a breath that you blow into the can. Let your gaze move over the colors, shapes, and symbolic messages on the watering can and see them light and awaken. As you water the plants, feel for their gratitude, and listen for what they need. Think of the enchanted stakes as wands and

staves that you are sharing with or gifting to the plants and the land. When you place them in the ground, feel the stakes grow spirit roots into the ground. As often as you like, put your hand on the stakes and draw energy down from the sky and up from the ground. Feel free to create spells and spoken charms to welcome the power of life.

Further Reading

Zakroff, Laura Tempest. *Sigil Witchery: A Witch's Guide to Crafting Magick Symbols*. Woodbury, MN: Llewellyn Publications, 2018.

Color Magic

Charlie Rainbow Wolf

THE SPRING EQUINOX MARKS the arrival of Ostara. It is the time when the sun enters into the astrological sign of Aries. It will fall around the same date in March, but it will vary from year to year because of the solar calendar. Easter, on the other hand, follows the lunar calendar, which is why sometimes Ostara and Easter are close together, and other years Easter is earlier or later than Ostara. Many deities are honored at this time, including Eostre, Freya, and Osiris.

Ostara is the beginning of spring on the Gregorian calendar, but here at The Keep, I always see it as the second of the spring festivals, with Imbolc being the first. By now, many of the spring flowers are peeking through the ground or even blooming, the snow has usually passed until the autumn (but not always), and there's a buzz of excitement and readiness as gardeners and farmers alike start to prepare for the growing season.

The Colors of Ostara

When I think of Ostara colors, my mind goes to pastels. There's a wonderfully light color returning to the sky. The blue that was washed out in the winter starts to return to a lovely azure. Many of the spring flowers are shades of pink and yellow and violet. Where the colors of Yule were deep and intense, to me the colors of Ostara are brighter and more lighthearted, somehow. The equinoxes are a time of balance, when the days and the nights are of equal length. This balance can be applied to any area of life: work and play, dark and light, masculine and feminine. Colors that might be found in the sunrises, such as pink, yellow, or white, are part of the Ostara palette—as is bright green, representing new vegetation and growth.

Green is the color of preparation. Actors or guests on a television show go to the "green room," waiting for their call. Someone with a green thumb is someone who is good at gardening and growing things—and flora needs adequate preparation to grow well. Traffic signals change to green when it is time to go and continue the journey. People who leave a job for another, or one location for another, often talk about going to "greener pastures," and there's a proverb about the grass always seeming to be greener on the other side of the fence. It's the color of hope, anticipation, and new beginnings.

In Yule, I spoke of green being a heart chakra color and how it forms a bridge between the physical chakras and those pertaining to the spiritual side of things. At Ostara, this bridge marks the balance of the seasons. Pink is another heart chakra color and represents the gentler side of red. The artist makes pink by adding white to the primary red, making it softer and more approachable—some might even say more pure or innocent. When I was young, it was customary to dress young girls in pink (and boys in pale blue), and while these old traditions are sometimes falling by the wayside now, it's not hard to see that pink could represent the young goddess, the maiden and her fertility.

Pink is also meant to represent tenderness, and this, too, echoes the vibe of Ostara. The most tender parts of the body—and those associated with intimacy and love—are pink. In the garden, the young growth is tender and susceptible to damage from frost and hungry predators looking for a springtime feast. Pink is an optimistic and happy color for the most part; even in language, people talk about being "tickled pink" when happy or "in the pink," meaning feeling fine.

Yellow is also prominent during this season of new growth and early spring flowers, which can be found in the palest creamy yellow of the breaking dawn to the intense brightness of the blooming daffodils. Yellow is a primary color, thought to elevate the mood and bring cheer. It is the color of spring and confidence, and it is one of the easiest colors for the human eye to see—which is why many traffic signs and school buses are painted bright yellow, and why those working at the local grain mill have to wear a "safety yellow" shirt at work.

Due to its potential intensity, too much yellow isn't a good thing. It is jarring, like a light that is too bright, or like the yellow bile Hippocrates associated with a cranky temperament. Perhaps this is why someone who displays cowardice is thought to be "yellow" or "yellow-bellied" and why "yellow journalism" is a term for irresponsible reporting.

Violet—another color associated with Ostara—is a lighter shade of purple: a secondary color created by blending blue and red. Its pale softness and subtle tone embraces red's strength and blue's integrity. In *You Are a Rainbow*, the author describes violet as "the world of the imagination and the unconnected, illogical images, magic, and whim" (Hills, 1979, 59).

Violet is associated with the crown chakra. While there are some spring flowers in this tone, it is not a particularly prominent color in nature. Perhaps that is why it is often associated with the higher mind, royalty, and spirituality. It elevates the vibration of purple and gives it a lighter and more refined energy. This seems to nicely complement what I was taught by my medicine elder about the scent of the lilac flowers being appealing to the ancestors.

Taking any color and making it into a pastel will help make it more gentle, and there's really no hard rule of thumb as to how to interpret a pastel color. Just like a bright color calls to mind something that is vibrant and intense, a softer hue is softer on the eye and less assertive. The meaning is still the same. Blue is still blue.

Celebrating Ostara

One of the beauties of working with pastels is how easy it is to blend their energies. Add a bit of light green to a soft blue to get a delicate teal or cyan. Add a touch of pink to a gentle orange to get a light peach shade. Marrying the colors also adds interest to any magical work using those tones.

The pastel colors of Ostara are often reflected in the candies and eggs that adorn the aisles of the shops at this time of year. I have very fond memories of dying eggs with my mum when I was a child. She bought the commercial dye kits, but as an adult when I have dyed eggs, I've tried to make my own dyes from onion skins and beetroot and other natural dyestuffs. The muted shades echo the soft tones of the festival and make a wonderful family activity during an Ostara celebration.

When it comes to Ostara stones, I like to use something that echoes not just the colors of the Sabbat but also its energy, and with that in mind, I choose watermelon tourmaline. With its soft pink and green shades, it immediately lifts the spirit. This is a stone whose emotional healing properties are said to "pull weeds while it plants seeds" (Raphaell, 1991, 133). How appropriate is it that the inner work for this season matches the outer work being done in the yarden (yard + garden = yarden)!

Reference

Hills, Norah. *You Are a Rainbow: Original Insights into the Work of Christopher Hills by Researchers Practicing His Theory of Nuclear Evolution.* Boulder Creek, CA: University of the Trees Press, 1979.

Raphaell, Katrina. *Crystal Enlightenment: The Transforming Properties of Crystals and Healing Stones.* Crystal Trilogy, vol. 1. New York: Aurora Press, 1991.

Ostara Ritual

Mickie Mueller

THIS IS A RITUAL working to bless new beginnings. The spring equinox is a perfect time to bless any project or undertaking that is on the horizon for you. It might be a new job, a creative project, looking for a new home, starting a family, beginning therapy or any type of healing journey, redecorating your home, starting or revitalizing a relationship—whatever you're beginning in your life. It's easily adjusted for either a solitary celebrant or a group of any tradition. I've done variations on this one through the years, both in my covens and on my own, and it never fails to bring positive change.

Egg Ritual for New Beginnings

Decorate your altar in any way that speaks to you of spring and new beginnings. Be sure to include a basket or bowl large enough to hold one egg for each participant and a small slip of paper and pen for each. Many people like to decorate the altar with colors of spring such as pale blues, lilac, light greens, and yellow. Some people also like to work with black and white to bring in the aspect of balance. You might like to add flowers, either fresh or silk, such as daffodils, tulips, or hyacinths, but don't feel limited to the traditional flowers that we think of this time of the year. You can also step outside into your yard or anywhere in nature to see what's blooming. Maybe some weeds (ahem, wildflowers) are in bloom, and you can put together a small bouquet for your ritual space that resonates with the energy of the land you live on. Other altar décor may include, but is not limited to, representations of rabbits, hares, snakes, nests, seeds, chicks, and eggs. Floral- or honey-scented incense is a nice addition, and if you enjoy working with stones and crystals, you might add quartz, selenite, moss agate, aquamarine, bloodstone, or any stones that you feel drawn to.

You'll also need a blown egg, prepared in advance, for every participant. This is accomplished by simply poking a tack or pin in the top and bottom of an egg to make small holes. Use a toothpick to gently "peck away" and make the holes a bit bigger, slightly smaller than the size of a pea. Use the toothpick to break the yolk within and mix up the egg a bit. Back in the day, we used to hold the egg over a bowl and blow in one hole with our mouth so that the contents of the egg would be forced out the other end and into the bowl. These days, I've discovered a cleaner and safer way: a brand-new bulb nose aspirator found in the baby section of the pharmacy works great (instead of your mouth) to blow the contents of the egg out and into a bowl. These eggs can then be used for scrambled eggs or in baking. Run water through the empied eggshell under the faucet until the water runs clear, and set it aside to dry. If you're vegan, you'll probably prefer to purchase or make hollow papier-mâché eggs on a balloon form, which will work just as well.

Before the ritual, each participant chooses a prepared eggshell and may decorate it with symbols of the season and include colors, runes, sigils, or any other symbols that represent the new beginning that they are focusing on for the ritual. You can provide eco-friendly markers, natural dyes, earth-friendly plant-based school glue, pressed flowers and leaves, and other biodegradable notions that the eggs can be decorated with. If adding herbs corresponding with your goal, crystal chips, etc. inside of the egg, you might wish to seal up one end with a small sticker, paper, and a bit of natural glue or beeswax so that the contents don't fall out, but make sure to leave one hole open. As the egg is being decorated, focus your mind on a positive outcome for your goal, adding your intention as you work.

Once the eggs are decorated, you can bring your egg to your altar space. Open the ritual with the usual methods according to your own tradition—some people cast a circle and call in elemental quarters and deities, some traditions use a method called laying a compass, while others might simply purify the area with sacred smoke, asperge with water, or visualize the space as sacred. Just use the method that works best for you.

The group leader (or you if you're working alone) may set the intention for the ritual with a statement of purpose in their (or your) own words or use this suggestion:

[We/I] welcome the energies of the spring equinox, a time of balance, potential, and new beginnings. The wheel has turned, and the earth once again is bursting forth with new life. At this moment in time, the days will become longer than the nights as the season of growth begins. We witness the warming of the earth as flowers burst forth and life stirs into action; we recognize that we are part of the earth and share a sense of oneness with all that is growing around us. We harness that energy of potential in all things to bless our new endeavors that await us on the horizon. May we bring these seeds of hope for the future into fruition and achieve the new beginnings we bless on this sacred day.

At this point each participant should be given a small slip of paper and a pen and may write the intention for their new beginning that they intend to undertake on the paper. Be sure to write the statement in such a way that assumes it will be blessed and manifest positively. As an example, "My search for a new home is blessed and will succeed in the best outcome for myself and my family." Once the petitions are written, they may be rolled up tightly and slipped into the hole in the end of the egg.

Each participant may now whisper more details of their goals into the hole of the egg and program it with their intentions. Really feel as if the goal is in reach and the energy of potential of this special day is supporting you and blessing all your efforts toward the goal. Be mindful to keep thoughts of roadblocks out of your mind, only focusing on the positive outcome. You don't have to be able to see it in your mind, but you should summon up the thoughts and feelings you anticipate having once the outcome is achieved and use those to program the egg.

One by one, each person may place their eggs in the basket as they make a statement such as:

From this egg, the future is born.

At this point, the individual or group may raise energy by any method according to tradition or preference. Singing, dancing, clapping, or any method you like. I love all these methods, and I also often include a simple chant that can be repeated over and over as the energy builds, such as:

Bless [our/my] beginnings, making a start, bringing it forth, with mind, body, and heart!

When the energy is feeling very full and can be sensed in the room, end the chant. If you're not on your own, be sure to designate the most energetically sensitive person in your group in advance to cue the group when it's time to end the chant and send the raised energy. If you're on your own, listen to your intuition, and you'll know when the time is right for you. At the moment the chant stops, all participants should channel the energy raised using the open palms of their hands aimed at the basket of eggs sitting on the altar, thus charging them with all the energy raised with the chant.

Often after raising energy, a short grounding and centering exercise is necessary and can be accomplished by imagining roots extending from the participants' feet into the ground and exchanging energy with the earth to regain balance.

The ritual may be closed in the way of your tradition, and refreshments may be shared. Eating, drinking, and celebrating will further ground personal energies. Each participant will take their egg off the altar at the end of the gathering; if you're alone, you may leave it there overnight. The eggs will now be planted beneath the earth by everyone in their individual gardens or containers, or even under a grassy lawn if you don't have a green thumb. Either seeds or a plant should be placed on top; don't worry if the egg is crushed in the soil during planting. The physical egg and the magical energy it holds will fill the soil and feed the plant as it grows. As it thrives, so grows and thrives the outcome of the project you blessed on the spring equinox!

Notes

Notes

Notes

Notes

Beltane

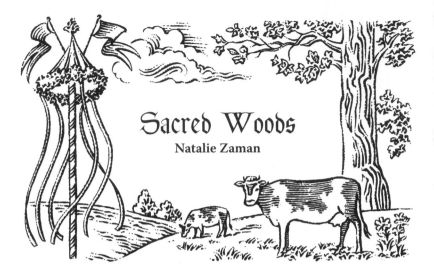

Sacred Woods

Natalie Zaman

WHO DOESN'T LOVE TREES—ESPECIALLY old ones, towering tall with gnarled trunks and twisted, hoary branches. Trees can be curmudgeonly, graceful, and definitely magical, and so, an essential element of Beltane celebrations. The root, in fact. It's widely accepted that the word "Beltane" means "bright fire," wood being the desired fuel. In many magical and esoteric circles, May Day (or any day) ritual bonfires are built from nine sacred woods, each bringing its particular energies to both flame and ash:

Tree	Magical Properties
Birch	A tree of regeneration and reincarnation, the birch is often the first tree to grow back in a forest after a disaster.
Rowan	A protective wood for many reasons, not the least of which is the star (pentacle) shaped blossom that can be seen on the underside of its red berries.
Ash	A masculine wood, ash is a tree of knowledge. (Norse mythology says that the first man was created from an ash tree, and the first woman, a rowan.)
Alder	Often found near water, the alder has a foot (root) in two worlds and so is good for divination and making choices, especially spiritual ones.

Tree	Magical Properties
Willow	Another "watery" tree, the willow's wood is flexible and filled with healing properties. It is also a symbol of mourning in America and many European countries.
Hawthorn	A heart tree, hawthorn is, literally, cleansing; its berries can help drainage and reduce fluids.
Oak	Oaks represent strength and many other things, including wealth, luck, and success—oak does it all!
Holly	Another protective wood, holly is one of my favorite trees, not only because of its associations with Christmas and Yule, but because J. R. R. Tolkien "planted" two holly trees at the entrance to Moria (to protect it?) and named the area "Hollin" after them.
Hazel	Sometimes called the, "Tree of Wisdom," hazel is used for divination and protection.

Once burned, ashes from Beltane fires may be sprinkled over land to protect it or induce growth and abundance, brushed around doorways and windows to protect or transport those who pass through them, or blended with water to create magical inks.

Like all things—plants, stones, colors, etc.—trees have multiple meanings, symbolic associations, and magical properties; what you see in the table above are but a few. It should also be said that this is *one* list of the nine sacred woods; there are others that include apple, grape (vine), and elder and omit holly, ash, and alder. The point is that there are many traditions, and all of them are valid.

I'm very familiar with the trees on this list (especially apple and grape, as I grow them), and for me, living in the northeastern United States, it's fairly easy to find any of them. Their magical and spiritual uses are steeped in (mostly) Northern European traditions—but what about other parts of the world? My travels have taken me to places where the trees are different—taller, wider, spikier … stranger. What about trees that grow in places where the environments and growing conditions are, well, pretty much the *opposite* of the temperate, season-changing zone where "the nine" sacred woods thrive?

And why *nine*? Why not two (Beltane is about partnerships)? Or three (symbolic of the goddess, celebrated at this turn of the wheel), or four or five sacred woods? Nine is a magical number, and the *Wiccan Rede* references it. However, there are ancient texts and poems that reference any number of sacred woods. (Tara Sanchez wrote a lovely article about it on her blog, *Temple of Hekate*.) I would like to offer the thought that when building a sacred bonfire, personal numerology should play a part. For Beltane, the numerology of the day, in this case, is May 1, 2023:

$$5+1+2+0+2+3$$
$$6+2+5$$
$$1+3$$
$$4$$

Perhaps there should be *four* sacred woods in this year's Beltane fire. But which? (Woods, that is.)

All trees are magical. Tropical trees, desert trees, and mountain trees each have their own beauty and medicine to share. I remember being dazzled by the trees, shrubs, and vines of Florida when I started spending serious time there: the various palms, flowering bushes with thick, glossy leaves, and the massive banyans that swallowed fence, building, and sidewalk. When I first thought about these as sacred woods, I tried to make direct correspondences—like substituting ingredients for a recipe. While trees certainly do share attributes (i.e., many are protective or healing or both...), each variety, subgenus, and so on has its own special magical qualities, and so I felt I needed to appreciate them for their own merits, not as understudies. What follows is a very short sampling of possibilities for alternate sacred woods.

Tree	Magical Properties
Mangrove	Mangrove trees are resilient, adapting to life in the harshest of conditions. Growing in clusters with roots deep into sandy soil, they protect against coastal erosion, making them ideal partners in defense magic. They literally "walk" on water and seem to grow out of it, rather than the more solid ground under the surface. They are deeper and more complex than they seem.
Banyan	Sacred in Hindu culture, the Banyan's wood and ash are used in Ayurvedic medicine. Banyans expand outward as well as upward by sending down shoots from their branches that plant themselves, then grow and merge with the central trunk. It's no wonder that these trees are symbolic of immortality and longevity.
Palm	Which one? There are literally over 2,500 varieties of palm trees, from low-growing, fan-shaped shrubs to the slender, bushy-crowned stalks that line Hollywood Boulevard. Called "palm" because their leaves resemble a palm with fingers, palm trees conjure up visions of tropical beaches and desert oases—making them wonderful for peace and vitality magic.
Sequoia	Giants of the forest, sequoias are magical just to behold and true "evergreens"—know that when you're standing in front of one, you're in the presence of a being that is potentially thousands of years old. Their size (your average sequoia grows to just under 300 feet in height and has a trunk girth of 20 to 25 feet!) and flame-resistant bark make them god trees; they're nearly indestructible. Sequoia's vibrant red bark (from which the term "redwood" comes) will bring power to any working.
Acacia	In the US, acacias can be found in the Southwest, where it is hot and dry. Like palm trees, the acacia is sacred in many cultures, including that of ancient Egypt, where it was linked to funerary customs. Acacia is useful in psychic work and connecting to those who have passed from this world.
Joshua Tree	The Joshua tree is a tree in disguise. Even though it grows like and looks like a tree, this Mojave Desert native is a succulent and a species of yucca. No one really knows how the Joshua tree got its name, but an often-told tale is that Mormons crossing the desert came upon the tree and thought it resembled a person with their arms raised in prayer—and they named it after the story of Joshua in the Bible. Joshua trees are endangered and should not be touched, as they are fragile plants. Stand in a Joshua tree's presence to celebrate and honor your own uniqueness.

Tree	Magical Properties
Magnolia	Native to the Southeast, magnolia trees can be found as far west as Texas. Magnolias are feminine trees; their soft, fragrant blossoms bring peace and comfort, and all parts of the tree can be used in healing magic of all kinds, both spiritual and physical.
Saguaro	Found throughout the Sonoran Desert, the saguaro is a giant cactus, but one that is certainly treelike. I have a vivid memory of driving through a saguaro forest and then up Mount Lemmon in Tucson. I watched in wonder as—with the change in elevation and temperature—the saguaros magically morphed into pine trees. Saguaros are sacred to the Tohono O'odham nation. Large, many-armed saguaros are ancient; they grow their first arm between 50 and 100 years old. Because they provide food for bats and homes for owls, and their flowers bloom when the sun goes down, they are guardians of the night.
Piñon	I read about piñon pines in Willa Cather's *Death Comes for the Archbishop* long before I experienced them years later when passing through the lobby of an Art Deco hotel in Delray Beach, where a fire of piñon logs was burning in the hearth. The scent transported me to distant deserts with golden sands and rose-colored sunsets. Native to Mexico and the Southwestern United States, the wood of the piñon pine burns with a fragrant incense that repels bugs and leaves little ash. Its scent is both warming and cleansing and is good for clearing rituals and fresh starts.

You'll notice that some of the brief descriptions of these alternate sacred woods contain personal stories—memories that made these particular trees special to me. I would encourage you to do the same; I have found that personal connection is a powerful element to any magical or spiritual endeavor. Make it your own!

What are your nine—or five or three or four—sacred woods? I encourage you to pursue your own research and follow your senses to find what works best for you. While anchored in tradition and knowledge, magic is, ultimately, adaptable. When finding the sacred woods for your Beltane fire, it's just a matter of making connections—and they're probably closer than you think.

(It is important to note that some of the plants mentioned [and others that are not] may be endangered, and endangered and protected species lists are constantly updated due to new research and changes in environment. Do not cut trees or remove live branches; gather fallen wood, seeds, and leaves where and when it is permissible. Be sure to check the rules for harvesting even fallen wood. Sometimes an entire area is protected because even fallen material can be part of a delicate ecosystem.)

Reference

Kynes, Sandra. *Tree Magic: Connecting with the Spirit & Wisdom of Trees.* Woodbury, MN: Llewellyn Publications, 2021.

———. *Whispers from the Woods: The Lore & Magic of Trees.* Woodbury, MN: Llewellyn Publications. 2006.

Sanchez, Tara. "The Nine Sacred Woods of the Need Fire." *Temple of Hekate* (blog). WordPress. April 30, 2018. http://www.temple ofhekate.net/blog/the-nine-sacred-woods-of-the-need-fire/.

Tolkien, J. R. R. *The Fellowship of the Ring.* New York: Ballantine Books, 2012.

Whitehurst, Tess. *The Magic of Trees: A Guide to Their Sacred Wisdom & Metaphysical Properties.* Woodbury, MN: Llewellyn Publications, 2017.

Cosmic Sway

Daniel Pharr

THE SECOND MOST IMPORTANT High Holiday of the Pagan liturgical calendar, Beltaine is spelled many ways and, like Samhain, has different methods of setting the celebration date. Beltane, Beltain, Beltaine, Beltine, and Ceitean are a sampling of the spelling and names for Beltaine. There are many more. An overland calendar was used by the ancients of the Celtic Isles since about 8,000 BCE, constructed with pits and standing stones or poles and used for about four thousand years to track solar and lunar cycles. The first evidence of transcription is on bronze tablets with holes next to the days in about 200 CE. A wooden peg was moved daily from hole to hole to track the date. Calendars evolved over millennia with additions and alterations of observed seasonal, lunar, and solar information as the Celts tried to synchronize the solar and lunar cycles with the seasons. This also explains why there are varying ways to choose the date for Beltaine, as is so with the other cross-quarter days.

Solar Beltaine

The simplest means of fixing Beltaine on the calendar is the solar method: May 1, with the balefire being lit after sunset the night before. The Moon will be in Virgo until 7:53 p.m. on May 1, at which point the Moon will void its course and enter Libra at 2:09 a.m. on May 2. The Beltaine celebration will likely be under the Virgo Moon on April 30. The Virgo Moon will exert a certain exactness to the rite preparations. Planning an event and being prepared for any eventuality is consistently better than a spur-of-the-moment rite, but sometimes the best outcome is from an unplanned, everyone-tuned-to-the-same-channel surprise. This Moon promotes consistency. Waiting for the Libra Moon may not work as well since the planning was influenced by the Virgo Moon. The Libra Moon will want beauty and charm, and the Virgo energy is more about efficiency.

Cross-Quarter Beltaine

May 6 at 2:11 a.m. is the calculated midpoint between Ostara and Litha. The Moon this night will be in Scorpio, the perfect Moon for a sexually charged ritual night. The Beltaine balefire symbolizes the beginning of summer, but the celebration is far more festive than just the arrival of a new season. Beltaine represents fertility for the coming year. Sexuality is at its peak and, as such, is often celebrated with matches and marriages and a Great Rite. The balefire was an important aspect of the Beltaine celebration. Individuals jumped the fire to bring fertility and purification. Couples jumped the fire to pledge themselves to one another. Cattle and farm animals were driven through the fire or between two fires to cleanse the animals of diseases and protect them in the coming year.

Pleiades Beltaine

A bit earlier than the cross-quarter calculation, the Beltaine Full Moon is May 5 at 1:34 p.m. Beltaine is always the seventh Full Moon in the cycle and marks the halfway point, and it is always in seductive Scorpio.

Mother's Day

Mother's Day is on May 14 this year, always the second Sunday. The Moon in Pisces will make Mom feel special. Lots of love and caring and acts of connectedness will show Mom she's always loved. A little creativity in showing Mom how special she is will be long remembered.

Black Moon

May 19 at 11:53 a.m. will mark the Dark Moon in Taurus. The Taurus Moon will also be shining the night before. A Blue Moon is often talked about as the second Full Moon in a month, called a monthly Blue Moon. The second Dark Moon in a month is known as a monthly Black Moon. Whereas a seasonal Black Moon is the third Dark Moon out of four occurring between a solstice and an equinox or visa versa. This night's Dark Moon is a seasonal Black Moon, which only happens every few years. This Moon will not be conducive to gatherings and teams. Taurus in the twelfth house is about withdrawing and time for the self. The Black Moon is going to enhance the desire for isolation. Security is found in privacy. Maybe this night's festivities should be a candle and a salt bath, ritual food and drink, and journaling. Volunteering may feel right in the moment, but expressing emotions may be misunderstood.

Full Moon

Sagittarius influences the lunar energies beginning June 2, and the Full Moon on June 3 at 11:42 p.m. The increased intensity of the Full Moon will boost the spontaneous Sagittarian influences to feel far more random and erratic. Conversations might jump from topic to topic in rapid succession, purchases might be made on a whim for something never previously considered, and the honesty displayed in all things may become honestly brutal in a twisted stretch for fun.

Dark Moon

The Dark Moon arrives on June 18 at 12:37 p.m. in Gemini and goes void-of-course two hours later at 2:24 a.m. The Dark Moon will promote introspection, especially where relationships are concerned. The charm associated with the Gemini Moon will be challenged, and darker traits may be examined. Boredom could be an issue, and when enhanced by the Dark Moon, boredom could turn to disinterest or neglect.

Father's Day

The Cancer Moon on June 18 for Father's Day is a nice gift for the family. Cancer influences are usually experienced in the positive aspects of home and hearth. In this Moon, emotions are more easily related. Nurturing of family and love relationships may be the focus this Father's Day. This should be a wonderful day for remembering the good times, the vacations, the weddings, the births, winning the lottery—all of the happiness that Dad has experienced. Take care not to slip into a murky hole of negativity. This is an emotional Moon, and sentimentality will arise from the depths. It could bring the laughter of memories, or it could bring tears of loss, breakups, deaths, angry moments. Try sticking to safe subjects and to gratitude and nurturing. Let Dad know you care and have always cared. Maybe even apologize for being difficult during the teenage years, and before tears start flowing, joke about how insane childhood felt.

Tales and Traditions

Kate Freuler

BELTANE IS BEST KNOWN for Maypole dances, fertility rites, and celebrating sexuality. It's the time when the god and goddess come together to consummate their relationship and conceive a new season of fruitfulness of the land. Beltane is a time for the blossoming of the fruit trees and the first phase of planting in the fields. Many rites centered on encouraging these new seedlings to take hold and flourish.

Spinning and Weaving

A lesser-known activity that was celebrated on Beltane was sheep shearing. At this time of year, wool was harvested to be spun into yarn, which would be knitted into clothing, woven into textiles on a loom, or knotted into nets for fishing and hunting. Wool and the many everyday tools it was used for were almost as important as harvesting food.

Sheep's wool, spinning wheels, and weaving looms have gathered immense amounts of folklore, appearing in fairy tales and mythology around the world. When you consider how the Maypole is draped in ribbons, which are then woven together by dancers during Beltane celebrations, some interesting connections can be drawn. While the Maypole dance was a fertility right, it also brings to mind the idea of weaving together all creation.

In the past, spinning wool was generally considered "woman's work," which meant its technicalities were somewhat mysterious to men. Spinning and weaving—like childbearing, midwifery, love, and death—was just one of the many important things that were considered women's business. Since wool was a necessity for survival in some cases, it had great power. Like many things women were in charge of, it became associated with witchery, which could explain its appearance in so many fairy tales. Spinning and weaving often took place in groups, and so involved a circle of women talking, exchanging information, and otherwise getting together for a good cackle, which as we know historically led to suspicion.

In mythology, spinning and weaving wool almost always represents the creation of life, the weaving of fate, and the snip of death, mirroring the cycle of existence.

In Greek mythology, the three Fates, called the Moirai, were the spinners of destiny. Clotho spun the yarn on the spindle, deciding when a person was born. Lachesis then measured the length of yarn, determining their lifespan. Atropos decided when death would come by snipping the yarn with shears. These three spinners determined the fate of every human being from the moment they were born until the second they took their last breath.

The Greek goddess Athena rules over spinning and weaving (along with war and wisdom), and features heavily in the myth about the origins of spiders. Spiders are naturally master spinners, weaving webs for survival much like spinning wool and weaving on a loom were essential to peoples' lives. The word "arachnid," which means "spider," comes from the tale about a young woman named Arachne who crossed paths with Athena. Arachne was known far and wide for creating beautiful tapestries on her loom and was very proud of her work. However, she refused to acknowledge that her great weaving skills were a gift given to her by Athena and claimed full credit for her work for herself. Hearing of this disrespect, Athena was offended. She took on the form of an old woman to confront the bragging, brazen Arachne, warning her that she should give more credit for her talent to the gods lest she invoke Athena's wrath. Arachne dismissed the old woman's warning carelessly, declaring that if Athena was such a great weaver she should come and prove it. Athena, furious, revealed herself, and a competition between the two weavers began. Athena wove a tapestry showing the gods doing heroic deeds. Arachne also wove a scene depicting the gods but portrayed them as mean and angry. When she saw Arachne's woven tapestry, Athena exploded with rage, beat her with the shuttle of her loom, and then turned her into a spider. Arachne and all her future children were doomed to weave forever in hidden dark corners, ignored and without praise, in the form of spiders.

In Norse mythology, there were weavers called the Norns, who took the form of giantesses. The Norns wove the fate of all things, including that of the gods, which rendered them especially powerful and terrifying. Usually, there were three Norns. One was the past, one the present, and one the future. Together they fabricated the destiny of all beings, pre-determining all of their life experiences and, of course, their demises. It was said that it was futile to petition the Norns to change your fate, and you just had to accept what they had given you. However, people did attempt to give offerings to them by making a special porridge with very specific ingredients. This porridge was fed to women just after they'd given birth in hopes that the Norns would incorporate good health into the tapestry of the child's life.

Wool, spinning, and weaving play a huge role in mythology, superstition, and mysticism. On Beltane, honoring the source of wool—sheep—was important and celebrated, since wool was such an intrinsic and necessary part of life.

On Beltane, the ribbons of the Maypole are intertwined as the participants move over and under one another in a dance celebrating fertility and creation. The weaving can be seen as unifying the god and goddess, of course, but one could also consider the action a means of creating fate while weaving a fertile future.

On May 1, consider weaving or knitting some wool into an offering for the Fates or as a symbol of blessing the fertility of the land. Simply braiding some brightly colored yarn together while imagining what changes you wish to see conceived in your life or your destiny is an interesting way to mark the celebration of Beltane.

References

Close-Hainsworth, Freyalyn. "Spinning a Tale: Spinning and Weaving in Myths and Legends." #FolkloreThursday. June 22, 2017. https://folklorethursday.com/folklife/spinning-a-tale/.

"Arakhne." Theoi Project. Accessed November 30, 2021. https://www.theoi.com/Heroine/Arakhne.html.

Beasts and Treats

Gwion Raven

FROM FLOWER CROWNS TO Maypole ribbons to bonfires, Beltane is an explosion of colour and creativity and fire! These recipes commemorate the kick off of summer and festivals and family gatherings and the promise of frolicking about without a care in the world. As you make these recipes, notice all the colours. It's easy to imagine a meadow of springtime flowers.

Grilling adds an element of the bonfire to the meals as well. Beltane fires have been lit as celebrations of life, community, and the onset of summer for thousands of years.

Enjoy as one meal or separate dishes.

Grilled Asparagus and Parmesan (GF & Vegetarian)

Fresh green asparagus, bright yellow lemons, silky olive oil, and parmesan cheese come together to make this tasty, grilled starter. Cooked on a barbecue grill or griddle pan on the stove, this is quick, easy, and ever so delectable.

Prep time: 5 minutes
Cooking time: 10 minutes
Servings: 4

16 asparagus spears, bottom inch removed
4 tablespoons lemon juice (1 large lemon)
4 tablespoons olive oil
Salt and pepper to taste
2 tablespoons fresh parmesan, grated or shaved

Fire up your outdoor grill or heat your griddle pan. When the surface is really hot, add the asparagus spears and cook until they have deep grill marks. It's important to cook the asparagus without any oil. Cook them dry.

When they're done, pull them off the grill and put them straight on a platter. Pour on the lemon juice and olive oil. Season with salt and fresh ground black pepper. Add the parmesan. I like to shave my parmesan rather than use grated, but both work perfectly well. If you use shaved parmesan, you'll need a little more.

Divide amongst four plates or let everyone dig in to the platter!

Beet Salad with Blueberry-Agave Dressing (GF & Vegan)

Sometimes when I cook, I look at what's on the plate and just delight in what I see. This is one of those dishes. It's just visually appealing, and you know the old expression about eating with your eyes first! I bet you've got a can or two of sliced beets in your cupboard and have no idea what to do with them. You might not even remember buying them! Check the expiration date, and if all is good, get ready to make this tempting side dish.

Prep time: 5 minutes
Cooking time: 10 minutes
Servings: 4

2 big handfuls arugula
2 15-ounce cans of sliced beets (roasted fresh beets are great too)
⅓ cup walnut pieces
1½ cup blueberries
2 tablespoons vegan blue cheese crumbles

½ cup extra-virgin olive oil
¼ cup red wine vinegar
2 tablespoons agave nectar
1 clove garlic, peeled and halved

Pile the arugula in the middle of a big serving platter. Open the cans of beets, drain completely, and arrange the slices around the arugula. Keep plenty of paper towels or tea towels handy—beet juice gets everywhere and easily stains. Sprinkle on the walnuts, ½ cup blueberries, and blue cheese crumbles over the salad and beets.

Add the remaining cup of blueberries to a small saucepan and cook over medium-high heat for 8 minutes or until they begin to burst open. Transfer the softened blueberries to a food processor along with the olive oil, vinegar, agave nectar, and garlic. Pulse for 30 seconds until combined. Pour the contents into a small jar or bowl. Drizzle the dressing over the beet salad. You can make the dressing ahead of time and refrigerate if you'd like to. It will keep in the fridge in an airtight container for 3 days.

Oven-Roasted Tri-Tip with Dry Chimichurri Rub

Let's bust out our own Beltane bonfire!

Okay, it's a propane grill on the back patio, but you get the idea. In ancient times, cattle were driven through two Beltane fires to ensure a bountiful harvest and plenty of food for everyone. Today, we can light our grills as a way of recalling those ancient practices. It's important to honour what we eat and where our food comes from, and to give thanks to all who made this meal possible.

Prep time: 30 minutes
Cooking time: 40 minutes
Servings: 4

2-pound tri-tip
3 tablespoons dried oregano
3 tablespoons dried basil
2 tablespoons dried parsley

2 tablespoons salt
2 teaspoons garlic powder
2 teaspoons dried crushed red pepper
1 tablespoon black pepper
1 tablespoon smoked paprika

Bring the tri-tip to room temperature by leaving it on the counter for approximately 30 minutes. While the beef is coming up to temperature, make the dry rub.

In a large mixing bowl, combine all other ingredients. Mix well until everything is incorporated. Evenly coat the tri-tip with half the rub. You'll use half of this rub for one tri-tip. Save the rest in an airtight container in the cupboard for up to 1 month.

Preheat the grill to medium-high. Grill the tri-tip fat-side down for 5 minutes. Don't move the steak for the entire 5 minutes. Turn the tri-tip and cook for 8 more minutes. Move the meat to indirect heat, like a top rack or edge of the grill and continue cooking until the internal temperature is 130–135°F for medium rare. Depending on the heat of your grill, this could take another 10–15 minutes. Let the meat rest for 10 minutes. Then slice thinly, against the grain.

Serve on a big wooden platter or cutting board. It doesn't do anything for the taste, but it sure looks great!

Lemonade with a Twist (Vegan)

The bees are hard at work collecting pollen and nectar for their hives. We'll let them keep their honey and use agave nectar instead. A little whiskey and a few sprigs of basil give this lemonade a little something extra. I'll be totally honest with you, I usually quadruple this recipe, because there's nothing I like better than lazing about on long, sunny Beltane afternoons with friends. I've been known to enjoy a few ice-cold glasses of this lemonade. Although most often associated with Scotland and Ireland, the roots of whiskey may go much further back, possibly 4,000 years ago to Mesopotamia.

Prep time: 2 minutes
Cooking time: 20 minutes
Servings: 4

½ cup agave nectar
1 cup boiling water
2 ounces whiskey
5 lemons
1 bunch of basil

Add agave nectar to a small bowl. Pour over 1 cup of boiling water and stir until the agave dissolves. Set aside for 15 minutes. Pour the agave into a 2-quart pitcher. Add the whiskey. Juice 4½ lemons (1 cup of lemon juice) into the pitcher. Fill the pitcher ¾ full with ice. Add cold water to fill the pitcher up completely. With a long wooden spoon, give everything a good stir.

Slice the remaining ½ lemon into slices and add to the lemonade. Pour into glasses and add a sprig of basil to each. Remember to rub the basil leaves between your thumb and fingers to release the oils.

Crafty Crafts

Ivo Dominguez Jr.

THE IMAGE OF DANCING around a Maypole or bonfire is often the first thing that springs to mind when thinking of Beltane. I also strongly associate flowers in bloom everywhere and floral crowns on revelers with this holiday. You may not have the opportunity or access to these sorts of festivities. You may have neighbors that would look askance at a backyard Maypole, or you may not have a backyard. This craft project gives you a way to tap into the joyful, life-affirming energy of Beltane that combines a circle dance and a floral crown.

A Dancing Crown

I've made a few variations of this over the years to use in small, usually indoor, rituals. The essence of it is a wreath decorated to look like a floral crown with equally spaced cords attached to its metal frame. Four to eight people can hold the cords taut and lift the floral crown wreath. As they circle in a slow dance, they symbolically turn the Wheel of the Year. With each full turning of the circle, they wrap some of the cord around their wrists. As the circle turns and shrinks, the power builds just as it would with a Maypole dance. There comes a point where everyone is packed close, and the dance

ends with free-form toning or a shout. After you've used it in the circle dance, the dancing crown can be put on a table or altar with a candle in glass placed in its center.

Materials

Wreath frame, metal or very sturdy willow
Materials to wrap it with, ribbons, flowers, etc.
Glue, or something else to affix the materials to the wreath frame
Colorful cords
> *Cost:* $0–$20
> *Time spent:* 2–3 hours

Design Ideas

A metal wreath frame is best and will determine some of your design options, so buy that first. A metal frame or a strong wooden one is needed because you will be tugging on the cords. In most settings, a frame that is between 12–18 inches works well. The materials you use to decorate the dancing crown will depend on whether you want to make a new one every year or reuse the one you are making. Fresh flowers and foliage are beautiful and in tune with the power of the season, but they will fade quickly. Dried flowers will last longer than fresh ones, and paper or silk flowers can last for years if stored properly. As a compromise, you can add a few fresh flowers into the crown with silk flowers, but make sure you remove them before they start to fall apart and cause stains.

The goal in this project is to capture the look and feel of both a Maypole and a floral crown. In between the flowers and foliage, you can weave curls of ribbons. Along the perimeter of the wreath, you can create a fringe of trailing ribbons. The color palette can be whatever evokes the beauty of nature in bloom. You can also add a string of beads, pearls, costume jewelry, or anything else that suggests the jewels of a crown. If it feels right, add fake feathers, birds, bees, or other symbols of spring's fullness.

The cords used for the circle dance can be made from thick colored cords, braided ribbons, or braided thin cords. The colors can alternate as they go around the dancing crown or be a rainbow, a random arrangement, or just one color. The length for the cords will be determined by how much room you have for the dance. They should be long enough for some to dangle from your hand and for some to be used in tying it to the wreath frame. For example, a cord that is five feet long gives a useful length of four feet. Since there are two cords opposite each other, plus a dancing crown in the center, the space needed to circle is around ten feet.

Construction Tips

Depending upon the floral decorations you've chosen, you will be attaching them to the wreath frame different ways. Floral wire or wired ribbon work well on most materials. To add more control with fresh materials, try using a needle and sturdy thread to bind things together. If you are using artificial flowers or dried flowers that have wired stems, those can be bent and intertwined to hold fast. Do not be afraid to shorten stems to a manageable length to tuck them out of the way. Hot glue is useful, though not always good with fresh materials, so test it on a bit of stem first. After everything is in place, I add a few drops and dabs of white glue, like Elmer's, wherever I think some reinforcement is needed.

To prevent fraying, the ends of the cords should either be lightly dabbed with glue or carefully seared with a lighter. You can tie the cords directly to the metal wreath frame where the hoops meet the spokes. Another option that gives you more flexibility is to use metallic book rings or loose leaf binding rings. These can be tied to the wreath frame or opened and slipped onto the frame. You can open and close the rings to add, subtract, or replace the cords easily. The rings are available in several colors.

Using the Dancing Crown

You can use the dancing crown as an addition to your usual Beltane celebrations or as a standalone ritual. Start with everyone taking a cord and taking a few steps back until the dancing crown is suspended in the center. If you have an odd number of people, someone should try to hold two cords with their arms spread to help keep the dancing crown level. Get comfortable with the feel of it and then step clockwise. Start circling slowly and begin to chant if you like. There are many chants for Beltane to be found online. If you have a friend on the side drumming or clapping, all the better. Keep your eyes and energy focused on the center. Each time you come full circle, wrap some of the cord around your wrist so it becomes shorter. You'll be speeding up with each full circuit, but keep it slow with building intensity. When the dance peaks with a shout, slowly lower the wreath to the ground. Putting the dancing crown in a place of honor for the merriments that follow is part of the ritual. Let it be a focal point for the energy throughout the holiday.

Reference

Skidmore, Melissa. *Beautiful Wreaths: 40 Handmade Creations throughout the Year*. New York: Skyhorse Publishing, 2019.

Color Magic

Charlie Rainbow Wolf

BELTANE IS NEXT ON the Wheel of the Year, another festival falling between an equinox and a solstice. It is celebrated around the beginning of May. Even today, many participate in the time-honored traditions of well-dressing and dancing around the Maypole. The deities of Beltane are those associated with fruitfulness and abundance, like the Green Man, Persephone, and—my favorite—Sheela-na-gig.

When I think of Beltane, I immediately think of bonfires and fertility. To me, Beltane is the first of the summer festivals, when nature is busy working hard to produce bounty and abundance. It is the halfway point between the equinox and the longest day, and it's when we're busy here at The Keep planting the seedlings and tending to the herbs and flower beds.

The Colors of Beltane

It's easy to see why green comes up again as a color for Beltane. Bright foliage is now on the trees, it's time to begin cutting the grass again, and the veggie starts have set their main leaves. Sometimes green is associated with money, too, and if you're anything like I am, it is easy to get carried away when shopping for new yarden additions.

Green represents fertility and growth. Just as it resonates with all that is green and growing in nature, it can also be applied to life's own desires and how to grow them. Wearing green clothing or jewelry, burning green candles, or celebrating with a feast of green and growing foods, such as salads and other leafy veggies, are all ways to show the universe things are being done in earnest now.

The season of fertility often means that love is in the air, and the heart chakra is green, after all. Of course, it's not all hearts and flowers, for when the heart chakra is out of balance and romance gets a bit tilted, that's when the negative side of love comes out in the form of jealousy, attachment, and control. It's not by accident that envy is colored green!

The power of the Green Man is at its height during Beltane. The Green Man can be found in many forms throughout history, obvious in some places and hidden in others. He symbolizes the life cycle of birth, death, and rebirth, and is usually depicted as a face surrounded by green leaves, often with them sprouting from his mouth. I like to think of him breathing life into the greenery. Some might even say he is the Holly King, who remains evergreen even while the seasons change. More recently, the Green Man has become a symbol of nature conservancy.

Red reappears as a Beltane color. It's echoed in the red of the bonfire flames, and it's the color of love, sexuality, and passion—very appropriate for a festival of fertility! Red is assertive and energetic, and being a root chakra color, it embodies the need to procreate for the survival of the species. It's the color of blood, the color of action, and the color that signifies warning.

It's said that red has the potential to stimulate circulation, improve respiratory rates and metabolism, and enhance productivity. Passion is usually associated with lust and intimacy, but the definition of passion is a "strong and barely controllable emotion," as in the violence and anger associated with a crime of passion. Red symbolizes both Cupid's love and an adversary's danger.

White is perhaps the Beltane color that resonates the least with me. White is symbolic of peace and tranquility, which seems at odds with the frenzy of the Beltane fires and other May activities! However, it could be said that these activities are possible because people feel safe and at peace with their surroundings, and I can resonate with that. It's hard to feel fully present during great sex when you're worried about what might be going on elsewhere!

Celebrating Beltane

Fire is at the heart of most Beltane festivities with its leaping red flames and the white-hot embers that dance at its source. Fire is purifying and cleansing, and farmers of old would often pass their herds near the smoke of the fire to cleanse them and ensure fertility and bounty. Jumping over the fire is said to bring good fortune, happiness, and gain in the coming year. You don't need a bonfire to jump the fire, though! You can reenact this with a red or a white candle, or even over the images of a fire if needed. Your mindset plays the biggest part in the success of this activity.

The community where I lived in the late 1970s might not have been outrightly Pagan, but their old traditions were still celebrated. The village held a huge fete on May Day, where the May King and the May Queen were crowned. There was a Maypole erected with multicolored ribbons where the children danced, and there was always some kind of a gala or fair with plenty of food and drink and music. Frivolity and love were very much in the air, and I've seen more than one romance start as the result of a May Day event!

We don't replicate the full jubilee here in central Illinois, but we do still celebrate in our own way. I make a lush green salad with homemade bread and fresh strawberries served with cream. We're often outside until sundown, and it is pleasing to come inside knowing that a light yet refreshing repast is waiting for us at the end of the busy day.

For a red stone at Beltane, a good choice would be ruby. Even though ruby is considered to be a gemstone and can be expensive, a small piece of low-quality, unpolished ruby won't break the bank and is easy to obtain. Wearing ruby is supposed to help prevent exhaustion, and some people believe ruby to be an aphrodisiac. No one wants to rise to a passionate encounter only to become too tired to do anything about it! When worn during intimacy, it is believed that ruby will heighten the experience and, because it stimulates the sexual organs, it may even help to promote conception (Frazier, 2017, 46).

Reference

Frazier, Karen. *Crystals for Beginners: The Guide to Get Started with the Healing Power of Crystals.* Althea Press, 2017.

Beltane Ritual

Natalie Zaman

YEARS AGO, A FRIEND introduced me to a British cooking show, *River Cottage*, which follows the adventures of Hugh Fearnley-Whittingstall, a journalist-chef, who conducted the experiment of giving up life in London for the slower pace to be found in Dorset. The Christmas special, which featured geese, real mince pies, and *maron glacé*, also included a side trip into the forest with a hedge witch to look for Yule logs. Wandering in the woods, they came across a semi-fallen ancient apple tree that was still bearing fruit. Each collected a fallen limb with a promise to the tree to come back, gather apples, and plant the seeds to continue his (the tree's) legacy.

Finding Your Grove

Finding sacred woods for your Beltane fire (or, depending on your area and situation, a sacred grove) can be accomplished in much the same manner as on *River Cottage*. All you need is some time, a journal and pen to record your experience, a sealable plastic bag or two to gather tree leavings, and a wood in which to (safely) wander.

1. **How many woods are *your* sacred woods?** The Beltane fire is often referred to as a *need fire*: the sacred woods burned in it will bring you what you need. This year, think about personalizing that number. Make a list of the attributes and qualities you want to bring into your life at this moment— what do you need? Use your favorite reference to determine the trees with whom you should partner. (Remember to take accessibility into account!) You can also use numerology to determine the number of woods you will need. The number of woods for this year's Beltane would be four:

$$5+1+2+0+2+3$$
$$6+2+5$$
$$1+3$$
$$4$$

You can also use your birth date or the birthday of a loved one to determine the number, or that birthday this year. Make it your own!

2. **Find a forest.** Where can you find a wood near you? Public parks are a great place to start, but keep in mind that these are public places with rules and advisories to follow. You can find green spaces everywhere. Check your town, municipal, or county websites for parks and publicly accessible open space in your area. Websites such as the National Forest Foundation and Discover the Forest are helpful tools for locating green spaces—simply enter your zip code, and you'll be in the green before you know it!

3. **Let go and let goddess.** Hugh's quest for sacred wood described previously didn't take him much farther than his own backyard. His Yule log suited his lifestyle and came into his hands as he let his senses and the universe guide him. When you are in your green place—whether it's close to home or far away—let go and let your senses be a compass; let the goddess guide your steps. *That said*—letting go doesn't mean

abandoning caution. You can let go and still be safe, which is important when you go into the woods! Here are some safety precautions I've taken on my travels into green and wild places:

• Don't go alone—there is safety in numbers; go with a friend (or three).
• Use common sense when visiting both new and unknown areas. Be aware of your surroundings.
• Dress for the weather and terrain.
• Know your mobility limitations.
• Have an exit strategy, especially if you're going off trail or off road (do *not* do this if you are not experienced or have issues with accessibility!). In other words, make sure you know how to get back to your car, civilization, etc., and bring a GPS.
• Respect and keep your distance from wildlife. Heed warnings regarding wildlife.
• If available, check in at the ranger station for directions and advice—this will also make the park staff aware of your presence in the area should something go wrong.
• Do not consume *any* plant. If you have doubts about what the plant is, don't even touch it. (I learned this the hard way with poison ivy. Note that the secretions of some plants can get on clothes, and you can have contact that way; it is important to be aware.)
• Check for any bites (especially ticks if they live in an area where you are going to be!) and contact with thorns or potentially poisonous plants.
• Worth repeating (from page 173): It is important to note that some of the plants mentioned (and others that are not) may be endangered, and endangered and protected species lists are constantly updated due to new research and changes in environment. Do not cut trees or remove live branches; gather fallen wood, seeds, and leaves where and when it is permissible. Be sure to check the rules for harvesting even

fallen wood. Sometimes an entire area is protected because even fallen material can be part of a delicate ecosystem.

4. **Know your trees, and get to know your trees.** Trees are living beings, and even though their names are things that we humans have created for them, knowing their names and as much as you can about them—both magical and mundane—acknowledges their uniqueness and makes them better magical life partners. Some great free resources for identifying trees are the Arbor Day Foundation, the Tree Musketeers (great for beginners!), and Treehugger (also great for beginners). I have included a list of books about the magical properties of trees that I have used; you can also use your favorite resources. Once you've ID'd a tree that you're drawn to, one of the nicest ways (I think) to get to know that tree is to speak with it—just like J. R. R. Tolkien, who famously loved trees. Tolkien's method was to literally hug the tree, placing his forehead against the bark, eyes shut. But there's no "one way" to talk to a tree. You know what you are comfortable with, and once in a tree's presence, follow your instinct. (Sidebar: Talking is one thing—taking is another. Trees leave us all sorts of gifts: fallen leaves, seeds and twigs, and shed bark. There is no need to pierce, cut, or take anything that is attached to a tree, unless you are picking ripened fruit.)

Ritual

Under the boughs of any tree, the simplest ritual becomes layered in magic and majesty. Hopefully the steps above and this simple working will help you find and begin your relationship with your personal sacred woods. Once you have identified and communicated with your trees in their natural habitats, see what they've left at their roots for you to take (if permissible): a seed, a fallen leaf or limb, or some bark that has been shed. Gather these and place them in the sealable bags, being sure to label them so that you know what trees they've come from.

What can you leave as a token of gratitude? Nature wants nothing save respect and protection. Leave with a promise and a puff of your breath to seal it:

Roots that go deep,
Leaves to the sky,
My thanks for the gifts
That at your feet lie.
I leave you my breath
And a promise to keep:
[Insert your personal pledge to the tree].

Take three deep breaths, exhaling onto or in the direction of the tree to seal your promise.

You will probably have a jumble of items to bring home with you. Identify each in your journal, perhaps with pictures you've taken or drawn. Once home from your adventure in the forest, bundle the gifts from your sacred woods in a natural cloth, such as cotton or linen, and tie it with string of the same. These will represent your sacred woods in your Beltane blaze, be it in a firepit under the trees and stars, a fireplace, or a tiny cauldron on a tabletop.

Bright-fire blessings!

Resources

The Magic of Trees: A Guide to Their Sacred Wisdom &
    Metaphysical Properties by Tess Whitehurst
"The Nine Sacred Woods of the Need Fire." Tara Sanchez, *Temple*
    of Hekate (blog). http://www.templeofhekate.net/blog/the-nine
    -sacred-woods-of-the-need-fire/
Tree Magic: Connecting with the Spirit & Wisdom of Trees by
    Sandra Kynes
Whispers from the Woods: The Lore & Magic of Trees by Sandra
    Kynes

Helpful Sites

Arbor Day Foundation: www.arborday.org

Discover the Forest: https://discovertheforest.org

National Forest Foundation: https://www.nationalforests.org
/who-we-are

Tree Musketeers: www.treemusketeers.net

Treehugger: www.treehugger.com

Reference

Grotta, Daniel. *J. R. R. Tolkien: Architect of Middle Earth: A Biography*. Philadelphia: Running Press Books, 1992.

Notes

Notes

Notes

Litha

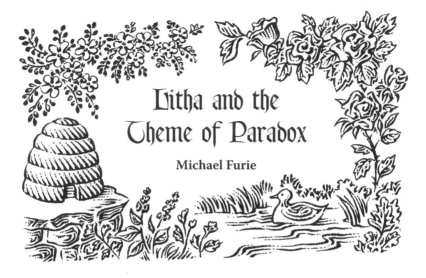

Litha and the Theme of Paradox

Michael Furie

CONSIDERED TO BE one of the most magical nights of the year, the summer solstice, also known as Litha or Midsummer, is the day when the sun is considered to be at the peak of power. From the moment of the winter solstice six months prior, the hours of daylight have increased by approximately one minute per day, reaching the pinnacle of light on the summer solstice, the longest day of the year. The night of Litha is legendary in its magic; even Shakespeare wrote about this special time in *A Midsummer Night's Dream*. Much like the sabbats of Beltane and Samhain, the summer solstice is a liminal (transitional, threshold) time with a strong otherworldly power; it is like a doorway through which spirit and the Fae can move freely and through which we can gain greater understanding of their natures.

Even with all of its mirth, merriment, magic, and madness, the summer solstice carries in it a paradox: the peak of power also initiates its decline. Even though this solstice is the beginning of the season of summer, it is the midpoint of the growing season and the "light" half of the year. One of the names for the summer solstice holiday is *Midsummer* because an older reckoning of the year is to divide it in two: the "light" summer half and the "dark" winter half.

The beginning of the summer half of the year is Beltane; therefore, the midpoint of this half is the summer solstice. This being the case, Litha is a turning point, a shift toward the waning of the heat and light. The solstice shift is a critical component of life on earth because though the light and warmth of the sun are crucial elements of the growth cycle, unrelenting heat and light would destroy the very life it helped to create.

Since this day is such an important point in the year, it is very much worthy of all the joy, celebration, and fanfare that have been attached to it over the centuries. One of my favorite legends of Litha, which also happens to perfectly illustrate the powerful paradox found here, is that of the Oak King and the Holly King. The Oak King is the embodiment of growth and the light half of the year, and the Holly King is the embodiment of decline and the dark half of the year. Some see them as a light and a dark twin, while others see them as the changing face of the same being, but either way, their key days are the summer and winter solstices. On these days of power and transition, they come together (and in most views, battle), with one king emerging as the sovereign to rule over the next half of the year. In the winter, the Holly King is deposed by the Oak King, and he rules the time of growing light until the summer solstice when he is defeated by the Holly King. In a romantic version, the two kings battle for the hand of the goddess of the land, and the winner initiates the change of season.

The lore of the two kings has some parallels with the Scottish lore of Bride and Cailleach, with Bride as the spring maiden being held prisoner by the Cailleach as Queen of Winter. Upon Bride's escape, the light half of the year begins. There are also parallels to the Greek lore of Persephone and Demeter, with Persephone as goddess of both spring and the underworld. In the yearly cycle, Persephone travels to the underworld on the autumnal equinox, and at that time, her mother, Demeter, as the goddess of harvest, blights the land in angst at the loss of her daughter for half of each year. When Persephone reemerges to the upper world, she and her mother go about energizing the land, and the seasons of growth and light commence once more. Of these three examples, only the tale of the Oak and Holly Kings is usually tied to the summer and winter solstices, however. In most versions, Bride and Cailleach are linked to Beltane (and Imbolc) and Samhain, and the journey of Persephone is usually linked to the spring and autumnal equinoxes. Each of these tales speaks to the relevance of seasonal tides and balance as well as the significance of specific sabbats and their contrasting days of power in marking these key environmental shifts.

Being integral components of the larger framework, each sabbat is not merely a standalone holiday, but rather a hub of an energetic relay circuit that gathers the preceding energy in the year and transforms it into a new form, releasing this new energy into the world to develop the next phase of the cycle. For Litha specifically, this means that the power of the season of growth, the length of daylight hours, and the influence and energy of the sun has reached its peak for the year and will now begin a barely perceptible shift toward longer nights, the bounty of harvest, and the onset of the season of decline. The Oak King has reached maturity and is now deposed by the youthful Holly King, who shall now begin his reign and thus preside over the time of harvest, late summer, and the season of autumn. Though this solstice is the beginning of the season of summer, it is also a doorway into the rich abundance of the agricultural harvest time (which we all depend on in one form or another) and what lies beyond.

A useful way to relate the paradox of Litha to magical work is to become aware of both sides of the energy and how it manifests. Scientifically speaking, the first law of thermodynamics states that the amount of energy in the universe is constant and that every natural process transforms and moves energy but cannot create it from nothing or reduce it to nothing. This is considered to be one of the immutable laws of physics. Applying this to magical concepts, this gives a new perspective to the season of decline. The energy that brought the light half of the year did not cease to exist (it cannot), but instead is transformed into a new state of being. Those long summer days need to shift into long autumn nights, in part, because those bright solar and vibrant earthly energies transform and then become manifest *as* the harvest. This is part of the nature of magic. Personal magic draws upon the same essential forces as the transformations that occur in the larger yearly cycle of the earth. We can utilize this power in our own individual lives in spellwork with similar results.

A good example of utilizing the power of Litha in magic would be in the building of prosperity. To channel the peak energy of growth, a ritual is best conducted just prior to the actual solstice. As part of a sabbat celebration, appropriate candles, herbs, and other ingredients can be charged with the power of the sun and the earth with the intention that this energy will remain in these items until it is released to bring prosperity. In this way, spell components can be charged when the time is best and then put to use later when a specific need arises. Once the spell is cast using the charged items, the energy will be released to complete its transformation as an abundant harvest; in this case, the "harvest" would be in manifesting the result of your prosperity spell. Generally speaking, the herbs, colors, and other spell components that are naturally aligned to the sun and the earth (which are a main focus of Litha) are also linked to prosperity, success, growth, and strength, which make for a wide range of specific magical intentions.

As an example, a yellow candle can be anointed with cinnamon oil to bring in the energy of the sun, and a gold cloth charm bag can be filled with grains of rice and wheat kernels for the energies of both the sun and the earth, and to this can be added a small scroll on which you have written out your specific intention for prosperity. The bag can then be tied shut and anointed with a bit of the cinnamon oil as a verbal spell is stated to seal in the magic. To specifically call upon the power of Litha, the verbal spell can be tailored to fine-tune this intent. One option could be:

The magic of growth has reached its peak, on this Litha, a boon I seek;

The power is harnessed to forge the charm, abundance bring, without harm.

Grains of the earth, by the sun you are blessed, unleash your magic for success.

Golden prosperity gathered for me, as I will so mote it be!

This is just one possible example, of course; there are endless possibilities to call upon the power of the sabbat, such as candle spells, cord magic, or even potions and brews. Not everyone chooses to perform magic on the sabbats; there are some that prefer to keep the holidays as purely devotional and celebratory, but even in such a case, items can be charged with the power of the sabbat during the celebration and used in spellwork at a later time.

The sabbat of Litha is such a powerful time. The sun is at its peak of power, the length of the daylight hours have reached their maximum point, and the earth is at its most vibrant with the richness of the land fully manifested. The cosmic dance between the sun and the earth, which results in each of our seasons, is such an incredible dynamic; if not for this interplay, the world as we know it would not even be possible. As the earth spins in orbit around the sun, the planet tilts back and forth much like a spinning top. The magical part is that this is all structured in such a way that it is balanced and the shifting occurs (essentially) steadily. We are not burdened with an erratic or unpredictable orbit, but instead are blessed to live in a world with a relatively stable cycle of ebb and flow and growth and decline.

Unfortunately, it appears that humanity's actions are disrupting the natural balance of the planet and are creating much more pronounced and severe atmospheric shifts than we were meant to bear. As magical people, we recognize that our actions can have a direct impact upon the greater framework of life. When we choose to celebrate and connect with the spiritual beings and forces that underlie physical existence, we are strengthening our personal connections to not only those specific beings, but also to the cosmic web as a whole. I feel that this gives us a heightened level of awareness, but also gives us a certain level of responsibility to help maintain the greater balance. Keeping the sabbats is not only a chance to celebrate and honor the powers of the sun and earth; we can also impart our energy and vision at this time *into* the yearly cycle, and this action can be channeled into helping to heal the earth. This is one aspect of "turning the wheel" of the year. It is an active role in which we become participants in building the future transformations of the unfolding progression of life rather than simply observing.

Each of the sabbats carries within it a unique energy. At the time of Litha, the summer solstice, we are given the opportunity to attune to the energy of growth at its strongest. While much of the focus lands on utilizing some of this power for our own benefit (which is perfectly acceptable), part of the paradox of this day is that with the benefit of being able to draw upon this increased energy comes the responsibility of giving back some energy as well in order to replace that which was taken and restore the balance.

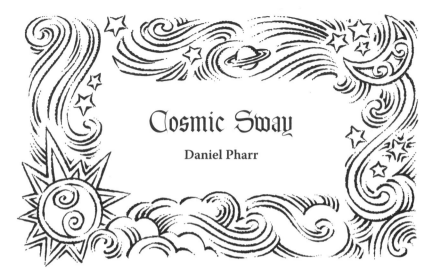

Cosmic Sway

Daniel Pharr

THE SOLSTICE, WHEN SPOKEN of in an offhand manner, is usually said to be on June 21. Most folks know this calendric placement moves around a few days in both directions. In the Northern Hemisphere, the summer solstice falls in a three-day range, June 20 through June 22, and by comparison, the winter solstice has a four-day range, December 20 through December 23. The Summer Solstice, the midpoint of summer, halfway between Beltaine and Lughnassadh, is on Wednesday, June 21, precisely at 10:58 a.m. under the influence of a Leo Moon. Considering that for many this day is a work day, some thought should be given to preparing for the rite so that being late for work is minimized. The fire holiday during the fiery Leo Moon seems right, where the night or day before would be in a Cancer Moon. Water on a fire holiday could mean steam, or the fire could be doused.

The Leo Moon will inject the fire energy into all aspects of life, but especially the ones that are in tune with Leo, like consciousness, compassion, generosity of time and money, and of course, leadership. Use this rite to set in motion goals for the next six months, especially those goals that prepare for the darkening days and colder nights to come. Advancing the quest from Yule will be a good use of the Leo Moon. Prepare not only the self but those that depend on help to make it through. There is also the aspect of recognition that might roar forth to be noticed. Helping others has its own reward, as does preparing oneself. If the need to draw attention to personal efforts and actions should rise like smoke from a flame, show others respect and fan the smoke away instead of choking on it. If you do receive some recognition, be gracious and grateful for the opportunity to serve.

Full Moon

A Capricorn Moon arrives July 3 at 7:39 a.m., meaning the rite will most likely be held the night before on July 2, which is also a Capricorn Moon and the eighth Moon in the cycle. The lunar influences of this Moon will promote ambition and will be a wonderful time to set big plans in motion or make big progress on goals already in play. Enjoy the Full Moon rite whenever is convenient, but if waiting for the actual moment on the West Coast at 4:39 a.m. and staying up all night, consider how the Capricorn lunar energies will treat the participants. When folks are tired, their innate feelings sneak out uninhibited. Exhaustion under a Capricorn Moon will promote nihilism, irritability, and indifference.

Independence Day

July 4 is a Tuesday. The Moon moves into Aquarius at 1:30 p.m. Barbeques and fireworks, food and friends, in the city or in the country, this is a holiday celebrated in one way or another by all Americans. Regardless of the manner in which the holiday is celebrated, the Aquarius Moon can bring out the uninhibited and free-spirited. These feelings, when expressed with hilarity, will bring joy to everyone. Costumes are fun under this Moon: Uncle Sam, your favorite president, or even your favorite dessert. Everyone loves an apple pie costume. Fireworks are wonderful, and huge displays of fireworks are perfect. If fireworks are going to be a private affair, be sensible about them. This Moon will bring out the innovators and the nonconformists and could be the cause of accidents or fires.

Dark Moon

July 17 at 2:32 p.m. is the moment of the Dark Moon in Cancer. That same night at 12:39 a.m. on the eighteenth, the Moon moves into Leo. The Dark Moon ritual will probably be planned for the night before, July 16. The Sun is in Cancer. Cancer is ruled by the Moon, and the Moon is in Cancer, so the solar and lunar influences will be strong. Emotionally sensitive people will be far more so. Those not usually sensitive will be weeping watching movies. Humanitarianism will peak due to the increased sensitivity. Donate to a charity, rescue a pup, or clean a beach. Hearth and home will be calling. The garden always needs work this time of year. If the party is at someone's house, pull weeds in their garden while enjoying a beverage. Channel the sensitive humanitarian insights into good for the community. When speaking, unless the goal is to incense a crowd, be careful of the words chosen and the tone and force with which they are presented. Mercury will be in Leo, which can impart loads of charm and charisma, but the fire can also burn.

National Avocado Day

Behold the avocado, one of nature's perfect fruits, and July 31 is its celebration. The avocado, when eaten, helps to lower bad cholesterol and can be used to replace unhealthy saturated fats with healthy unsaturated fats. Under the Capricorn Moon, foods best eaten are raw fruits and vegetables. Fashion a nice big salad with leaves of lettuce and add sliced avocado. Or, better yet, make some guacamole. Scoop out the flesh of two or three avocados, small dice two slices of onion, fine chop one jalapeño or serrano pepper, and mix it all together, smashing the avocado. Stir in salt, chopped cilantro, and garlic powder. Dice one Roma tomato and fold in with a squirt of lime for freshness. Voilà.

Full Moon

The Full Moon is the ninth Moon in the cycle and will be in Aquarius on August 1 at 2:32 p.m. The Moon enters Aquarius on July 31 at 11:58 p.m., and before that the Moon will have been in Capricorn. Assuming the Full Moon rite will be on July 31, choose to be under the eccentric and uninhibited Aquarian influence throughout the rite after 11:58 p.m. or under the sensitive and disciplined Capricorn influence until 11:58 p.m. If Capricorn is chosen, serve guacamole. And if the event is to cross the cusp, prepare the food before the Moon ritual. If grounding is needed at any point, the guacamole will do the trick. This Full Moon night will also be considered Lughnassadh using the Pleiades system of fixing the High Holiday dates on the calendar.

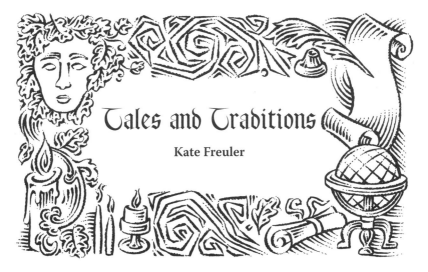

Tales and Traditions

Kate Freuler

THE SUMMER SOLSTICE IS the longest day of the year in the Northern Hemisphere. The sun blazes hot in the sky at its fullest power. After this date, the wheel begins to turn toward the waning length of days and the coming darkness. While the sun will still reign for quite some time, Litha marks a time to acknowledge the sun and all the bounty it has helped produce. Traditionally on Litha, also known as Midsummer, it's said that the goddess is heavily pregnant, much in the same way the earth is loaded with the bounty of upcoming harvests on the cusp of full fruition. Rituals focus on nurturing the growing gifts of the earth, such as vegetables, fruits, and grain. In honor of the sun, sometimes fires are lit for a full twenty-four hours in celebration.

The Lore of Lavender

The summer solstice is a traditional time to gather herbs for use in medicine and magic. One such herb that is still extremely popular today is lavender. Lavender is burned on Midsummer to honor the god and goddess and is mixed with other fragrant herbs to attract the favor of the Fae, who are known to be especially active on this date. Lavender is often included in summer handfasting rituals, where it is both burned as incense and included in floral bouquets. Lavender is best known for its associations with love, but if you dig back into history, it turns out lavender has been used for almost everything, including very practical applications. Lavender was burned in sickrooms to cleanse the air, and small cloth bundles of its dried flowers were stashed in chests and drawers to prevent moths from nibbling on clothing and linens. The essential oil is antiseptic and anti-inflammatory and can be used to treat minor bug bites or burns. In aromatherapy, it treats anxiety, depression, and insomnia.

Stories about lavender's powers and uses can be found around the world. When the tomb of King Tutankhamun was opened, lavender bundles were discovered inside that still held their scent after thousands of years. It's unclear if the bouquets were placed in the grave to ward off the smell of death, as an offering, or both.

Lavender also pops up in the stories about Cleopatra, an Egyptian ruler famous for her beauty, intelligence, and ruthlessness. She was known to wear the scent of lavender while seducing both Julius Caesar and Marc Antony. The snake that eventually killed Cleopatra is said to have been hiding in a lavender bush just before striking. Perhaps it's because of Cleopatra that the fragrant herb gained its popular association with love and attraction.

In the fifteenth to seventeenth centuries, young Tudor women would brew a tea from dried lavender to divine who their future lover would be. They would drink the herbal infusion before bed and chant: "St. Luke, St. Luke, be kind to me. In my dreams, let me my true love see." The identity of their true love would come to them in a dream. It was said that putting lavender inside a mattress or under the pillow of a spouse would ensure a happy marriage.

In medieval times, the scent of lavender became associated with sex workers. In some folklore, it says this was to advertise their profession and to provide protection in an often dangerous line of work, but the origins of this belief are far less magical in nature. During this time, poverty was overwhelming, especially for women. Many worked in underpaying jobs during the day, often as laundresses, and did sex work at night to make ends meet. Washer women often used lavender in cleaning and scenting laundry, which is possibly how the connection was formed.

This diverse herb is even said to have come to the aid of thieves. The story says that during the bubonic plague, there were four thieves who made a habit of plundering the homes of the ill, and in some cases, the dead bodies and graves of the deceased, making off with jewelry and valuables. When asked why they themselves never caught the lethal illness, the thieves attributed their health to a brew made of lavender, vinegar, and other herbs that they rubbed on themselves before their robbing sprees. In some versions of the story, the thieves were captured and convinced the judge to grant them their freedom in exchange for the powerful recipe. In another version of the tale, four thieves were arrested and sentenced to bury plague victims as punishment; they invented the brew so they wouldn't contract the disease from the corpses. This potion is known today as "Four Thieves' Vinegar." You can find recipes for it online or purchase it ready-made. Four Thieves' Vinegar is used as a household cleaner and sometimes for medicinal use. In magic, some people associate it with purification and breaking curses. The specific role of lavender in the brew was probably a combination of its medicinal qualities and to mask the less-than-pleasant odor of vinegar and garlic with its strong floral scent.

On Litha, the sun is at its most powerful, and so are the herbs harvested beneath it. Try growing some lavender and gathering it at Midsummer to harness all its many wonderful properties. Lay some out for the Fae, burn some for the god and goddess, and keep some for yourself to bring love and attraction into your life. You can fashion sachets filled with dry lavender out of pretty cloth and ribbon to keep with your clothing, both to avert pests and attract love. Try making a batch of Four Thieves' Vinegar, or keep a sprig of dried herb in your pocket to bring calm and tranquility. You can even include food-grade lavender in cookie and muffin recipes to bring some of its calming, protective, and loving energies to all who eat them.

Containing the power of the blazing Midsummer sun, the lavender you harvest on Litha will retain its power all year round.

References

Cunningham, Scott. *Cunningham's Encyclopedia of Magical Herbs.* Woodbury, MN: Llewellyn Publications, 2013.

"Lavender-Part2." Our Herb Garden. Accessed July 29, 2021. http://www.ourherbgarden.com/herb-history/lavender-part2.html.

Sedgwick, Icy. "Lavender Folklore: The Tales Behind The Calming Plant." Icy Sedgwick. March 8, 2018. https://www.icysedgwick.com/lavender-folklore/.

Peterson, Tina. "A Treatise on Lavender in History." Lady Violette. June 8, 2002. https://ladyviolette.com/tag/history-of-lavender/.

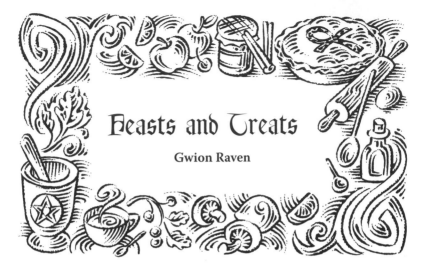

Feasts and Treats

Gwion Raven

THE SUMMER SUN IS at its highest point in the sky. Summer vegetables are available everywhere from farmer's markets to back gardens to planter boxes on apartment balconies. As a cook and a Pagan, this is my favourite time of year because there's so much fresh produce to choose from. Warm evenings beckon us to shared meals, shared stories, and conversations that last into the wee hours. These recipes are light and cool and quick.

Summer Solstice Squash and Tomato Salad (GF & Vegetarian)

When I think of summer vegetables, yellow squash, green zucchini, and red tomatoes come instantly to mind. With the addition of fresh herbs, this salad is incredibly refreshing and simply stunning.

Prep time: 10 minutes
Cooking time: 30 minutes
Servings: 4

1 medium yellow squash, thinly sliced
1 medium zucchini, thinly sliced
½ cup red onion, sliced
2 cups cherry tomatoes, halved

4 fresh basil leaves, chopped
4 fresh oregano leaves, chopped
¼ cup olive oil
¼ cup white wine vinegar
¼ teaspoon salt
¼ teaspoon black pepper
Shaved parmesan

Place the squash and zucchini slices on a large dinner plate. They can overlap a little. Don't worry about making this look perfect because you're going to scoop it all into a serving bowl in a little bit. In a mixing bowl, add the rest of the ingredients and gently fold them together. (Quick note about the basil and oregano: I like to chiffonade them into ribbons. The easiest way to chiffonade is to place the basil leaves on top of one another, then add the oregano. Roll the herbs into a cigar shape and thinly slice. It's easy and looks great in the dish.)

Spread the tomato mixture all over the squash and zucchini. Let it sit for 30 minutes. Transfer everything into a serving bowl and shave fresh parmesan on top.

Chicken with Preserved Lemon Aioli Wraps

When I was quite young, my family would go on summer picnics. We'd find ourselves in a field by a stream. My dad would fish for a while and my mum would butter bread, chop an apple or two, slice cheddar cheese into big chunks, pull apart a chicken breast, and pour mugs of tea from a thermos flask. This is my updated homage to summer picnics and hot days and blissful memories.

Making your own aioli, which is basically garlicky mayonnaise, is easier than you think and so very worth the effort. Preserved lemons, a Middle Eastern staple, bring a surprisingly unique sweetness to the dish. The apple is there for crunch and tartness. The whole meal takes about 10 minutes to prepare, and you get to use a mortar and pestle! If you're having guests over, double or quadruple the recipe.

Prep time: 5 minutes
Cooking time: 15 minutes
Servings: 4

1 clove garlic, halved
Pinch of salt
1 tablespoon preserved lemon peel, chopped
1 egg yolk
½ tablespoon lemon juice
½ cup olive oil
2 cups cooked chicken breast
1 medium green apple, peeled and cubed
¼ teaspoon salt
¼ teaspoon pepper
2 cups spring mix
2 whole wheat tortillas or wraps

Mash together garlic and salt in a mortar and pestle. Add preserved lemon and mix to combine.

In a small bowl, combine egg yolk, lemon juice, and garlic paste. Add 3 drops of the olive oil and whisk slowly. Keep adding the oil a few drops at a time until the mixture starts to thicken. Once you have incorporated half the oil, pour the rest in a steady stream, whisking all the time. Set aside.

Combine the cooked chicken and apple in a bowl with the salt and pepper. Gently fold in the aioli.

Lay out a tortilla. Add ¼ cup of spring mix, slightly off-center. Add ¼ cup of chicken, apple, and aioli mixture on top of the spring mix. Tightly roll the tortilla. Repeat with the other three tortillas. Cut through the center at a slight diagonal.

Serve on small plates with the Summer Solstice Squash and Tomato Salad.

Summer Watermelon and Basil Skewers (GF & Vegetarian)

I can't decide if this is a starter, a main dish, or dessert. I think it's all three neatly served on a wooden skewer. Whatever it is, you won't be able to get enough of this summer treat.

Prep time: 15 minutes
Cooking time: 15 minutes
Servings: 4

2 pints seedless watermelon, about 16 cubes (I get it right from the grocery store, but feel free to cut up your own watermelon.)
16 fresh basil leaves
12 cherry tomatoes
12 chunks of feta or mozzarella cheese
¼ cup balsamic vinegar
¼ cup sugar

Starting with a cube of watermelon, fill a wooden skewer with basil, then cherry tomato, then cheese. Plan on 4 watermelon cubes per skewer. Repeat until you have four nicely filled skewers. Refrigerate.

In a small saucepan, add the balsamic vinegar and sugar. Cook over medium heat until the sugar is dissolved, stirring occasionally. Turn off the heat and set aside to cool for 15 minutes.

Serve watermelon skewers on a platter and, using a teaspoon, drizzle the balsamic glaze all over the skewers. The taste is divine!

Blueberry Lemon Tea (GF & Vegan)

Here's another quick recipe celebrating the ripe fruits of summer. It's colourful, easy to make, and oh-so-very refreshing!

Prep time: 2 minutes
Inactive: 15 minutes
Servings: 4

4 cups boiled water
6 green tea bags
½ pound fresh blueberries (frozen works too)
1 cup water
¼ cup fresh lemon juice
2 tablespoons agave nectar

Bring 4 cups of water to a boil. Add the teabags and steep for 5 minutes. Remove the teabags and discard.

Using a small saucepan, combine the water, blueberries, and lemon juice. Bring to a rolling boil, then reduce the heat and simmer for 6 minutes.

Pour the blueberry mixture into a sieve over a bowl, capturing the juice. Use the back of a spoon to gently mash the blueberries so you get all the juice possible. Discard blueberries. Stir the agave nectar into the blueberry juice.

In a large pitcher, combine the tea and blueberry juice. Refrigerate until cooled.

Serve the tea over ice. Feel free to add a lemon slice and any leftover blueberries to make it look wonderful.

Crafty Crafts

Ivo Dominguez Jr.

YES, THE SUMMER SOLSTICE is about the peak of the sun and the longest day, but my best memories of Litha celebrations are of the summer nights. Spending time with friends in the relative cool of the evening by a firepit is perhaps the best reward of the season. We talk, sing, chant, dance, and drum under the stars.

Shawl

This is a craft project to make a shawl or hip scarf with dangles that jingle, tinkle, or click for a wearable percussion instrument. You can dance with it or use it while you sit and shake it as an accompaniment. Although this project may remind you of the dance scarves worn by belly dancers, the appearance and the sound are very different.

Materials
Scarf, shawl, or materials to make one
Items to dangle and jingle
Ribbons and cords
A sewing kit and thread
    Cost: $0–$30
    Time spent: 2 ½ hours

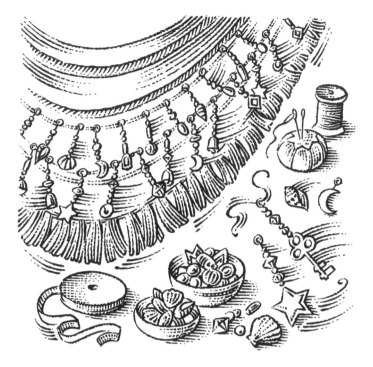

Design Ideas

If you love to sew, you can start by making the scarf from scratch. The most useful shapes are a triangle, a long rectangle, or a rectangle with a half-circle bump in the middle. If you make the scarf, you can choose the colors or patterns that you prefer, and it will be the perfect size for you.

It is also perfectly workable to start with a shawl or scarf that you already have or buy for this purpose. Whether you buy or make a scarf, be sure to add a cord, grosgrain ribbon, or cloth belting to the top edge with enough length to make it easy to tie around your waist or over your shoulders. The cloth you choose may be light and airy, warm and sturdy, or something in between. However, if the fabric is light and thin, then the decorations that you attach must also be light enough not to pull too hard on the fabric or they will pucker it or distort how it drapes.

Design As You Go

The sounds for these dancing shawls are produced by dozens of small objects attached in a way that makes them jostle, rustle, and collide against each other when there is motion. The first step is to collect an array of small objects that make sounds you like. The following items are some of the best little noise makers:

- Tambourine jingles come in various sizes and colors
- Small loose clam bells or jingle bells
- Shell beads and drilled shells
- Wood or bone beads
- Small metal objects like keys or charms
- Links or scales used in making chain mail or scale mail

The items are strung, sewn, or knotted onto cords or ribbons that will be attached to the dancing shawl in parallel or zigzag lines that are horizontal to your waist. The color for the cords or ribbons is another design choice. It is usually three tiers of dangles; you may want more, but never less than two tiers. Don't forget that you are adding weight with the dangles. Periodically heft all the parts to check if the weight is reasonable and that the dancing shawl or scarf won't be too heavy.

Before attaching the dangles to a cord, put three or four in your palm. Cup your hands together and shake them lightly to see if you like the sounds. With a bit of experimentation, you'll find the combinations that you like best. Put the combinations into small bowls or tubs to keep organized as you make your choices.

When it comes time to attach the dangles to the cords or ribbons, you must take their shape and size into consideration. They need to be spaced far enough apart so that there is a small gap between them. If the goal is a rustle or soft clink, make the gap around ½ inch. If the goal is a louder or more precise clink, then make the gap between ½ and one inch. The length that it dangles from the cord should be long enough so that it can easily swing to hit its neighbors, but not so long as to encourage tangling. Attach the dangles with sturdy and slippery thread, like silk beading thread or something similar, to the cords.

The cords with dangles can run the full length of the shawl or scarf. You can also vary their length to make a design, such as a triangle, a diamond, a chevron, or a lightning bolt. Before sewing the cords onto the shawl or scarf, do a test run to see if you like the look and the sound of your design. Take straight pins or safety pins and temporarily attach the cords. Then pick up the dancing shawl and shake it several ways to see if you like the sound. Move things around until it is just right and mark the locations with some chalk or a sewing pencil. Then sew the tiers of dangles in place.

Now that the sound-making elements are done, look at the piece again to see if you want to add any design elements in the open areas. It may already be perfect, or you may see some places where you want to add sequins or beads, draw something in a design with fabric markers, and so on. Another option is to add fringe to the lower edge of the shawl or scarf below the last row of dangles. A zigzag stitch is the best way to attach the fringe so that you maintain flexibility in the fabric as it moves when in use.

Construction Tips

You may have noticed that glue has not been used in this project. If you use the shawl or scarf to dance or as an instrument, it will move and shake. Glue tends not to hold as well with the countless repeated tugs from the dangles. You can use glue for adding things like sequins and other decorations that are not under stress, but they, too, may give way. In doing the sewing, add as many stitches and knots as you think are needed to make this a durable piece. It can last for years if it is well-made.

Using the Dancing Shawl

You can wrap it around your waist, hips, or shoulders and dance, but there are other possibilities. While sitting, you can hold it behind your head or in front of your chest and shake it. You can also dance solo, without drums or songs, and let the rhythm of your dancing create the sound that inspires your dance. It is easy to trance out moving to a sound created by your motion.

Color Magic

Charlie Rainbow Wolf

LITHA IS A SOLSTICE ceremony, when the days are the longest in the Northern Hemisphere. It is celebrated when the sun leaves Gemini and moves into the sign of Cancer. Litha always falls in June, but the exact date varies according to that year's ephemeris. The deities linked with Litha are those associated with the sun.

The Gregorian calendar says Midsummer is the start of summer, but to me, it is the middle of summer—it says so right in the name! It is the time when the sun is at its apex, when the hay is being cut and stored for the colder months, when Mother Nature and all those who work in harmony with her seem to be at their busiest. On our little postage stamp of land, we always seem to be working hardest in the hottest weeks of the year!

The Colors of Litha

It's hard to pin down colors for Litha because nature seems to be full of every color imaginable. Primary colors are blue for the sky or the coast, yellow for the blazing sun, or red for the seasonal berry fruits like raspberries or strawberries. Secondary colors might include green for the vegetation, or orange and purple for the flowers.

Bright or pastel, it seems all kinds of everything are present during this solstice! I tend to gravitate toward solar colors at this time of year. Creamy white, like the watery sunshine that dances on the water or is found in the fresh cream poured over the seasonal fruits, is one that comes to mind. Wearing white is cooler than wearing darker colors—something that might be a factor when out in the hot summer sun.

Ivory, ecru, and perhaps even beige fall into this color category. These hues resonate with the understanding and sincerity of white, but they're softer, more sophisticated, and less harsh. Where white might be too blinding and cause headaches for some, ivory is easier on the eyes. It's relaxing and calming, but it doesn't have to be dull. It will accentuate complementary colors, and it will also enhance their energies. The ivory-white berries of the mistletoe plant are believed to be at the height of their energy during Litha.

Gold is also linked to Litha, and it's hardly surprising, with gold being associated with the sun and Litha marking the longest day. Gold can be bright and light and playful or more serious and classic. Like the sun, it is associated with light and illumination, with life and prosperity, and with riches and treasure.

The metal gold is considered to be precious, and many have lost their lives at the hands of others who pursued gold for material gain. Gold features a lot in everyday language, and it seems to have a dual meaning. A "gold digger" is used to describe someone who is just after money, while a "golden child" is said to do no wrong. A "gold standard" is a high quality of excellence, while "fool's gold" is a term used to describe something that looks good but is actually worthless.

The blue I associate with Litha is the pastel sky blue. Call me crazy, but I swear the sky blue of Midsummer and Midwinter is not as bright as the sky blue of the equinoxes! I see Litha blue as very watery and thin, perhaps blinded a bit by the bright light of the sun.

Pastel blue also makes me think of open spaces, meadows full of summer wildflowers, coastlines, and the skies that hang over sandy beaches. It still has the qualities of any shade of blue—tranquil and relaxed, sincere, trustworthy, and inspired—but these are mellow, more low-key and soothing. Blue is the color of the throat chakra, the energy center that has to do with communication. At Litha, it is good to remember that real communication involves listening as well as talking. Listen to Mother Nature and really hear what she is telling you.

Green makes yet another appearance at Litha. Like blue, it's now starting to become more muted, because the vibrancy with which it first appeared in springtime is giving way to maturity as it prepares for the coming of the autumn. (For those in the Southern Hemisphere, this will be backward, with the pastel green starting to intensify rather than intense green starting to fade.) Also like blue, the pastel shades of green embrace the qualities of all shades of green, but they're softer and gentler.

Green at Litha is represented by the Oak King, who is at his peak during this festival. His leaves will soon start to change color as he surrenders to the Holly King for the winter, but he's not ready yet. Obviously one of his colors is green, and he also reflects the gold his leaves are about to turn and the brown of his tree trunk. Brown is the color of the soil, the wet sand, and the potter's clay.

Brown might not be one of the colors that first springs to mind when celebrating Litha, but it is in the brown earth where the crops and other growing things sink their roots. It is the color of nuts and seeds to be saved until the following spring, and of the firewood that is thrown onto the bonfire or gathered to heat the home in the coming long nights. Its energy is grounding and earthy, wholesome and homey, stable and reliable.

Because it is the color of the earth, brown is a good foundation color for other energies. It adds security and sustainability as well as providing a warm and cozy ambience. It's protective and balanced, but not quite so intense as black. It's a good color to use when looking to fit in or to help someone feel like they belong. It goes well with ivory, the characteristics of one enhancing the characteristics of the other.

Celebrating Litha

Food is an important part of all the festivals here at The Keep, and Litha is no exception! This is when we have a fire in the firepit and fill the table full of finger food. We lay out all kinds of fruit and salad vegetables and homemade bread, and I bake a two-tone oat and chocolate brownie. If we're lucky, there's fruit wine from the previous summer fruits to wash it all down as well as mead—the golden honey embracing both the color gold and the association to the "honey moon," or the full moon closest to Litha.

The stone that sits on my incense altar at this time of year is a small piece of amber given to me by a Druid priest at a solstice festival in the West Midlands back in the mid-1990s. It's inconspicuous, but it is the memory attached with it that is important—and this actually makes it *more* appropriate, because of the energetic properties associated with amber (anyone who has seen the resurrection of the dinosaurs in *Jurassic Park* will get it). Amber isn't actually a stone; it is fossilized resin, sometimes with insects or other organic matter preserved in it. Its muted gold color is soothing and relaxing, while still reflecting the light and life from the sun.

Litha Ritual

Michael Furie

FOR THIS RITE, we will make a potion to gather some of the magical essence of this sabbat so that its energy can continue to enhance our magic for the rest of the season. The ritual will call upon the Oak and Holly Kings to honor them for bringing the shift of season.

The Essence of Summer

Using a sabbat candle, we will also release some of our own energy into the magic of the holiday to maintain the cosmic balance and impart our own intention into the season. Finally, it will conclude with a small sacrifice of part of the ritual meal in gratitude for the power of the earth, sun, and light in our lives.

Items Needed
Chalice

Athame

Altar decorations (such as oak leaves or flowers for the right side of the altar, and holly leaves, mistletoe, or sprigs of rosemary for the left side)

2 white altar candles

1 light green candle (for the goddess of the earth)

1 offering dish

1 yellow candle (for the sabbat candle)
1 brown candle (for the Oak King)
1 dark green candle (for the Holly King)
Lighter or matches
Round loaf of bread (either homemade or store-bought)
Cauldron (or cooking pot with at least 1-quart capacity)
4 cups water
1 tablespoon chamomile
1 tablespoon black tea
1 tablespoon peppermint
1 orange, sliced
Preferred sweetener (sugar, stevia, honey, etc.)
Ladle
4 tokens, one for each of the elements (bowl of salt for earth; stick
or cone of frankincense incense for air; a red candle in holder or
a sunstone for fire; and a bowl of water for water)

Lay out the altar first, with the chalice on the left and the athame on the right side, each surrounded by decorations in a pleasing manner. The white altar candles are placed to the back of the altar, one on the left and one on the right. The light green candle is placed at the back of the altar between the altar candles. Set the offering dish in the center and the yellow sabbat candle directly behind it in an appropriate holder. Place the brown candle in a holder directly to the right of the dish and the dark green candle directly to the left. Have the loaf of bread on a plate nearby but not directly on the altar.

Next, begin making the potion. Fill the cauldron with water, placing it on the stove over medium heat. As the water begins to warm, charge the ingredients by holding each of them in your hand (or holding your hands over their containers) and mentally sending energy into them with the intention that they will be filled with the growth and prosperity energies of Litha. Envision a golden light surrounding each one. After all of the ingredients are charged, begin adding them to the cauldron one by one. As they are added, a short chant can be repeated over the cauldron to focus the magic, such as, "Herbs of solstice, potion of growth, Litha's strength now drawn forth. Into this potion the energy fills, to harness the magic that I will."

Stir the potion slowly, heating it until right before it boils. Turn off the heat and cover the potion with a lid for at least fifteen minutes so it can cool down. Once it has cooled to a desirable level, ladle some of the potion into the chalice, sweetening it as preferred, and take the chalice back to the altar. Once everything is ready, begin the ritual. Cast a circle in your preferred manner, or you can use the following method.

Litha Circlecasting

Four tokens, one for each of the elements, can be placed at the four cardinal directions of the working area. After the tokens are placed, light the altar candles, then, starting and ending in the north, use the athame to trace a circle of power surrounding yourself and the working area. As you form the circle, say, "This magical circle shall now be formed to draw in blessings and protect from harm."

After the circle is made, the elements can be invoked at each of their quarters. Begin in the east. Reach out with your feelings and call to the power of air, "Sacred air, on this solstice at this hour, enchant this circle with your power." Move to the south, reaching out, and as you light the red candle, call the power of fire, "Sacred fire, summer heat warm and bright, enchant this circle with your light." Move to the west and call out to the element of water, "Sacred water of lake, sea, and storm, enchant this circle with your charm." Finally, move to the north and call to the power of earth, "Sacred earth, strength of land and vital essence, enchant this circle with your presence."

Ritual

Once the circle is complete, return to the altar and light the light green candle, saying, "The wheel has turned and the sabbat of Litha is upon us. The power of light has reached its peak and shall soon begin its decline. Goddess of the land, mother of all, bless and protect us with your power divine." Light the dark green candle, saying, "The battle resumes for the yearly crown, with the Holly King poised to take the throne. I call to you in gratitude, asking that this season be blessed and filled with joy and good." Light the brown candle and say, "To the Oak King, I bid fond farewell in thanks for your power of growth and light. As you prepare to surrender your reign, I honor your sacrifice and remember your might." Gazing at the light of the candles, ponder the seasonal shift that is now underway and envision the two kings battling for the crown of the year and the blessing and favor of the goddess.

Pick up the chalice of potion and hold it up in salute, first to the dark green candle and then to the brown candle, and say, "Oak and Holly meet tonight, commencing the shift through mystical fight; they each bring balance to life and land, from the peak to decline now close at hand. With this potion I do now drink and take in the power that I seek; enhancing my magic through Litha's energy, for highest good, so mote it be." Drink some of the potion and feel its power increasing your own. Pour a little bit of the potion onto the offering plate in thanks. It is now time to charge the yellow sabbat candle.

When you feel ready, pick up the yellow sabbat candle and hold it in both hands. Envision the unfolding summer season and see how you want it to be; in other words, build your personal vision of how the summer shall go. See your own life unfolding, but also visualize the earth and see the land healing and the weather balanced. Build this vision strongly, and mentally pour this into the candle through your hands as an emerald green energy. Once you feel the candle is fully charged, place it back into its holder. Light the candle, saying, "The wheel has turned and the new season unfolds; into this energy a vision I mold: to restore the balance, bring healing and peace, this magic I cast, the power released. For good of all things, with harm to none, so I say, this spell is done."

Finally, pick up the plate of bread and point the athame at it with your strong hand, saying, "May this bread nurture the body, mind, and spirit. From seed to sprout to grain progressed, gift from earth be truly blessed." Break off three small portions of the bread and place them in the offering bowl for the goddess of the land, the Oak King, and the Holly King. Next, eat at least one piece of bread to take in the blessing of the season.

Closing

Give thanks to the goddess and both kings, saying, "Goddess of the earth, I thank you for your blessings. Oak King, I thank you for your power of growth and your sacrifice. Holly King, I thank you for your power of transformation." Release each of the elements, starting in the north, then move counterclockwise around the circle. At the north, say, "Sacred earth, thank you for attending this rite; you are now released with my blessing in love and light." At the west, say, "Sacred water, thank you for attending this rite; you are now released with my blessing in love and light." At the south, say, "Sacred fire, thank you for attending this rite; you are now released with my blessing in love and light." At the east, say, "Sacred air, thank you for attending this rite; you are now released with my blessing in love and light." Back at the north, draw the energy of the circle into the athame, saying, "The circle is open, merry meet, merry part, and merry meet again. This rite is done." Extinguish the candles in reverse order of lighting them.

Notes

Notes

Notes

Notes

Lammas

From Flowering to Fruition

Lupa

SUMMER IS WINDING ITS way through the clouds and the forests, dancing along lowered streams and sun-warmed berries. It throws brief but powerful storms across the land now and then, bringing a bit of respite to parched land along with the risk of lightning strikes and fire. Lammas is settled within this cauldron of challenges and blessings, and through it all, life continues its efforts to not only survive but thrive.

This sabbat signifies the first harvest of the year, or so every 101-level book on Wicca says. But what does that really mean? Most Pagans aren't farmers or gardeners, and given that so many seasonal foods can now be found in grocery stores year-round due to international distribution, a lot of people no longer have a day-to-day connection with where their food comes from. So while we understand "the harvest" from a theoretical perspective, it's not as easy to imagine the relief of knowing that your food for the winter is assured as months of hope and hard work pay off in the form of berries, vegetables, grains, and more.

As someone who has spent the past few years living on a farm, I have some understanding of the release of tension that occurs when sifting through strawberry patches yields more ripe, red berries than anticipated, or when a sheep's five-month-long pregnancy results in healthy twin lambs who immediately begin to nurse. But these are only supplemental forms of food here; they are not the mainstay compared to the grocery store. So how can those of us who are not subsistence farmers—or foragers and hunters, for that matter—make the idea of the first harvest more relevant?

We've had to look at traditional themes in more abstract manners as we've become more urbanized. The effort that was once contributed by everyone in the community toward bringing in the harvests is now funneled toward jobs and businesses by most working-age people. And while the harvest has traditionally been seen as a physical reward for one's efforts, even our ancestors appreciated the more subtle payoffs, whether that was improved relationships with the land and spirits, or better status within one's community. So it is that we also now harvest not only physical goods but also social power, personal growth, and new knowledge and wisdom.

Lammas and Lughnasadh are also often conflated into one celebration. Lughnasadh is a celebration of the Irish Celtic god Lugh, who is known for having mastered a great number of skills. This ties in surprisingly well with the idea of a more abstract harvest, as the time and effort invested in a particular skill or tool may be celebrated once a certain milestone or accomplishment is reached. Therefore, Lammas can be a good time to reflect on one's growth in reaching fruition, even if there's still room for more expansion and development, whether in a practical sense or in a more abstract part of your life.

And that's an important thing to remind ourselves of: Lammas is only the first of three harvest celebrations. There are two more to come, and a lot can happen in that time, both good and bad.

Harvest Is a Process, Not an Event

Here in the United States, the dominant overculture has a strong tendency toward linear thinking, with hard and nonnegotiable boundaries that often take the form of boundaries like "yes/no," "win/lose," "succeed/fail." Yet real life is a lot messier than that, which is in and of itself a mercy. After all, not every experience or situation is going to be all good or all bad; often there are some positives and negatives, which achieve a sort of balance. Perhaps the negatives have some room for improvement, while the positives may fade away if not properly tended to.

Historically, farmers would grow a variety of crops and raise multiple species of animal. This not only offered them a greater variety of food for their own pantry, but it gave more possibilities to sell surpluses to others for extra funds. Yet many farmers today set their sights on one particular cash crop throughout the year, particularly as corporate agribusinesses have consolidated many small farms under their control. And reliance on that one crop to pay the bills for a year means there's that binary "make it or break it" approach. Once it's done, it's done, no matter how it unfolded this particular year. That lack of diversity means that these farmers are incredibly vulnerable and have more difficulty leaving a system in which even the seeds themselves may be patented and not collected for next year's sowing. Harvest becomes a one-time event rather than a multiple-focused process.

While "the harvest" being referred to in Pagan sabbats coincides with autumn-fruiting plants like grains, many fruit trees, etc., there are potential harvests to be had year-round. Many crops can be planted in winter for spring harvest, especially in milder climates. And, of course, there are many wild foods like some berries and roots that are ready to be eaten at various times of the year, not just late summer and fall. And each of these individual crops and foragings can be varyingly successful; it may be that one year the salmonberries offer a spring bumper crop, but later in the season the huckleberries don't do so well due to a fungal infection. Or perhaps a disease kills a number of laying hens in the flock, which reduces the number of eggs available, while a young cow giving birth for the first time successfully has twins, both female. Unless it's a truly abysmal year, a varied harvest allows more mitigation of risks and more opportunities for success even amid failure.

This is important, because Lammas comes at a very risky time of year. Summer has dragged on long enough that many places are parched, and drought can ruin a crop weeks or even days before harvest. It's the thick of wildfire season too, which has expanded and worsened due to climate change in recent years. Having a successful harvest in spite of these dangers can bring even more gratitude and relief, even as we know we aren't out of the woods just yet.

It Ain't Over 'Til It's Over

Lammas is not the end, but only the beginning of the harvest. It is a sign that your efforts are starting to pay off, and perhaps some things you were working on are complete. But you still have some way to go before you can truly rest. That means you need to pace yourself and not rely too heavily on one particular part of the process.

It's very easy to feel discouraged when something doesn't go well, even if everything else is going according to plan. That binary thinking I was talking about often pushes us to see anything less than perfection as an abysmal failure. Unfortunately, many people had this harmful message pushed on them from a young age by those who were tasked with helping to guide young minds, whether parents and other family, teachers, or other authority figures. We also tend toward a laser focus on success and winning, with the single champion being lauded as the only one worth paying attention to, and anyone else is an also-ran to be ignored and forgotten.

No wonder, then, that we can become distraught whenever something isn't going as we had hoped. Yet Lammas is the perfect time to remember that setbacks are not the end of the world, and we often have more chances to see things through to a better conclusion. Moreover, even when one part of our lives may be difficult right now, we have other areas that are more successful, even if we take them for granted because we're so used to their stability.

For example, let's say a project at work didn't pan out, or a relationship with a coworker is making the workplace stressful. Chances are these are both temporary situations, and things will resolve in the future one way or another. Even if the very worst happened and you had to leave that job, that may well be setting you up for something better down the line. Moreover, even if your professional life isn't looking so hot right now, maybe your home life is better, with people who care about you and support you. Or maybe you have a hobby or other interest that gives you a break from the stresses of everyday life and allows you some recovery time.

That's similar to how a diversified farm is. Not only are there many different crops to tend to, but the farmer can't afford to fall apart if one of them doesn't do as well as they'd hoped. Not only do they still need to pay attention to the needs of the plants and animals on the farm, but by spending some time with these other beings, they can be reminded of the fact that not everything rides on one particular harvest and that there are other opportunities ahead that may very well make up for this one, single loss.

For me, Lammas is a time to both celebrate the victories and mourn the losses, all while still having hope for the future. It helps to keep me from the sort of tunnel vision that says my efforts are all-or-nothing. Most importantly, it reminds me that it's okay for me to spend some time celebrating my accomplishments as well as what I've learned from my setbacks, and that I can still think well of myself even if I am an imperfect being (like pretty much everyone else!).

The Seven of Pentacles

Of all the cards in the traditional tarot's seventy-eight, the one that I most associate with Lammas is the Seven of Pentacles. It signifies a time when your efforts are beginning to pay off, and while the work isn't done, you can at least sit back and appreciate your success so far. This allows you a moment to get some context for what you're doing. You aren't just looking at the details of your day-to-day efforts, but the larger pattern they're a part of and the overall direction you're headed in.

When I created my first deck, the Tarot of Bones, I was inspired by imagery from the Rider-Waite-Smith deck. I placed seven vertebrae, the bones that I found most analogous to pentacles, within a wall of greenery and flowers. I wanted the viewer to feel as though they were looking directly upon a garden that was lush and full of both the bones (pentacles), which represented manifested spiritual energy being funneled into this agricultural effort, and the flowers, which were yet to fully come to fruition. The garden had come a long way from the seeds first sown in the soil months before, and there was now something really worth looking at! But it happened because of the gardener's intent being brought into reality through effort and persistence, an energy that is represented throughout the suit of pentacles.

Yet the Seven of Pentacles is also a reminder that nothing is guaranteed, that outside forces beyond our control can still rise up and knock us off course. The thing is, not every harvest is successful. When the Seven of Pentacles is reversed, it may signify that something has gone wrong in spite of your best efforts. Perhaps insects devoured something in your garden, or unusually high temperatures scorched your plants even with frequent watering. Or the problem might be within you: perhaps you didn't have the time to properly care for your garden due to other obligations, or you underestimated how much work might be involved. Either way, the success you were hoping for eludes you.

So what do you do from there? Just because things aren't working according to plan doesn't mean that all is lost. This is only the first of the three harvest festivals; there's time yet to turn things around.

Cosmic Sway

Daniel Pharr

SOLAR LUGHNASSADH IS CELEBRATED after sunset on July 31 and extends through the daylight hours of August 1. Simple. Easy. Giving lunar holidays solar-based days in the calendar does make knowing when to observe a High Holiday much easier, although the ancients were not overly concerned with ease replacing accuracy.

The Aquarius Moon will shine its inspirations upon the celebrants. Offbeat self-identification may be the underlying energy for the evening. Personal feelings can be intricate, and when everyone's emotions compete in complexity, communication can be an issue. Mostly, people will want to free themselves from self-imposed emotional bonds.

Cross-Quarter Lughnassadh

The calculated cross-quarter date for Lughnassadh is August 7 at 6:54 a.m. under a Taurus Moon. However, the Moon will move into Taurus at 2:25 a.m., only four hours earlier. Before then, the Moon will be in Aries. Since the High Holiday will likely be celebrated on August 6, plan for fiery influences of the rite. Aries helps to uncomplicate any situation by promoting direct action. This may help to make the High Holiday a simple task in both preparation and execution. Typically a balefire, or any ritual fire, will be integral to the festivities, and what better Moon than a fire Moon to assist?

Pleiades Lughnassadh

The full and ninth Moon in the cycle will be in Aquarius on August 1 at 2:32 pm. The Moon enters Aquarius on July 31 at 11:58 p.m. and goes void August 2 at 5:15 p.m., and before that will have been in Capricorn. Since High Holidays were often set on the Full Moons, partly for the practical reason of having the Full Moon light to see in the darkness, Lughnassadh may be celebrated on the nights of July 31 or August 1. High Holiday festivities often last late into the evening, if not the next morning, so Capricorn will be involved to help plan and prepare for the event, and Aquarius will help to pull it off.

Harvest

Lughnassadh (*lew-nass-ah*) is also spelled Lunasa and Lughnasadh, and is known by other names. The Christians call this day Lammas or Loaf Mass Day (August 1) in reference to the Holy Communion. The Pagans celebrate this day as an honoring of Lugh, the fire god. On this day and night under a Full Moon, the harvesting of the first ripened grain was also celebrated by baking loaves of bread. Lughnassadh is a time to give thanks for the abundant harvest, eat seasonal fruits and vegetables, and bake breads and wheat-based foods like pies. Identify the abundance of life in all ways and give thanks, not just for food, but love, work, and joy. The harvest rite can also be a plea for assistance to increase abundance in all aspects of life. Lughnassadh is the first harvest festival and is often celebrated with an outdoor feast under the Moon.

Books and Laziness

Book Lovers Day is August 9, and the Moon is in Gemini. National Lazy Day is August 10, and the Moon is still in Gemini. The Gemini Moon encourages an inquisitive mind and contemplation. There will not be a better time to stay home, brew some tea, enjoy a book, and consider universal truths. The boss is sure to understand.

Dark Moon

The Dark Moon arrives on August 16 at 5:38 a.m., but it will have been in Leo the night of August 15, so light a candle in the darkness at your leisure. The Dark Moon rite is a wonderful time to commit to something new, maybe even exciting. The fire energy of Leo will help make a great start. And as with taking on anything new, to preserve balance, release something old that has been taking your energy.

National Dog Day

August 26 every year is National Dog Day. This year the Moon is in Capricorn, so celebrating the dog, man's best friend, seems only natural. Dogs give their love freely every day; giving back to them is important. Order a cake from a dog bakery and have a dog party, or just buy a doggie donut and have a private celebration. Maybe take a long walk, have a game of fetch, or go somewhere special like the beach. Volunteering at the shelter is time well spent and will help many dogs. The Capricorn Moon will support these efforts nicely. The sensitivity of the Capricorn Moon will enhance connecting with a dog, and the loyal energies will make play last longer than planned.

Blue Moon

The Full Moon in Pisces is on August 30 at 9:36 p.m. This is the tenth Full Moon in the cycle and, as it is the second Full Moon in August, it is a monthly Blue Moon—the second Blue Moon in a calendar month, which is, of course, a solar calendar construct and occurs yearly. An astrological Blue Moon is the second Full Moon in an astrological sign, such as Aquarius. This is not an astrological Blue Moon; the first Full Moon of August was in Aquarius and the second in Pisces. The seasonal Blue Moon, the Blue Moon recognized by the ancients, is the third of four Full Moons between a solstice and an equinox, or visa versa, which happens only once about every three years. Regardless of which type of Blue Moon, the Blue Moon represents bounty. Blue Moons are opportunities to find closure from the preceding month's trek. Emotionally aware and magically sympathetic, the Pisces Blue Moon will enhance the ability to see into the future and to predict the path of least resistance. Sympathetic magic will also be fully formative in the desired result. Clairsentience, the sensing of emotions, will be livelier than normal, perceiving clearly that which has not been revealed.

Dark Moon

September 14 at 9:40 p.m. brings the Dark Moon in Virgo. This will be an enjoyable day to visit friends or meet new ones. Virgo's kindness and humility will soften the demeanor, allowing for an easy chat with a new person. In ritual, light a candle or have a fire, set intentions, and begin something new. Further the quest. Let go of something that is no longer found useful, but this is not the time to cut out anything cherished.

Tales and Traditions

Kate Freuler

LAMMAS, OR LUGHNASADH, IS known as a grain festival. Lammas marks the season of harvesting wheat, corn, and grains that would have been used for baking bread and other dietary staples. Lammas is the first of the three harvest celebrations. There were still many other crops growing and coming to fruition, and the goddess is still heavily pregnant, so Lammas festivities contained elements of fertility rites to ensure the earth's bounty would continue to flourish in the coming months. Some covens perform the Great Rite on this date, preferably in a fertile field. A feast is often held, featuring the harvested grains like corn, wheat, and oats, followed by dancing, celebration, and merriment. Thanks are given to gods and goddesses of the fields, and sacrifices are made in their honor. A traditional way to do this was to burn or bury the first piece of grain cut during the harvest and dedicate it to the deities. Additionally, a single corn or wheat stalk can be left standing in the field after the harvest as an offering to nature spirits.

Bread and ale were the two most common products made from grains, so these featured heavily in Lammas ceremonies. In fact, *Lammas* comes from the Anglo-Saxon words "loaf-mass."

Bread represents the harvest, home, and hearth. For many, the smell of freshly baked bread brings to mind coziness and comfort.

As it rises during preparation and while baking, the smooth, warm dough is reminiscent of an expanding pregnant belly, which could be where the idiom "bun in the oven" comes from. These qualities make bread a symbol of growth and potential.

Sacred breads are sometimes baked with the fresh grain and shared within a coven in celebration of Lammas. A loaf of bread is passed from person to person within the circle. Each participant states something for which they're thankful, pulls a piece of bread from the loaf, and eats it. Then the loaf is passed on to the next person. This can be seen both as a sacrifice and an act of gratitude to deity.

Baking bread is a particularly unique process. It's different from all other forms of baking because it requires a chemical reaction to take place between the yeast and other ingredients and needs precise conditions for this to happen. This chemical process literally transforms a few everyday materials into a completely different object: life-sustaining food. But for this transformation to be successful, all of the ingredients and conditions must be just right.

Baking bread and working magic have a lot in common. In both cases, you're taking some very basic natural elements that, when combined, transform into a completely new state of being or experience. When baking bread, you create the perfect balance of heat, moisture, timing, and ingredients. When working a spell, you factor in lunar and astrological timing, the magical properties of herbs and other ingredients, and how you plan to direct energy. If something is off during your working, such as your intention is wavering or you get distracted, the success of your spell will be affected. But when the elements and energies in your spell come together just so, they transform into something new, manifesting your will.

Bread baking follows several basic essential steps to make a good loaf of bread, and a magical working is very similar. No matter what kind of ritual or rite you perform, there are some universal things to consider.

1. **Timing.** With bread baking, the ingredients are often adjusted to fit the temperature and climate. The elements of your magic function the same way. Bread rises best in a warm, humid environment. It will still rise somewhat without those conditions, but it definitely does best at the right time and temperature. In magic, doing your spell during the right moon phase and astrological time isn't absolutely necessary—it won't make or break your spell—but it certainly helps.

2. **Raising energy.** After mixing bread ingredients, the dough has to rise. The yeast and sugars work together, producing gas, which makes the mixture expand. This chemical reaction creates heat as the dough slowly doubles in size. This process can be likened to how when you bring together intention, energy, and tools, they amalgamate to transform your ideas into reality. During a working, you raise energy and, using concentration, make it grow and take shape. When a spell is done just right, this gathering and increase of power can be keenly felt.

3. **Practical work.** Kneading bread is the laborious part and takes some muscle. After the dough has finished rising, you have to mash, push, and fold it for a set amount of time. If you skip this part, the bread won't rise properly during baking. The physical exertion of kneading is comparable to taking practical measures to achieve your magical goal. For example, if you do a spell for money, you must combine it with actions such as sending out your resume or asking around for jobs. If you skip the practical, hands-on part of your working, your spell isn't going to succeed.

4. **Patience.** After kneading, the dough is set aside to rise some more, allowing further development as perfect bread dough is formed. It's tempting to skip this part and put it right into the oven, but to do so would ruin the end result. This waiting period is similar to the time that comes after your spell has begun working and you've taken practical measures to reach

your goal. The magic, or the chemical reaction, is still taking place. For now, you have to just stand by and allow it to happen. At this time, you should try to forget about the spell you cast and allow results to come to you. Obsessing over your working after the fact will interfere with what you've set in motion.

5. **Manifestation.** Last but not least is the end product! While bread dough bakes, it solidifies into its final delicious form. This is the final step between thought and matter as your desires manifest in your physical life. Energies (or raw ingredients) begin to solidify, becoming the end product or result. At this time during a successful magical working, you might start getting calls for job interviews or find an unexpected check in the mail. It's time to enjoy what you have created!

If you bake bread this Lammas, try thinking about it a little differently. Fill each step of the process with intention, turning the baking of bread into a spell in and of itself. Whatever you manifest, gratitude is key. Lammas is all about honoring the source of our nourishment and giving thanks. So regardless of how you celebrate, remember to acknowledge all that you have to be thankful for and where it comes from. And if you can, share!

References
McCoy, Edain. *The Sabbats: A New Approach to Living the Old Ways*. St. Paul, MN: Llewellyn; Enfield, 2001.

Feasts and Treats

Gwion Raven

LAMMAS ALWAYS CONJURES IMAGES of long, hot days, shared meals, and enjoying the fruits of our labours. Traditionally a harvest festival, Lammas is a time to rest once the wheat is in and before other crops are harvested. We can learn a lot from stopping partway through the year, assessing our accomplishments, and recognizing the work left to do.

Rather than focus on baking bread, a lovely pastime to be sure, these recipes draw their inspiration from simple, seasonal ingredients reminiscent of rustic foods eaten in the fields by hardworking people. If you can, serve these in wooden bowls on a blanket outside. Eat with your hands, and wipe your mouth with your sleeves.

Where I live, blackberries are abundant in August, so they are heavily featured!

Quick Flatbread with Blackberries and Goat Cheese (Vegetarian)

Whenever I make this, I always say I'm going to cook it over an open fire, but rarely do. I think there's something quite romantic about going berrypicking along the hedgrows, making a little campfire, and filling my belly with bread, fruit, and cheese. It's possible

I'm part hobbit. If you do prepare this over an open fire, make sure it's in a proper firepit and you practice extremely good fire safety.

Prep time: 5 minutes
Cooking time: 30 minutes
Servings: 4

1½ cups flour
1 teaspoon baking powder
½ teaspoon salt
1½ tablespoons olive oil
½ cup ice cold water
2 tablespoons olive oil, for frying
8 ounces blackberries
8 ounces goat cheese
½ red onion, sliced

Preheat oven to 350°F.

Combine the first three ingredients in a mixing bowl. Pour in the oil and water and mix until you have dough. The dough should be a little wet and not overly sticky. Cover with a paper towel or plastic wrap and set aside for 15 minutes.

Divide the dough into four equal pieces. Add a sprinkle of flour and slowly flatten the dough balls between your palms until they are ¼ thick.

Put a cast-iron skillet or frying pan over medium-high heat for 2 minutes. Add 1 tablespoon of olive oil. Heat for 1 minute. Add the flatbread to the skillet. Cook 2–3 minutes per side until golden brown.

Top each flatbread with blackberries, cheese, and onion. Drizzle with a little olive oil and pop in the oven on a baking sheet for 5 minutes, or until the cheese has melted.

Serve on a wooden cutting board. Cut it if you must, or tear it and share it for more fun!

Summer Sausages and Tomatoes over Bread

I first ate this meal when I worked for a winery. We'd spent the day harvesting grapes. We weren't the professional pickers, but the winery required every employee to spend at least 4 hours in the vineyards each year so we understood what it meant to do the backbreaking work of harvesting. After a long, hot day of picking grapes and hauling containers to and fro, I was ready for a hearty meal. A half a dozen of us sat around a table of upturned wooden crates. We quaffed red wine, voraciously ingested sausages, and mopped up the leftovers with fresh-baked bread.

You can make this dish with your favourite sausages and whatever fresh tomatoes you have on hand. I like to use mild Italian sausages because they often contain fennel, which I adore! For a vegan option, add plant-based sausages and cook only for the last 20 minutes.

Prep time: 5 minutes
Cooking time: 60 minutes
Servings: 4

3 pounds mixed tomatoes, stems removed. I recommend smaller varieties like cherry tomatoes
2 bay leaves
1 sprig rosemary
1 tablespoon dried basil
2 cloves garlic, peeled and minced
8 sausages
1 tablespoon olive oil
1 tablespoon balsamic vinegar
1 crusty loaf of bread

Preheat the oven to 375°F. Arrange tomatoes, herbs, garlic, and sausages on a rimmed baking tray, preferably in one even layer. Drizzle with the olive oil and balsamic vinegar. Using your hands, gently toss the ingredients to evenly coat. Roast in the oven for 30 minutes. Open the oven and turn the sausages over. (If you're using vegetarian sausages, this is when you add them.) Shake the pan a little. Cook for another 20 minutes. The tomatoes will render down to something like sticky jam.

Cut 4 thick slices of bread. Warm in the oven for 5 minutes.

Serve on warmed plates or bowls. Heap the tomatoes, sausages, and any sauce onto a bread slice. Add a little fresh ground black pepper and salt if you like.

Blackberry and Apple Crumble (GF & Vegan)

When my children were quite young, we'd head out to a local park ringed with blackberry bushes. We'd come home with stained fingers, plenty of scratches, and pounds and pounds of fresh blackberries. Blackberry bushes grow pretty much anywhere, and they produce so much fruit. If you're lucky enough to live where blackberries grow, there's something lovely about heading out with a couple of big bowls and returning home with hundreds of wild blackberries—minus a few to snack on, on the way home, of course.

Prep time: 15 minutes
Cooking time: 60 minutes
Servings: 4

Berries

5 cups blackberries
¼ cup granulated sugar
2 tablespoons arrowroot powder
2 tablespoons agave nectar

Topping

2 cups gluten-free 1-to-1 flour
¼ cup brown rice flour
1 cup sugar
1 cup almond milk
¼ cup coconut oil, melted
1 tablespoon baking powder
1 teaspoon salt

Preheat the oven to 350°F. In a large bowl, mix the fruit, sugar, arrowroot, and agave and set aside.

Using a stand mixer, beat together the ingredients for the topping. Mix until all ingredients are incorporated. The dough will be a bit crumbly.

Grease a 2-quart baking dish and then pour in the blackberry mixture. Drop large spoonfuls of the dough onto the blackberries. Bake for 45 minutes or until the topping is golden brown. Let cool for 15 minutes.

Serve in bowls with a sprig of mint, drizzle on a little more agave, or top with your favourite whipped topping.

Blackberry Iced Tea (GF & Vegan)

With so many blackberries, there's always something else to make. The colour of this tea is a rich, deep purple, almost like red wine. Mint leaves, lemon, and a few fresh blackberries serve as delicious garnishes.

Prep time: 5 minutes

Cookie time: 10 minutes, plus 3 hours to cool

Servings: 4

2 cups fresh blackberries (frozen works too)

3 tablespoons granulated sugar

5 cups boiled water

4 bags black tea

3 cups cold water

1 lemon, sliced

4 sprigs of mint

Grab a big bowl. Add the blackberries and sugar. Mash the fruit with the back of a spoon and mix. Set the macerated fruit aside.

Boil 5 cups of water. Add tea bags and steep for 6 minutes. Remove the tea bags.

Pour tea over the blackberries and stir everything together. Set aside for 1 hour to cool.

Get a sieve and a serving pitcher. Push the mixture through the sieve, mashing the fruit to get out as much juice as possible. Add 3 cups of ice-cold water. Refrigerate for 2 hours.

Serve in tall glasses filled with ice. Add lemon slices and extra blackberries, top with mint sprigs. Then sip it. You'll want to gulp it, but savour it like the summer sun.

Crafty Crafts

Ivo Dominguez Jr.

IT IS THE SEASON of the first harvest and the honoring of sacred sacrifices. John Barleycorn, Lugh of the many talents, abundant fields, and the smell of baking bread are all evocative of the holiday. One of the sacrifices that is sometimes overlooked is the clearing away of forests to create farmland. Tailtiu, Lugh's foster mother, cleared the land so that there would be food for the people and, in so doing, died of the effort. Tailtiu was a goddess of place, so she truly sacrificed herself in the felling of the trees. Lugh created funeral games and a harvest festival to remember her. This craft project is in honor of her and the forests that became farmland.

Face of the Forest Mask

We'll be making a foliage-covered mask to represent the Green Man, the Green Woman, or a nongendered Face of the Forest. What you create is up to you and your preferences. The mask will be wearable, though it can also be hung on the wall or placed on an altar. I have also hung masks from trees or put them atop poles stuck in the ground for outdoor rituals. It is not that difficult to make a beautiful and personally meaningful mask, and you may find yourself making several.

Materials

Premade mask, unless making from scratch
Various scraps of cloth, rags, yarn, and cords
Paper, newspaper, shop towels, tissue paper, and paper towels
Floral wire, pipe cleaners, or other objects to use as stiffeners
White glue
White masking tape or duct tape
Stapler
Scissors
Gloves
Paints to finish the project
Mixing bowl, one that is not used for food
Protective cover for your work area, as it will get messy
Optional: a blow-dryer, heat gun, or electric fan
   Cost: $0–$25
   Time spent: 3 hours, plus drying time

Design Ideas

You can make some choices and plan some details, but the best masks seem to emerge straight out of the process of making them. Making a list of facial features that you want to include and what kinds of leaves, flowers, fruits, etc. that you want to add is useful. Do you have a particular facial expression or mood that you want the mask to convey? Knowing what colors you plan to use before you go shopping for supplies is always a good idea. This project can take a few days because of drying time, so give yourself some leeway before Lughnasadh to get it finished. The technique resembles papier-mâché but primarily uses cloth instead of strips of paper. If you are an experienced mask maker, you might consider building the mask, but in most cases, I suggest starting with a blank, premade half or full mask from a craft store. Whether or not you need all of the items on the materials list or additional items depends on what you are trying to create.

Making the Mask

The first step is to cut out some leaf or petal shapes from the cloth that you have. Have a strip of cloth from each shape that extends like a short stem. Experiment with different arrangements of these on the premade blank mask. This will give you an idea of the sizes and shapes that you need. Take note of where you want the leaves, flowers, etc. to attach to the mask. At those spots, tape down pipe cleaners folded in half, or some other flexible wire, to create anchors for the leaves and such. Do as many as you like, because if you have any leftover, they are easy to hide. If your plans call for leaves, twigs, tendrils, and such that extend beyond the edges of the blank mask, add some pipe cleaners that have been twisted together that extend outward as supports.

Mix two-parts white glue to one-part water in a mixing bowl. Then dip the largest leaves one at a time in the mixture and wipe off some excess glue. Begin to place them on the mask. Bend, twist, and shape them to give them life. Wrap their cloth stems around the pipe cleaners to attach them to the mask. Periodically bend and shape the cloth and the wire as you work to make it look good. To speed up the process, you can use a blow-dryer to stiffen the glue enough so you can continue working. When you are not using the glue-water mixture, cover it with clear wrap to keep it from drying.

You can use ripped-up pieces of paper dipped in the glue mixture to smooth or fill in the joints between different parts. You can also crumple and apply paper to create textures like bark or stone. Small bits of wet paper are almost like clay for creating some details. Some petals or flowers are easier to construct by folding and stapling paper and then dipping it. Small paint brushes, tweezers, and old makeup sponges can be used as shapers as well.

After the mask has dried completely, you may paint it. The paint also acts as an adhesive to solidify the whole piece. I prefer acrylic paint for these masks. It is usually best to start with the darkest base colors and work your way out to adding the highlights last. A bit of roughed-up sponge is great for dipping into paint to apply a mottled or dappled effect to the foliage. Making some parts look drier or wetter by using a clear gloss or matte medium makes them look more real. If you have time, paint the inside of the mask as well. If the whole mask is covered in paint, it will hold up in wet weather outdoors.

Construction Tips
While the mask is still wet, place pencils wrapped in foil through the holes where the cords for wearing the mask will go; this way, they won't close up. For letting the mask dry, you can place it on a sheet of foil. If it can't lay flat until it is fully dry, place a bowl upside down and use it as a form to hold the mask. After it has been

painted and dries for a second time, do a test fit. You may need to do a bit of trimming or sanding. You can also glue strips of felt on the inside of the mask to cushion rough spots.

References

Good, Jonni. *How to Make Masks!: Easy New Way to Make a Mask for Masquerade, Halloween and Dress-Up Fun, With Just Two Layers of Fast-Setting Paper Mache.* La Grande, OR: Wet Cat Books, 2012.

Color Magic

Charlie Rainbow Wolf

THE FESTIVAL OF Lugnasadh is another quarter festival, falling between the Midsummer solstice and the autumnal equinox. It marks the end of the growing season in the Northern Hemisphere, and the arrival of the harvest deities such as Lugh, Crom Dubh, and Ethne. Lugnasadh is usually celebrated around the beginning of August.

This is my favorite time of year. I see Lughnasadh as the first of the three harvest festivals. When I lived on the Lincolnshire farm, it was when we first started gathering in preparation for winter, and not just the harvest of fruits and vegetables, but also things like firewood from downed trees and yarn from the spinners to knit the winter's woolies.

The Colors of Lughnasadh

This is also my favorite color palette. When I think of Lugnasadh (Lammas), I think of the warm red of the glowing stubble fires, the yellow gold of the ripening grain, and the moss green of the tired foliage. Other colors for Lugnasadh include shades of orange and browns from the lightest tan to the deepest umber.

Because this is a grain festival, it's unsurprising that gold and harvest colors are the main theme. Here, the yellow isn't the bright light of the sun or the brilliant lemon of the spring flowers. At Lughnasadh, yellow takes on a straw color, more restful and easier on the eye and in keeping with the turn of the seasons as they start to slow down in preparation for the coming winter.

Orange is the marriage of red and yellow, both of which are Lughnasadh colors, but perhaps with yellow dominating, and that's okay too; there are many shades of orange. All shades encourage people to socialize and look after each other, which could be why there are so many successful harvest festivals starting around the beginning of August. It's associated with the sacral chakra, the center that governs creative energy and how it is used. Giving and receiving must be in balance in all areas in order to succeed, and working on this chakra will enable that to happen.

Giving and receiving play a big part at Lugnasadh, as the grain is given by the land and received by the farmers. Orange is a very giving vibration, and this reflects the story of how the sun god Lugh— as the living grain—is cut down so that he might sustain the village throughout the winter. Then, his seed is planted in the spring so the cycle of life, death, and rebirth might continue. I think this sums up the bittersweet vibration of this time of year perfectly. It's sad to see the summer ending and the fields being emptied, but it's also a time to rejoice in the harvest so freely given and the bounty and abundance that follows.

Orange is also associated with success, another aspect of the harvest. It's bold and giving and needs to be shared. It's not as passionate as red due to the influence of yellow, but it is still glowing and strong. Many shades of orange are muted even more at this time of year as the light fades while the copper-colored fruits ripen, awaiting their turn to be plucked from the vine.

I see Lugnasadh red as a bit of a conundrum, for although it is a muted harvest red, it's also still got some heat in it. I think of the glowing crimson around the cooling embers, or the fading russet of the stubble fires in the Lincolnshire fields. It's the red where orange finally surrenders the yellow, much the same as the corn finally surrendering the grain.

This is also the time when some of the first apples are starting to ripen. I find it interesting that they, too, reflect the Lughnasadh colors. Our old sheepnose tree is not ready to harvest yet, but its young fruit is starting to turn from gold to red. The quinces are going from green to gold. The leaves on the burning bush are starting to lose their vibrant green and welcome the bronze that will eventually lead to scarlet. Nature knows.

Aspects of red are associated with courage and energy: the energy to get through the harvest and the courage to face the coming winter. Wearing red is said to boost confidence and help to overcome apprehension. As a base or root chakra color, its theme is survival—and not just physical survival, but survival of the tales and traditions that go with it.

Lugnasadh brown is all about the bread: from cutting the grain to milling it, then raising the dough and baking it, to finally feasting on the finished loaf. Those who know me know I spent my early adult life near the village bakehouse, and I have been baking bread for decades—sometimes milling my own flour, first on a hand crank mill with grinding plates and later with an attachment for my stand mixer. There's something very satisfying about seeing the loaf through from grain to table. The bread echoes all shades of gold for Lugnasadh, from the lightest of gold in the flour to the deepest of brown in the toasted crust.

Celebrating Lugnasadh

Bread is just one way that we enjoy the harvest grain. Here at The Keep we make our own ale, and we celebrate that at this time of year with a dark brown stout brewed from malted barley. When we do "cakes and ale" at our house, they're made from scratch—and absolutely delicious! We often make "beer bread" at this time of year too.

The Lugnasadh stone on my incense altar is citrine. A stone of "new beginnings" might be a bit odd for a harvest festival when everything is being cut down for the winter, but the cycle of death *and* rebirth is part of Lugnasadh's magic. The citrine I use starts out a pale gold near the base and rises to a deep amber at its natural point. Citrine represents manifestation and helps to drive energy toward the desired outcome. According to Naisha Ahsian, citrine helps when focusing on desires (Ahsian, n.p.). Manifestation becomes easier because energy is not wasted pursuing things that will only delay the chosen goals from being met.

Reference

Ahsian, Naisha. *The Crystal Ally Cards: The Crystal Path to Self Knowledge.* East Montpelier, VT: Heaven & Earth Books, 1997.

Lammas Ritual

Lupa

THE THEME FOR THIS ritual is "the garden is full of flowers and the first fruits; your work is not yet full done, but you are beginning to see the results of all the effort you've put in." I've already discussed how nothing is guaranteed and how we can become too focused on what isn't going as well as we'd like. Here I would like to draw on the relief and joy that comes when the agricultural gamble pays off, as well as the Seven of Pentacles' invitation to look back and appreciate just how far you've come. Whether your efforts have been in the realm of practicalities like achieving financial security or improving your health, or more conceptual activities like creative expression and improving emotional connections with self and others, this is a time to celebrate what you've gained and prepare yourself for the next steps.

The First Harvest

First, thoroughly clean your altar and ritual area to the best of your ability. Then gather emblems and reminders of what you are currently trying to accomplish and what keeps you motivated each day. Perhaps there are pictures of the people you care the most about and who you want to benefit from your success (don't forget a picture of yourself, of course!). You might also include the tools of your trade or representations of hobbies and other leisure activities. Most importantly, you want to include any symbols of specific accomplishments or other milestones you've made along the way to represent the fruits of your efforts so far. Put these images of your progress in one part of your ritual space.

Have another spot set aside for representations of what didn't work out and setbacks you may have faced. Maybe you didn't pass a class or you didn't get a job you wanted. There may have been a breakup with a partner or a falling out with a friend or family member. You might even have had to completely restructure your life around an unexpected health problem. Even if the setbacks seem small or insignificant, if they had even a temporary effect on your progress, it's okay to include them.

Finally, create a space for reminders of what you haven't completed yet, the unfulfilled long-term goal of all this effort. Maybe you're saving up to buy a house or earn a new degree. Or your goal could be a healthier relationship with yourself or improved connections with those around you. Keep in mind that there's no such thing as a goal that's too humble or simple; not every harvest has to be focused on the big and the bold, after all. If it improves your life, that's a good enough reason to include it.

Put a candle in front of each of these three groupings, making sure to avoid any potential fire hazards. (A fire extinguisher is a perfectly reasonable ritual tool to have any time flames are involved!) Choose harvest-themed colors; plain beeswax candles are ideal for this. Bring in a few pieces of ripe fruit or other food that is currently in season and place one in front of each set of reminders. (If you have grown or foraged the food yourself, even better!) Then dress yourself in ritual attire or other clothing that helps you feel accomplished, competent, or otherwise extraordinary.

Open your ritual by calling the quarters, inviting in deities or spirit guides, or however you see fit. Then stand (or sit, if you prefer) before the altar and say the following:

I, [name], am immersed in the tides of Lammas, the first harvest. Through the previous seasons I have ridden the ebbs and flows of time, fortune, and my own energy, all of which have brought me to this point. I have walked this path of my own will, and today I take a moment to look around and see where it has led and where it may yet take me.

Now, face the reminders of what you are currently putting your efforts toward and what you've accomplished thus far; light the candle there. Take a moment to think about where you were a month ago, a year ago, and even further back. Remember where you were when you first began to walk this path and how much you've grown and learned since then. Consider that you may not even have had a specific plan at the time, but now you are seeing how everything fit together. Pick up the fruit or other food in front of this pile and hold it up, and say:

When I began this path, I wanted to achieve [name your various goals and hopes here]. And now here I stand, older and more experienced. In the time since I set foot to the path, I have learned and achieved [list off specific skills, lessons, and accomplishments]. I am grateful for all these opportunities, and I am proud of myself for making it this far. I celebrate this first harvest, where I am seeing my efforts come to fruition.

Take time to eat the fruit or other food slowly and mindfully, paying attention to the flavor and texture. Think of how much time and effort went into this very piece of food that now nourishes you and how it carries the energy of what you have accomplished so far. Allow yourself to enjoy a moment of respite and joy, and be proud of yourself as you consume the embodiment of your success so far.

Next, face the reminders of what did not go as well as you would have liked, the roadblocks and challenges that may have tripped you up or blocked you from a particular place, and light the candle there. Consider the factors that led up to these problems and then what you did to be able to address them to the best of your ability.

Allow yourself to mourn what has been lost but to also be proud of yourself for not letting these setbacks stop you entirely. Pick up the fruit or other food in front of this pile and hold it up, and say:

No path is without its risks, and even as I have found success, so have I also now and then encountered trouble along the way. I know that I have faced [name the setbacks and upsets you've been through on this path], and still I am here. From these experiences I have learned [list any lessons or new knowledge gained from working through these setbacks]. And in the future I plan to avoid them or mitigate their effects by [specific actions] to the best of my ability. In adversity I have found strength and wisdom, and I celebrate my resilience.

Take time to eat the fruit or other food slowly and mindfully, paying attention to the flavor and texture. Consider how the plant that grew it also had to overcome challenges for it to grow to fruition. Think of yourself as a plant that has produced flowers and is now preparing to turn these beautiful statements of fertility and potential into full results, ready to adjust to any setbacks along the way. Nourish yourself in celebration of making it this far in spite of the risks and losses.

Finally, face the reminders of what is yet to come and what your ultimate destination may be, lighting the candle in front of them. Think of how your goals may have changed and matured over time and how you have stayed motivated the whole way. Acknowledge the risks that may still trip you up and how even though nothing is guaranteed, you still hope for a positive outcome. Pick up the fruit or other food in front of this pile and hold it up, and say:

Before me the path stretches into new territory. I carry with me my hopes and my fears, the lessons I have learned, and the unknowns I have yet to explore. What I hope for is [name the goals and accomplishments you are working toward], and my hope is that through my efforts, the support of others, and the best possible fortune, I may see these come to a full and fruitful harvest. At this first harvest, I set my intent to see these through in the second and third and beyond if necessary.

Take time to eat the fruit or other food slowly and mindfully, paying attention to the flavor and texture. Enjoy the sweetness of the success you have seen so far, and anticipate how good future harvests may be. Imagine yourself standing in the midst of celebration and joy as you achieve what you have set out to do. Allow yourself the knowledge that getting there may have its difficulties, and you may have to change your course, but there will come another time when you get to taste this wondrous victory.

Meditate on your journey more if you need to, then say farewell to your guides, extinguish the candles, and close your ritual space.

Notes

Notes

Notes

Mabon

Mabon: Apple of Wisdom

Suzanne Ress

THE AUTUMNAL EQUINOX—SEPTEMBER 23 in 2023—falls within the seasonal sabbat period of Mabon: September 21–29. The word "Mabon" makes me think of apples; in fact, I think it would be an excellent name for an apple variety. But, actually, "Mabon ap Modron" is from Welsh and Arthurian legend, son of Modron, and a form of the dualistic male Horned God, also known as Cernunnos or Apollo. At this sabbat, we celebrate the second harvest, giving thanks and appreciation for all that nature and life has bestowed upon us throughout the growing season. The Autumn Equinox sabbat has apparently only been known as Mabon since around 1970, when it was named such by a leading Wiccan of the time, Aidan A. Kelly. At any rate, I think Mabon is a lovely name that expresses the feeling of this second harvest festival very well: "Ma," as the first part of *Malus*, the genus of all apples, and "bon," which means "good"—so, "good apple."

Across the Wheel of the Year from Mabon is Ostara and the first day of spring. Just after Ostara is when the apple trees bloom in my neck of the woods, creating a lovely fragrant, white canopy highly attractive to hungry honeybees. The apple trees' sweet blossoms at Ostara, pollinated by bees and other insects, have lost their petals by Beltane. The fertilized carpels slowly develop, growing under the sun and rain and warmth of Midsummer and Lammas to form Mabon's luscious ripe fruits. These fruits nourish us and many other creatures through the winter. Mabon signals the start of the darker half of the year, and from now until Ostara, the nights will be longer than the days. But for most of us in the Northern Hemisphere, September, especially the period of Mabon, is usually a pleasant, cooler, end-of-summer-feeling time—a sort of wrap-up to the joys of summer.

On my small organic farm, there is a fruit-tree orchard. There are plums, persimmons, cherries, pears, loquats, apricots, and apples. We planted many of the trees, but many more were already here when we moved in.

An apple tree can live as long as a hundred years, and there are three original large, old apple trees in our orchard: a red apple producing Grand Alexandre; a russet producing Reinette; and a green producing Gabiola. These are antique apple varieties I have never seen in any shop. Several times in years past, around this time of year, I have strolled through local apple festivals, observing all of the old varieties laid out with identifying labels on long, white cloth-covered tables, and that is how I know what these trees of ours are.

A low estimate of the number of apple varieties is around 7,000, but there may be as many as 30,000 different varieties of apples in existence; although, if you only saw the apples in grocery stores you might think the possible varieties were the commercially popular Gala, Granny Smith, Honeycrisp, Golden Delicious, and Pink Lady. Many of the less-common apple varieties are difficult or impossible to find for sale, so the only way to have them is to seek out a tree. Many of the older and less popular varieties are smaller than what you now find in shops and less perfect-looking, but what they lack in appearance is, at least in my opinion, made up for in complexity of taste and uniqueness of texture.

Our old Reinette apple tree has been especially prolific over the years, or, rather, every other year, as it, like many other apple tree varieties, is a biennial-bearing tree. So, if last year it produced thousands of apples, this year there will likely only be a couple dozen. On one side of the Reinette is the Gabiola, and on the other side is the Grand Alexandre, all in a well-spaced row on a south-facing terrace. All three of them are biennial-bearing, and they have synchronized themselves so that all three of them bear fruit in the same years and little or none in the between years.

On the copious years, there is so much fruit that loads of it fall down into the horse pasture below every night, and every day when I open the gate to let the horses out, they all rush to eat the windfallen apples under the trees—that is, all the ones left uneaten by the deer, roe deer, fox, field mice, and badgers.

I use my extendable pole picker to get several baskets full of apples at a time. Some of these will be given or bartered away to friends, and many of them we eat raw or I make into pie or add to salads, rice dishes, meat dishes—even slice onto pizza with gorgonzola. Many of them will be cored and sliced to dry in the food dryer, then stored in jars in the pantry for later use.

But there are always some apples left on the trees. Bats visit at night. During the day, wasps, hornets, and bees suck out the juice of the very ripe or rotting apples at this time when there are no flowers blooming, and birds will peck at the flesh of the ones bored into by the insects. Whatever is left will fall and be partially consumed by worms, larvae, and nematodes, while the remains will rot into the ground, feeding soil bacteria, until all that is left are the apple's seeds. Inevitably, we always have a few little sapling apple trees in the pasture the following spring.

The apple's seeds are arranged around its core in a pentagram shape when the fruit is cut horizontally—one reason why apples are considered the witch's fruit. The biblical forbidden fruit—the one that the world's first woman gave to the world's first man—was also called the fruit of the knowledge of good and evil, and is widely believed to have been an apple. One reason for this is that the apple has been around a long, long time—about 4,000 years. All the tens of thousands of varieties around now are descendants of the original wild apple (*Malus sieversii*), native to Kazakhstan.

There is something mystical, a little witchy, about apples. Apples are considered sacred to a number of fertility and love goddesses, and the trees have long been revered by Pagan people for their fruit, their beauty, and their wood. I would also add that apple trees, particularly the old ones, seem to me to resonate at a very pleasing frequency: The energy they emit is attractive! Applewood can be used to make powerful magic wands, and, more mundanely, it is used in smokers to give a slightly sweet taste to a variety of foods.

Many years ago, the first time I came to Italy, I was staying with a friend at his parents' home in Salerno. It was just after Yule time, and one evening, post-prandial, my friend's mother brought out a bowl of small red apples, announcing that they were, "Annurca" apples, highly prized and locally grown. I tried one, and yes, it was firm and sweet and tasty, and nothing like a Red Delicious. Annurca apples (*Malus pumila* 'Annurca') are thought to be the oldest cultivated apple variety still available today. They were mentioned by Pliny the Elder in his writings and have been in cultivation around Salerno, Italy at least since then!

Surely, the reason that apples have been cultivated for so long is because we love them. Discounting tomatoes, which are technically fruit but seem more like vegetables, apples are one of the most popular fruit in the world. Because they are so popular and have been around for so long, a lot of mythology has grown up around them. In Greek, Irish, and Norse mythology, there are golden apples that bestow immortality upon their eaters. In other tales and myths, apples symbolize beauty, love, healing, seduction, and trickery.

Are there really golden apples? Well, maybe they were russet Reinettes, which, when perfectly ripe, tend to take on a golden hue. Besides russet-colored, there are also white apples! The most famous is called the White Cloud, and it is creamy white outside and bright white inside. There are even black apples! The Black Diamond, cultivated in Tibet, has a black-purple skin and pure white flesh, and one called the Arkansas Black is a beautiful deep red-black outside. There are a lot of pink-fleshed apples. The Pink Pearl, Mountain Rose, Grenadine, and Thornberry are some.

When one of my relative's children were small, one of their favorite bedtime stories was a beautifully illustrated version of "Snow White." They would squeal with a combination of delight and fear when I read the lines of the witch/queen disguised as a peddler after Snow White expresses doubt that the beautiful (but poisoned) apple the peddler offers her is safe to eat: "I'll cut it in two. You eat the red half, and I'll eat the white half."

I'm not sure what it was about that particular line, but for years, whenever I offered those kids multitone apples, I'd say, "You eat the red half, and I'll eat the white half." It was an ironic joke between us, as if to say, "Do you trust me? Can you trust anyone? Can you even trust a beautiful two-toned apple?"

I mentioned previously that *Malus* is the genus name of all apples. Intriguingly, *Malus* in Latin also means "evil" or "bad." So Mabon could mean "good and bad" as well as "good apple."

Entering into the dark half of the year can be sad in some ways, even to the point of provoking anxiety in certain people. Summer is over, and the days will now grow shorter and shorter until Yule. The weather will turn cooler, then cold, and trees will lose all their leaves, and everyone in the Northern Hemisphere will seek shelter for many hours of each day. Less time spent outdoors in nature under sun or moonlight can tend to cause feelings of depression. Many people really do not look forward to short days and long nights.

It is essential to keep in mind that, just as this darker period of the year is necessary for trees and other plants to rest and regenerate, so it is necessary for us humans to have a period of forced contemplation, a time to draw yourself inward and take stock of what you are grateful for and what you might improve on. It is also a good time to exercise your memory.

The smell in the morning air around Mabon takes me back to my school days and all the excitement, anxiety, and little bit of sadness that I felt then, knowing the summer and my freewheeling lifestyle were over for a while and I was going to have to start wearing shoes again.

Toward the end of September, a couple weeks after school had started, my godparents would load us all into the station wagon and take us to a nearby farmers market. There were great bins of fresh-picked apples: green ones, red ones, yellow ones. We each chose the kind we wanted and got a paper sackful. My godmother's choice was always the little tart, green cooking apples. They were too hard and sour to eat raw. At home, she would cook them down in a cauldron to make applesauce. It was delicious, sweet applesauce with a pleasant tang. Compared to it, the store-bought applesauce has always tasted like cardboard to me.

So, is Mabon the name of an apple variety? Not as far as I know, but I think it should be!

I picture it as half red and half white, a perfect little package of life-giving energy and magical connotations. Its sweet, beloved flesh surrounds its pentagram arrangement of seeds, making it the ideal symbol for the Mabon sabbat and the start of the dark half of the year. Begin this season with plenty of reserve energy, built up over the lush days of spring and summer, and continue to fuel your spiritual needs as the nights turn longer and longer.

Reference

Snow-White and the Seven Dwarfs: A Tale from the Brothers Grimm. Translated by Randall Jarrell. Illustrated by Nancy Ekholm Burkert. New York: Farrar, Strauss, and Giroux, 1972.

Cosmic Sway

Daniel Pharr

THE AUTUMNAL EQUINOX IS on September 23 at 2:50 a.m. The Moon will be in Capricorn after 4:20 p.m. Energies will be in balance but leading to darkness away from light, to cold away from warmth. This is mid-autumn, halfway between the beginning of autumn on Lughnassadh and the beginning of winter on Samhain, and the second harvest, often celebrated as the Wiccan Thanksgiving. The days still feel warm and the nights a bit cool. Even the breeze has a hint of winter, but there usually aren't drastic changes in seasonal norms. The wheel turns slowly, as do the seasons and the weather. The last days of the summer deadlines are approaching. Soon the inward work and hibernation will be at hand. Spend time in nature.

Bring harmony into the home. One activity that never disappoints is picking apples. The apple is the perfect Wiccan fruit with an internal star. Apples are connected to spiritual workings, even in Christian liturgy. Gather apples to feed the family and preserve for the cold months ahead. Preparing for winter is another great activity. It brings thoughts and consideration of how life is lived, what food is eaten, what food is not, and how can food be used to bless the body. Connect with the night; hang out in the darkness. If the sky is clear, stars will abound. The same is true of gazing into the inner darkness. If the way is clear, the stars of the inner self will shine brightly.

Full Moon

September 29 at 5:58 a.m. is the Full Moon in Aries. This is the twelfth Full Moon in the cycle. In the ancient times, the second harvest festival would have been celebrated under the light of this moon. If the growing season was good and the growth cycle bountiful, the moon would have lit nighttime harvests. Aries is about straight-on movement, full-throttle speed, and no detours. Simple, practical, and getting things done. This lunar energy will be easily transmuted into similar action in both the physical and spiritual realms. This Moon will also help open a doorway to the inner workings of the self. Spend some time with a journal, maybe enjoy a salt bath, maybe both together. The Aries Moon will facilitate communication and bring forth the inner wisdom so badly needed in the world.

This Full Moon will also bring higher-than-normal tides to oceans and tidal-affected freshwater bodies. If access to a tidal body is available, sit for a bit and connect with the tidal movement. The length of this lunation may have seemed longer than normal, because this month was three-and-a-half hours longer than the average, allowing for three-and-a-half hours extra to make progress.

Solar Eclipse

October 14 at 1:55 p.m. is the Dark Moon in Libra. Normally, the idea of night before day moves celebrations to the evening before the actual event arrives in the daylight hours. In this case, that would be October 13. However, this Dark Moon will eclipse the Sun and would be best celebrated during the actual celestial event. The solar eclipse will show its totality in America from Oregon to Texas, across the Yucatán, along Central America, and then Columbia and

Brazil. The solar eclipse is a powerful force in the lives of the people it touches. An eclipse in astrology is a major event regardless of the proximity of the eclipse shadow being cast upon the earth.

The manner in which it connects with the planetary arrangement in the birth chart is most important. A solar eclipse always has the Sun and Moon conjunct, bringing the inner landscape and outer self together to live as one for the moment. It temporarily suspends reality in lieu of an alternate reality—one in which the Moon has the power to black out the Sun so the Sun doesn't shine during the day.

This exemplifies the power of the Moon and emotions—the unseen inner landscape—over the self that is shown to the world. A solar eclipse enlivens awareness, especially of life purpose and goals. The eclipse ushers forth a larger vision of life, and a vision likely not ever imagined. The eclipse steals the limited perspective that generally guides human life in the mundane world and replaces it with never-seen-before possibilities and opportunities. It offers a chance to consider life anew.

These changes that come from an eclipse might seem like a cataclysm, a seismic shift, a meteor impacting the earth, because letting go of the familiar, even if the familiar are chains that bind, can be jarring. Major sustainable spiritual growth can happen in eclipses when letting go of the familiar to follow a new path that presents itself in a new opportunity. Stay open to possibilities. A leap of faith may be required. The Fool card in the tarot is a perfect card for an eclipse. The depiction of a carefree or careless traveler about to step off a cliff could not be more apropos for an eclipse.

Full Moon

October 28 at 4:24 p.m. will be the Full Moon in Taurus. This is the thirteenth Full Moon in the cycle and, therefore, the first Full Moon in the next. Happy Pleiadean Samhain! This Moon is the first Full Moon after the culmination of Pleiades, when the cluster of stars was directly overhead at actual midnight, halfway between sunset and sunrise. The Moon is also the last Full Moon in the series of thirteen that began Samhain in 2022. Samhain is always graced by a Taurus Full Moon. Assuming the preference is not to celebrate Samhain based on the Pleiadean system, this Full Moon is just the last Full Moon of the year. Taurus will impart a grounding influence, as it always does, on the revelry approaching Witches' Night. Increased sensuality and appreciation of beauty will hopefully blanket the methodical energies of the Taurus Moon. The cross-quarter system calculates Samhain to be on November 7 at 12:38 a.m. under a Virgo Moon.

All Hallows' Eve

October 31 will have the Moon in Gemini. The Gemini influences will be all about the fashionable look for trick-or-treating and the ubiquitous Halloween party. If the solar calendar dates are preferred for the High Holidays, happy solar Samhain.

Tales and Traditions

Kate Freuler

MABON, OR THE FALL equinox, marks the second of the three harvest festivals. Fruit, squash, and more are collected and celebrated, particularly grapes which are made into wine. This sabbat is sometimes referred to as "Pagan Thanksgiving." Mabon is a time to consider what you have gained throughout the year and what you need to let go of.

Traditionally, Mabon activities center on gratitude, sharing, and showing appreciation. Sometimes a sacrifice can be made in the form of charitable acts or donating to good causes as an expression of gratitude. Some practicing covens will have a gathering on this day that's very similar to North American Thanksgiving feasts. In some Mabon festivities, a harvest queen and king are crowned to act as the vessels for the god and goddess during the celebration, which emphasizes giving thanks and prayers. In some parts of the world, people visit gravesites and burial cairns to honor the dead. Regardless of how you celebrate, it's generally a time to recognize the coming dark season and the change that comes with it.

Some modern Pagans argue that Mabon is a "made up" sabbat, because historically there is little evidence that Pagan ancestors had a name for the fall equinox. However, Mabon has been celebrated as a spoke on the Wheel of the Year by Wiccans, Witches, and Pagans in modern times for a while now and is mostly accepted as an important event.

On Mabon, day and night are of equal length. This parallel state of light and dark is an example of perfect balance, lasting only twenty-four hours. It's said that on this day all oppositional forces hang in perfect balance for a moment: the god and goddess have equal power, good and evil have equal influence, and life and death are simultaneously acknowledged. After this, the days will shorten bit by bit as the season of darkness takes over. In this way, Mabon is an occasion for transformation and change, acting as a gateway between two states of being as your spirit symbolically moves from light to dark, or day to night.

This is known as a liminal time. Liminal means "in-between" and is used to describe a place, situation, or experience in which one is suspended between an ending and a beginning, or balanced between two (often opposing) things. Liminality is a state of "not knowing," of waiting to see what happens next, of hope and sometimes apprehension, as a transformation takes place.

Liminal means "threshold," something that is both an exit and entrance. The same could be said about Mabon as the sun makes its exit and the colder months enter.

Physical liminal places are considered particularly powerful locations to do rituals or magic. A physical liminal space is anywhere the land or your surroundings change form: the meeting of earth and water on a beach, the occurrence of dawn or dusk, or even a cliff edge meeting air. There are human-made liminal spaces as well, like crossroads, tunnels, or gateways. These are all places where one thing transforms into something else or that fulfill two roles of being.

Liminal experiences happen in small ways every day, like the time between sleep and wakefulness when you're not completely in the dream world, but you're not quite awake either. They can also manifest as larger, major life changes, sometimes over which you have little control. Often when we're experiencing a liminal time in our lives, like a breakup, moving, or switching jobs, it can be unsettling or stressful. However, without these experiences, we would never progress.

Many times a broader liminal life experience is a rite of passage in some way, a personal journey that leads to growth. It can be disorienting and confusing, but at the same time very exciting, full of potential and hope.

Liminal experiences in life are perhaps some of the most defining moments of our existence. Many people say that their hardships are what shaped their character. Often those hardships were a transition or experience of liminality, like hitting rock bottom and having to start over from scratch. The most challenging part was the in-between, when they were unsure of what would happen next and had to be in a space of facing the unknown. Transition and growth happen when we relinquish control and let change run its course. Choices are made and courageous leaps of faith occur. Clinging to the past because of the fear of the liminal and the unknown stunts a person's personal and spiritual growth. It takes bravery to walk head-on into change, but if you don't, you'll eventually find yourself shoved into it by circumstance, flailing around in the darkness without a candle.

On Mabon, the act of giving thanks, and of letting go of what no longer serves you, is in many ways welcoming a state of liminality into your life. You're letting go of the past and stepping into the future. To flow with the liminal times that cycle through existence like the seasons is to willingly relinquish control and allow your soul to guide you.

The fall season itself is liminal. The leaves are beginning to shrivel, tinged by death, but the trees haven't fully entered dormancy. The earth is winding down and showing signs of preparing for snow and cold, yet still producing food for the final harvest. It's a season of being neither alive nor dead, warm or cold, as you wait for the weather to change but don't know exactly when it will occur. While we indulge in the life-giving fruit and vegetable harvest, we're beginning to simultaneously feel winter's deathly breath in the crisp air.

In your own life when you're unsure of what's coming next, or when you have an instinctive feeling that you're on the cusp of change, you are like the autumn in many ways. Parts of your inner self are dying, while other elements of the person you are becoming take form. Meanwhile, it can feel like you're scrambling around in the dark not knowing how to proceed. How you walk into the unknown is up to you. Embracing it and going with the flow will lead to opportunity and growth, but fighting against it could be as futile as willing winter not to occur. Instead, remember that within a liminal space you become your truest self, and you build your future based on what occurs during that time. In this way, times of uncertainty can be extremely powerful.

While Mabon is often seen as a time of perfect balance, it also heralds change. During your celebration this year, consider contemplating the positive power of the liminal and how important your own "in-between" times have been for your personal growth. Think about what you want to transform in your own life and what kind of risks might be involved. By taking the risks, you're stepping into the liminal, embracing the "in-between." Darkness may seem like a place of nothingness, but it's simultaneously a place where anything and everything could happen. Unlimited potential is just waiting for you to find it.

References

McCoy, Edain. *The Sabbats: A New Approach to Living the Old Ways.* St. Paul, MN: Llewellyn; Enfield, 2001.

Beckett, John. "Enough with the Mabon Hate!" *Under the Ancient Oaks* (blog), Patheos, September 11, 2018. https://www.patheos.com/blogs/johnbeckett/2018/09/enough-with-the-mabon-hate.html.

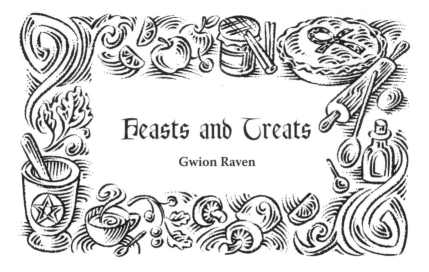

Feasts and Treats

Gwion Raven

THE AUTUMN EQUINOX IS a point of earthly balance. The day is as long as the night. It's likely to be warm, and echoes of summer are everywhere, but look closely and you'll see a yellow leaf here, a red leaf there, and the mornings may have just a little more chill to them. The cold nights of winter are just around the corner.

What I love about these dishes are the bold red, orange, and brown colours to remind me that autumn is here. Spices like cumin and cinnamon perfume the food and the whole kitchen. You'll find more sweetness than spicy heat here, which is another nod to the changing weather outside. Enjoy these dishes together as one meal.

Moroccan Stew with Sweet Potatoes (GF)

Cinnamon, cumin, apricots, sweet potatoes, and preserved lemons mimic the colours of fall. They also taste so phenomenal together. The secret to this dish, just like the equinox itself, is balance. Cook this slowly. If you can resist the urge to eat it right away, let it sit in the fridge overnight and let the flavours meld together … or, you know, eat it right away!

Prep time: 15 minutes
Cooking time: 20 minutes, plus 3 hours in the oven
Servings: 4

3 tablespoons olive oil, divided
1 pound beef stew meat, cut into 1-inch cubes
1 yellow onion, chopped
3 garlic cloves, minced
1 tablespoon paprika
2 teaspoons ground cumin
2 cinnamon sticks (or 2 teaspoons ground cinnamon)
2 cups beef broth
½ cup dried apricots, chopped
2 carrots, chopped into ½-inch chunks
1 sweet potato, peeled and cut into 1-inch cubes
1 15-ounce can garbanzo beans, drained
½ cup fresh cilantro, torn
Zest of 1 lemon

Preheat your oven to 250°F. In a Dutch oven or cast-iron enamel braising pan, heat 2 tablespoons of oil over medium-high heat for 1 minute. Add beef and brown on all sides, about 4 minutes. Remove beef from pan and set aside. Transfer to plate. Add another tablespoon of oil. Add the onion. Cook for 6 minutes. Add garlic and cook for 2 minutes more. Stir frequently. Add spices. Cook for 1 minute. Give everything a good mix. Pour in the broth, bring to boil, then simmer for 5 minutes. Add the beef and any juices to the pan. Cover and put in the oven for 2 hours.

After 2 hours, chop the apricots, carrots, and sweet potatoes. Drain and rinse the beans. Carefully remove the braising pan from the oven, remove the lid. If using cinnamon sticks, remove them and discard. Add the vegetables and beans, stirring until everything is combined. If the stew looks too thick or dry, add ¼ cup of water. Put the lid on and pop the pan back in the oven for 1 hour.

Serve in bowls. Top with torn cilantro leaves and lemon zest. Refrigerate leftovers and enjoy all over again the next day.

Cumin Yogurt (GF & Vegetarian)

This tasty sauce is perfect when it's dolloped on top of Moroccan stew, but it's also great as a dip for vegetables or falafel or pita chips. Also, it takes less than 2 minutes to make.

Prep time: 2 minutes
Servings: 4

½ cup plain Greek yogurt
½ teaspoon ground cumin
Pinch of salt
Fresh ground black pepper

In a bowl, combine yogurt and cumin. Season with salt and pepper.

To serve, add a tablespoon to stews or leave in the bowl and surround the dip with fresh vegetables.

Cumin Rice (GF & Vegan)

You can eat this all by itself in a bowl with a little pat of (vegan) butter on top or use as a base for Moroccan stew. The whole dish takes 30 minutes to cook.

Prep time: 2 minutes
Cooking time: 30 minutes
Servings: 4

1 tablespoon olive oil
2 teaspoons cumin seeds
1 yellow onion, diced
2 cups water
1 cup of white rice
1 teaspoon salt
Zest of 1 lemon

Heat a large saucepan on medium-high for 1 minute. Pour in olive oil and heat for 1 minute. Add the 2 teaspoons cumin seeds. Cook 1 minute, shaking the pan the whole time. Add the onion and cook for 5 minutes, stirring frequently. Add the rice and immediately add the water and salt. Bring to a simmer. Cover and reduce to low heat. Cook for 15 minutes. Remove the pan from the heat and set aside for 10 minutes. Leave the lid on.

Serve as a side dish or eat it just as it is. Garnish with the lemon zest right before you tuck in.

Cinnamon and Clove Tea (GF & Vegan)

There are two great things about this tea: The first is the taste, of course. The second is how my kitchen smells when I make it. The aromas of cinnamon and cloves soon punctuate the air, and before too long, I'm busy making more for folks who just happen to wander into the kitchen to see what's going on. Cinnamon and cloves are often used in recipes said to keep away colds, so there are added health benefits too. This tea is sure to warm you up. It's best with tea leaves but a tea bag works just fine too. Serve with or without your favourite milk.

Prep time: 2 minutes
Cooking time: 15 minutes
Servings: 4

2½ cups boiling water
½ cinnamon stick (or ⅛ teaspoon ground cinnamon)
2 whole cloves (or ⅛ teaspoon ground cloves)
1 teaspoon agave nectar
2 teaspoons loose leaf black tea (or two tea bags)
5 tablespoons milk

Boil water in a saucepan. Once at a boil, add the cinnamon, cloves, and agave. Cover and keep at barely a boil for 5 minutes. Add tea leaves and bring back to a boil for 1 minute. Steep for 3 minutes. Add the milk.

To serve, if using leaves and whole spices, pour the tea into cups through a tea strainer. If using tea bags and ground spices, just pour into 4 small cups.

Crafty Crafts

Ivo Dominguez Jr.

THE FALL EQUINOX IS the sunset of the year, and the world is filled with rich hues. The fruits, vegetables, and grains are ripe, and the leaves are beginning to glow with golden and ruddy colors. The air is filled with the fragrance of the season and a sense of accomplishment as the many harvests continue. It is a time to set aside enough of the bounty to make it through the winter and until the first harvests of the next year. It is also a good time to set aside emotional reserves and spiritual vitamins as well for the cold and dark.

Gratitude Box

This project calls for the creation of a decorated wooden box with strips of paper and a decorated pen or pencil. Every day from the Fall Equinox until Samhain, write something on one or more slips of paper that brought you gratitude, awe, wonder, or comfort and drop them into the gratitude box. If others live with you, you can invite them to join in the process as well. Then, as you pass through the dark half of the year, you take out a slip and read it to relive that moment and refresh your spirit.

Materials

Wooden box, pine ideally
Glue, white, super glue, and jewelry glue
Acrylic paints
Small piece of decorative cloth and cord
Shiny bits, old costume jewelry, beads, crystals
Sealant, polyurethane or polyacrylic
Pencil
Paper
   Cost: $0–$25
   Time spent: 3 hours, plus drying time

Design Ideas

There are a broad range of wooden boxes, chests, and coffers available at most craft stores. The box you pick should be large enough so that your hand can rummage through the slips to find the one you are meant to read. When in doubt, the larger box is probably the better choice. Boxes that are made of a soft wood like pine will be easier to decorate. It is also best if the box is bare wood, and you can give it a light sanding with 120- or 180-grit sandpaper.

What does a box look like that holds emotional treasures? That is the question to ask yourself as you plan how you will decorate the box. You could make it look fancy and worthy of holding heirlooms. You could make it very simple but elegant. Do you want a design with a celestial motif, a floral pattern, spirals, a cornucopia, or something else? The method described here attaches beads, crystals, or pieces of jewelry to the box. I always rummage through my collection of shiny things before I buy anything for a project. Stud earrings, brooches, hair pins, and all sorts of costume jewelry are great starting points as well.

Do you want to stain the wood or leave it plain? If you choose to stain the wood, skip the smell and expense of a commercial wood stain. Using acrylic paints, which you may already have, mix a dab

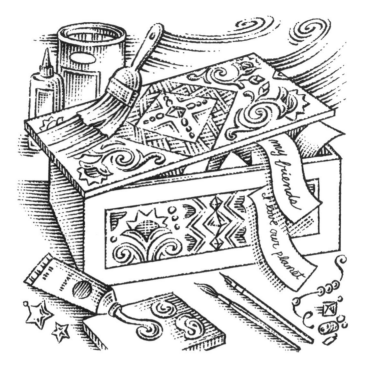

of brown plus a touch of a color you like with enough water to make a thin wash. Appy it to the box with the brush or sponge quickly to keep the tone even. It is absorbed quickly, and you can add a second layer to darken it. Consider a small amount of a metallic color in the last layer for some sparkle. Let the wood dry for an hour or two. You can do the same or something different inside.

For the bottom of the box, I like to cut a piece of felt or velvet and put a few dots of glue on the wood and press the cloth down. Take a piece of decorative cord, cut to the size of the interior perimeter of the box, and rub its whole length with white glue. Push the cord down so that it acts as a border around the cloth at the bottom. I use the eraser end of a pencil to apply pressure.

The details will vary according to your design, but the method I am describing will stay the same. With a pencil, I gently mark the pattern I will be creating on the box. In this case, I have a large mother-of-pearl stud earring I want to put at the top of the box as a focal point. I use a large nail or a nail-setting tool and a small hammer. With those, tap gently at the center of the top to make a dent in the wood, then test to see if the stud fits in the dent. If it does, put a bit of super glue or jewelry glue on the stud, in the dent, and on the edges where the earring will touch the glue when you place it. Depending on what you are attaching to the box, you may need a small drill to deepen the hole for the stud. When attaching some objects, it is easier if you have a rotary tool (like a Dremel) to create indents for some of the edges. Don't be afraid to use a small needle-nose pliers to shorten studs or add slight bends to make things fit better.

The same process can be used to attach small beads, crystals, and cabochons to create your design. You can also use ornamental upholstery tacks as decorations. Also, a broken necklace can be turned into a great border with upholstery tacks and a few links glued in place. It is easier if you start from the center and work outward on each of the faces of the box that you want to decorate. When you are done adding ornaments, add a coating of polyurethane or polyacrylic to give the wood some gloss and a protective layer.

To decorate a pencil, take thin cord rubbed with white glue and wrap it around to hide the surface completely. When it has dried, add a jewel, tassel, or a curled ribbon at the top.

Using the Gratitude Box

For this to work well, it must become a routine. Pick a time in your schedule that is consistent, such as a mealtime or some other activity. This will help ensure that you create a gratitude slip every day. The same is true when it is time to dip into this box of treasures. If you really need to renew yourself, you may be in no mood to do it. Create a scheduled routine to pull slips from the box as well. Read the slip several times and let its meaning and restorative grace sink in. I return the slips to the box after reading them and mix them up a bit. Most years, I continue to dip into the box until the Spring Equinox as the next balance point in the wheel.

Reference

Smith, Jeremy Adam, Kira M. Newman, Jason Marsh, Dacher Keltner, eds. *The Gratitude Project: How the Science of Thankfulness Can Rewire Our Brains for Resilience, Optimism, and the Greater Good.* Oakland, CA: New Harbinger Publications, 2020.

Color Magic

Charlie Rainbow Wolf

MABON IS THE QUARTER festival between the summer and winter solstices. In the Wheel of the Year, it falls between Lugnasadh and Samhain. It is marked by the sun leaving Virgo and entering into Libra, so even though it always falls toward the end of September, its exact date will vary from year to year. It's named after Mabon, the Welsh god of the harvest, although this is a fairly new term, attributed to Aiden Kelly around the 1970s.

Mabon is the second harvest festival and the penultimate festival of the year. It is the peak of gathering in the bounty for the coming of the winter and a time of the autumnal equinox, when the days and the nights are of equal length. Mother Nature's bounty is at her peak, and the last of the grain has been cut, the seeds safely stored for next spring's sowing.

The Colors of Mabon

The colors of Mabon are those of Lugnasadh, but they're richer, more intense, and more earthy. Perhaps you've seen the cornucopias filled with their harvest and noticed how everything is colorful yet subtle. Red gives way to maroon or burgundy, orange yields to copper or bronze, green becomes mossy or olive, and brown takes on the rich, warm tones from the lightest ecru to the deepest chocolate. These are echoed in the oven-baked bread, the rich, ripe berries, the moss starting to gather on the tree trunks and stone walls.

The burgundy red of Mabon is best described as a blend of red (a primary color) and purple (a secondary color). It has all the heat and passion of red, but this is subdued and elevated by the peaceful and dignified addition of purple. This combination creates serious and focused energy. Its strength and force might make it overpowering for some people; others find it stimulates their determination. It's not a color for demanding attention, though. Burgundy works tirelessly in the background toward the desired goal.

Maroon is similar to burgundy in that it mutes and dulls the energies of red, but it doesn't add the prestige of purple. It's thought to stimulate the appetite, which may be why so many restaurants choose this muted red for their table settings. Where bright red is related to assertiveness or potential aggression, passion, and the possibility of danger, maroon takes those qualities and mutes them, turning them inward on a voyage of self-discovery rather than outwardly flaunting them.

When orange presents itself as copper, much of the heat has been grounded in the same way that the metal copper is used to ground a current. This shade of orange might be seen as red mixed with brown rather than yellow. Qualities of stability and security are associated with copper. Like burgundy, it does not seek the limelight but is quite happy being left to its own resources to get things accomplished. Its earthy tones and the influence of brown help with focus and achievement.

As bronze, orange stays muted, and perhaps a little insignificant. The bronze medal is never quite so prestigious as the silver or the gold! Bronze is recognized as a soothing and restorative color. If the hustle of the harvest is starting to become exhausting, bronze will help to alleviate the stress.

The green of this time of year is subdued too. The chlorophyll that overpowers other colors in foliage breaks down and the green fades, letting other colors be seen. This is the color of trust, perhaps trusting that the harvest will be enough to get through until the next growing season, or that the warmth will return after the cold of winter.

Olive takes green and adds a touch of brown to it. It still embodies the energy of green—harmony, balance, and tranquility—but brings it down to earth with the dependability and consistency of brown. Olive green might also suggest hope; offering the olive branch is a term for seeking to resolve a dispute with someone.

Green is between the warmer shades (yellow, orange, and red) and the cooler tones (violet, purple, and blue). It is in the middle energy center of the seven chakras. Green builds a bridge, signifying a place to come together, a position where unity and peace might be found. With the seeds of the harvest being preserved for future planting, it is also a bridge between what was, what is, and what will be.

Lugnasadh's yellow is a muted, mustard yellow—and once again, it could be considered as yellow with a touch of brown added to it. All of these colors keep their natural energy, but with brown added, they seem to grow up somehow—adding maturity and solidity to their vibration. Added to the other colors, it increases the energy in what could be a bit somber or underwhelming.

Mustard might also promote creativity. Much of the harvest is suitable for making into incense or potpourri. Mabon activities include cooking, baking and preserving, and doing the autumnal cleansing—similar to spring cleaning—in preparation for the winter.

Celebrating Mabon

I feel very lucky to be born the week before Mabon, and I claim Mabon as "my" festival. This is the time of year when I swap from being busy in the garden to picking up my needlecrafts in the evening. Kitchen work includes making pear honey, apple butter, and other culinary delights to go on the homemade bread in the upcoming weeks.

I put an ametrine on my incense altar at this time of year and add clove to my usual smoke blend of sage, lavender, and cedar. Ametrine is a form of quartz that is part amethyst and part citrine. Mine is particularly enigmatic, as it also has an enhydros—a tiny bubble of water—trapped inside the stone. Some ametrines are man-made, with the stone being artificially heated; I find the energy of the naturally occurring stones to suit me the best.

The energy of ametrine is that of both amethyst and citrine. It takes the new beginnings and the focus of the citrine and blends it with the higher-mind energy of amethyst. Ametrine promotes the higher mind and the imagination, while providing the grounded energy and tenacity to make those visions a reality. It embodies balance and harmony—perfectly reflecting the energies of Mabon.

Reference

Kelly, Aidan. "About Naming Ostara, Litha, and Mabon." *Including Paganism with Aidan Kelly* (blog). Patheos. May 2, 2017. https://www.patheos.com/blogs/aidankelly/2017/05/naming -ostara-litha-mabon/.

Mabon Ritual

Suzanne Ress

THE PURPOSE OF THIS Mabon ritual is to embrace the duality of the season, of nature, and of ourselves. On the one hand, at this time of year we may feel relaxed and ready to tackle another cold season; we may welcome the cooler nights and still-beautiful, vibrant days. On the other hand, we cannot ignore that days have gotten, and will continue to become, shorter and colder, and we cannot predict what lies ahead.

Just as the autumn equinox occurs during Mabon, so our feelings about this gateway time may be both positive and negative, happy and anxious.

The Light Half and the Dark Half

The ritual may be performed in solitaire or in a group. It should take place on the evening of the equinox (September 23 this year) and outdoors as far from human civilization as one is able to travel in a reasonable amount of time. A city green space will do if nothing else is available; although, if the sky is clear, being able to see a good quantity of stars and the waxing moon would be a plus. In case of inclement weather, participants should come equipped with large black umbrellas.

All participants should be dressed in black, with no jewelry save a necklace in the form of a pentacle, if desired. No perfumes, scented creams, or other unnatural odors should be present on the skin.

For this ritual you will need the following items:

A black cloth, round or square

A red candle and a white candle in windproof lanterns or hurricane lamps

Cinnamon incense and an incense burner

A consecrated and charged athame, pocketknife, and wand

A green apple for each celebrant, covered halfway horizontally with red candy apple coating

A small cutting board

Cider, sweet or hard

An apple cake, or apple muffins

Additionally, each participant might wish to bring a small flashlight or headlamp.

When you have reached your destination, begin to set up your temporary altar by spreading the black cloth in a spot that feels receptive. It could be a picnic table, a tree stump, a bench, or just on the ground.

Place the two candles at the center of the cloth, with the incense in its burner between them. Place the sacred athame, pocket knife, and wand evenly around them, with the cutting board under the pocket knife. The coated apples (which should be in a basket or other attractive receptacle), the cider, and the cake or muffins should be evenly spaced in a larger circle around the tools.

All ritual participants shall stand around the black cloth altar. If there are only two participants or a solitary practitioner, they stand facing north with the altar in front of them.

The sacred athame is used now by the decided leader to call the quarters and close the circle to all possible negative influence. The candles and the incense are lit. Participants shall now walk around the altar deosil and chant, drum, play musical instruments, sing, or clap in order to raise the magical power of nature up from the ground all around them in a cone of beautiful, sparkle-flecked light. Once the cone has been raised, everyone shall stand still. If there are enough of you and you are close enough together, hold hands. The apples in their receptacle shall be blessed by the leader with a wand and these words,

Earth all around us,
Within us, amongst us,
All fruits of this season potent
With earthly power,
We increase our own power
and our knowledge
With this fruit,
Our connection to earth.

Each participant takes an apple from the receptacle with her left hand. The pocketknife and cutting board are passed clockwise, and each person cuts his apple in half horizontally, just above the candy line. This is best done kneeling or squatting down, with the apple on the cutting board and the cutting board on the ground, being careful not to cut your fingers. Once the apple is cut, the cutter says,

Who gets the red half,
Who gets the white?
Who will be charmed on equinox night?

The board and knife are given to the next person, who cuts his apple and repeats the magic chant. Each participant now has a red half and a "white" half.

The leader says,

The red half is dark,
Its knowledge is hidden.
The white half is light,
Its joy comes unbidden.
We now eat the red,

Ancient magic we seek.
We gift the white
To a friend we keep.
For luck and good fortune,
For fortune and luck.

Now, all together, everyone repeats,

For luck and good fortune,
For fortune and luck.

Each person takes a bite of their red half, then breathes upon the white half and gives it to the person on their left. (Participants should use discretion, either breathing on the apple while wearing an FFP face mask, or symbolically breathing.)

Everyone, in unison, says,

My breath is the breath of the universe,
Wisdom is mine.
I breathe positivity into the fruit of wisdom.

The white halves are to be considered charmed apples and are kept for after the ritual to be given to someone unknowing for whom you wish good fortune in the coming six months. If that person, when given the apple, shall eat it without hesitation, good fortune will be guaranteed. If the apple is rejected or not eaten, the charm will not work. But it is important that you do nothing to influence your friend either way.

Now, gazing at the pentagram of seeds inside the red half of their apple, each participant meditates for some moments on the knowledge and magical ability they will gain by eating the red, dark half. When they are ready, the apple half should be eaten in its entirety. This must be done in silence. Look at the moon, the stars, the two burning candles on the altar cloth, or close your eyes and visualize a bright and glowing violet pentagram. Do not look at the other participants if there are any!

Take as long as you like in this consummation of ancient knowledge. Savor the apple and chew it well.

When, finally, everyone has finished, each shall kiss the person to their left and wish them well. (Masks can remain on if desired.)

The leader will take the athame in their right hand and dismiss the quarters in reverse order, and then will lead the group widdershins in a circle around the altar cloth thirteen times in silence to bring the cone of light back down into the earth. The leader will extinguish the candles, and participants may turn on their flashlights or headlamps.

Cider and cake are now offered to everyone, and people are encouraged to laugh, chat, converse, and enjoy themselves in the normal convivial fashion for a spell, until it is generally agreed the time has come to adjourn the meeting.

Sometime within the next twenty-four hours, each participant must give the white half of the apple to their chosen beneficiary. It is encouraged to keep the apple-half refrigerated and covered with cling wrap, and even to trim off any browned edges if necessary, before giving it to your chosen person to increase its appeal.

Blessed be!

Notes

Notes

Notes

Notes

Notes

Notes

Notes